DATE DUE

2 8 AUG 1972 AR CH

9 DEC 1974 B A

DEC 1 1984

DEC 0 8 1984

OCT 1 6 1988

OCT 1 6 1988

DIALOGUE WITH ISHMAEL

Israel's Future in the Middle East

DIALOGUE WITH ISHMAEL

Israel's Future in the Middle East

AUBREY HODES

FUNK & WAGNALLS

NEW YORK

TO

DR. JOSEPH W. WUNSCH

engineer — humanist — visionary

I am grateful to the
Institute of World
Affairs, New York, for
a research grant which
greatly helped me to
write this book.

A.H.

Awalu al reiti katar—A torrent of rain starts with a few drops

—ARAB PROVERB

When brothers quarrel, strangers profit

—JOSHUA IBN SHU'AIB
CONSTANTINOPLE, 1523

Two neighbors' fields were separated by a wall. One side of the wall was painted black and the other white. One of the neighbors shouted to the other: "The wall is black!" and the other replied: "No, the wall is white!" In the end a fight broke out and they killed one another. But neither of them thought of looking at the other side of the wall. . . .

—FOLK TALE FROM THE
ANTILLES ISLANDS

CONTENTS

DIALOGUE WITH

ISHMAEL

1 ∎ *Bitter Olives*

THERE IS a moment when a Jew living in Israel becomes an Israeli. For me this moment came a month after I arrived in the country, when I was hiking in Galilee, on the road that runs north from Acre along the edge of the sea. In a cutting I came across an abandoned railroad track and decided to follow it as far as it would go into the mountains. The tracks teetered for a while on top of the cliff and then plunged straight toward the massive white chalk Ladder of Tyre.

Following it, I saw that it ran into a tunnel hewn in the chalk face. There it was blocked by a concrete wall. A new, hostile, ugly warning plug. On the other side of the wall was Lebanon. And in that moment—both luminous and filled with dread—I felt the human ring around us, the contours of hatred which hemmed us in, which pressed us against one another in our mutual need and dependence. I sensed the shock waves of animosity from the invisible people and places on the other side of the wall. At that hour I first attained the perception of life on a border, in the shadow of a frontier, which never leaves anyone who is genuinely living in Israel. And instinctively I looked back in longing at the sea, in gratitude for its freedom, its link across the open water with Europe and the lands of the Mediterranean.

Other places on Israel's borders give one the same uncanny feeling that political tension has been transmuted into landscape. The Jordan, dropping below sea level between Israel, Jordan, and Syria—the cave canyons along Ein Gedi—the dunes of the south—all these are chasms where opposing cultures glare at one another across a piece of earth as barren and arid as their own hostility.

The Great Rift Valley is a human fault, not only a geographical one.

The Israeli-Arab dispute is not an ordinary political conflict between states centering around specific issues. It goes far deeper than just the surface clash. Essentially, it is a conflict between two vastly different civilizations whom history has placed at one another's throats. At its fulcrum lies what Martin Buber called "existential mistrust"—a potent blend of suspicion and fear touching the irrational roots of being and bringing out submerged primitive patterns of behavior.

For the Arabs Israel is a dagger of progress aimed at the heart of a world which still moves at a pace far removed from that of the West. The Zionist influx awoke and liberated the stifled Arab feelings of inferiority in the face of twentieth century advances. Instead of gradually coming to grips with the challenge of Western concepts, Islam and the Arab world were forced to confront these concepts in the suddenly tangible form of a new, alien society whose very establishment seemed to set the seal on their own backwardness. The result was a "pathological antipathy"[1] toward Israel—which is "*in* the Arab world" but "not *of* the Arab world."[2]

For the Jews, Arab resistance to their national renaissance threatened the aim of the only movement which could provide an alternative to the estrangement and suffering of Diaspora life. The desperate survivors of Christian Europe had barely enough life force left to fling themselves onto their bridgehead in the Moslem East. There they were shocked to encounter a second attempt to annihilate them—this time by their prospective neighbors.

This situation, which came to a head in 1948, contained all the elements of tragedy. There could be no question of blame or moral judgment. The Arabs were acting as Arabs, and the Jews were acting as Jews. Each responded to the climactic test from the depths of its own experience. As always, the Arabs acted to keep out intruders; as always, the Jews acted to survive. Simply

1. Emile Bustani, *Doubts and Dynamite* (London: Allan Wingate, 1958), p. 13.
2. *Ibid.*, p. 54.

by being themselves, they were doomed to clash. Both the conflict and its outcome were unavoidable.

The resulting trauma led to a complete break in communication between the two sides. In most more specific political disputes the combatants continue to maintain some form of contact as, for example, the United States and Communist China do through the regular meetings of their envoys in Warsaw. Even arguments and mutual insults are a form of contact. But between the Arabs and Israel there is no genuine two-way contact at all. The dialogue has broken down completely. And the opposite of a dialogue is not two monologues, but silence. Silence is the only form of speech between Israel and the Arabs today. The meaning of this silence is not that neither side speaks but that neither directly addresses the other. The language in which this silence is conducted is propaganda and its lexicon is a classic compendium of bitterness, ignorance, and invective.

As Dr. Joseph E. Johnson has observed:

"For a decade and a half a state of armed hostility has been fortified by a communications relationship that permits the strident voices on each side to be heard by the other with shattering clarity, while cutting off all possibility of the kind of quiet, direct, face-to-face communication that is essential to the beginning of mutual comprehension."[3]

"One result of this tragic situation," the President of the Carnegie Endowment for International Peace added, "is that the only possible communication of ideas and true thoughts, as distinct from propaganda, must be carried on through intermediaries."[4]

Dr. Johnson himself served as one of these intermediaries during his 1961–1963 term of office as Special Representative of the United Nations Conciliation Commission for Palestine, in an attempt to resolve the Arab refugee problem. He noted ruefully that even when these intermediaries are disinterested, "even when—

3. Address to the 24th American Assembly, Arden House, Harriman, New York, October 24, 1963; published by the American Assembly, Columbia University, New York, p. 6.
4. *Ibid.*

which is seldom—their motives are not suspect," they "are bound to encounter a predisposition to disbelieve anything that runs counter to views, estimates and conclusions conditioned by separate cultures, by hostility, and by the strident voices."[5]

This total breakdown in communication since 1948 has exploded three times into war—another form of silence and the ultimate victory of the strident voices. But during the years between these wars both Arabs and Israelis retreated into a state of no-war, no-peace. No leaders met; no programs were announced; but both sides acted as if there was an agreed state of hostile coexistence, as distinct from the conscious (if uncomfortable) peaceful coexistence between Western and Eastern blocs. The tense equilibrium which existed between the second Israeli-Arab war in 1956 and the third war in 1967, for example, was arrived at by both sides' unwillingness to initiate new military actions, the clear knowledge that these would not be tolerated by an already impatient world, and the lack of courage to draw the logical conclusions from this walk along the tightrope. Before June 1967 it seemed that the Middle East was sinking into a gray, uneasy status quo, during which the strident voices were perhaps more muffled than before. But this status quo was always frenetic and uneasy, never a desirable period of cooling off before efforts to establish a more stable relationship.

Now that the Israeli-Arab War III has lanced the rising tension in the region and created a new uneasy status quo, both sides appear to be settling in for another restless period like the eleven years between 1956 and 1967. I believe this is the real danger facing Israel and the Arab states: that they may come to feel that this status quo is more convenient than any attempt to break it. In the absence of any real readiness to resolve the deadlock through mutual concessions, both sides appear to think that the present prickly truce can be tolerated for a time while they use it to build up their strength for an attempt to overthrow it.

Both sides would like to postpone any solution of their own differences until they have made more progress in solving their own domestic problems. Israel has to absorb and integrate hun-

5. *Ibid.*, pp. 6–7.

dreds of thousands of new settlers, while maintaining national
unity and averting any sudden drop in cultural and economic
standards. The doors have to be kept open for Jewish immigrants
from the West and, hopefully, from Eastern Europe and the
Soviet Union, and a new native-born generation has to be raised
to replace the ghetto-oriented generation of the wilderness. The
Arabs urgently need social and economic reforms. Islamic doctrine
on such matters as birth control has to be reconciled with modern
developments. President Nasser still hopes to export his revolution
to other Arab countries, and some near-feudal regimes are trying
to forestall this by introducing gradual reforms in time.

It is difficult to escape the conclusion that—apart from the three
times in the last twenty years when mutual threats escalated into
war—much of the saber-rattling is not meant seriously and serves
as smokescreens behind which the respective national leaders can
continue their internal policies, using the threat of the other side
as a lever for their own pressing objectives. It can be said, without
a hint of irony, that if Israel did not exist Nasser would have to
invent it, and the reverse is just as true.

A prominent Israeli journalist who talked to Arab students at
American universities reported that they feared Israel's economic
domination of the Arab world, because of the great imbalance
between the two societies. "In reality," they felt, "the present
situation of 'no peace and no war' is what creates the security belt
which the Arab countries need in order to develop their economies
independently. There was no reason why the Arab countries
should desire to change this situation."[6]

The students argued that the no-peace, no-war posture acceler-
ated the processes of economic development in the Arab countries.
"It creates the momentum and the desirable social fermentation,
as well as national unification, without leading to actual war. Arabs
are passive by nature, and conditions of at least 'almost war'
arouse them from their passivity to activity, while a situation of
'almost peace' inhibits the destructive tendencies of this fermentation. The pendulum oscillates from 'almost peace' to 'almost war,'

6. H. Benedict, "No War and No Peace?" *New Outlook*, January 1960,
p. 39.

moving from one to the other in accordance with local and foreign needs."[7]

In these students' opinion, there was "an identity of interests between Israel and the Arab countries in maintaining the present abnormal situation."[8] In other words, they felt that both sides could exploit the fear of the other hostile society to undertake the social changes each needed so badly. By preying on the fear of being outstripped by the other side, leaders could thrust both societies forward more quickly than would otherwise be possible.

The dangers inherent in this approach are obvious. Each side hopes to be able to control the no-war, no-peace bacillus, to manipulate it to meet local needs. But this political fermentation is taking place in a highly charged region, a focal point of international rivalries and pressures. It cannot be turned on or switched off at will. As in all explosive processes, undesirable side reactions can take place. And then, as happened on June 5, 1967, the delicate balance is upset and national passions drive the leaders on both sides over the brink.

Further, the no-war, no-peace situation is disastrous because it erodes the foundation of goodwill on which any future Israeli-Arab *rapprochement* will have to be based. Leaders come and go, but their populations remain. Unless we assume that this conflict will continue to plague us till the end of time, we must agree that negotiations will become possible at some stage. And when this happens the leaders on both sides will have to feel the mood of their public—a mood which is being molded and set harder by the strident voices. Each year that goes by makes it more difficult to bring about an understanding between the man in the street on both sides.

But there is a far greater issue at stake. The root of the clash between Israeli and Arab cultures is their disparate attitudes toward their respective national objectives. Civilization, in the Western sense, is the art of solving problems; in the Oriental sense, the craft of enduring their non-solution. Israel takes a determinedly Western approach. It is a *problem-solving* society. The Arab world, on the other hand, tends to be *problem-perpetuating*.

7. *Ibid.*
8. *Ibid.*, p. 40.

The Israeli regards a problem as a challenge, something to be tackled and overcome; the Arab, as something to be accepted and lived with.

This fierce, almost competitive desire to solve problems has inspired some of Israel's greatest achievements. As an Israeli, I am intensely proud of my country's daring and imaginative approach to agricultural pioneering, social experimentation, the integration of new settlers, scientific research, and language revival. But we seem to lose this daring and inventiveness when faced with our greatest problem: the apparently implacable Arab resistance to our national revival. We are puzzled by their enmity, baffled by their sterility. Like all problem-solving societies, we are acutely conscious of losing time, and we cannot comprehend how the Arabs can be so prodigal with their time and their human resources.

Faced with the blank wall of the Arabs, Israel has taken refuge in a fortress of isolation and distrust and adopted a defeatist approach. Some Israeli leaders have made dark references to "forty years in the wilderness" and to "no peace being possible in our generation." In doing so, we are playing into the Arabs' hands by moving from a Western to an Oriental posture. *We are behaving like a problem-perpetuating society, not a problem-solving one.*

In doing so, we run the risk of losing the Western-linked ethos which we claim to be transmitting to the Middle East and Asia. If Israel is to reinterpret the values of Western civilization in the country where these were born, it must display its ability to apply these values to the world it lives in and to its immediate environment. This can scarcely be done by abandoning the active role and taking on the quietist character of so many Middle East lands. This would be carrying assimilation to the region too far. Nor can it be done by relying solely on advantages gained by conquest and violence—another traditional Middle East way of solving problems.

It is because Israel has demonstrated its internal drive and will to solve problems that it should prove its ability to gain the goodwill of the hostile environment into which it has projected itself. Israel should take the lead in turning the Arab world into a problem-solving one and in helping it take, finally and irrevocably, the way of the West. Israel should understand and encourage those Arab leaders who are struggling to change their peoples' traditional thought patterns.

The man rooted in Western culture believes that the given facts of life and nature can be changed by human endeavor, and hence he acts to change them; the man rooted in Oriental culture does not really believe that anything can be changed by man's efforts, and hence he conceals inaction with talk. In such an existential clash between two cultures it is the duty of the more vigorous and action-orientated culture to set the lead and to demonstrate to the more passive society the truth of its basic thesis. *It is precisely because Israel is more dynamic that it should be more charitable.*

Israel cannot acquiesce in the status quo unless it is prepared to surrender its problem-solving imperative. It should have the courage to apply the dynamism which is its most striking characteristic to the gravest of its dilemmas. It should make a positive and constructive attempt to eliminate differences, not to entrench them. It should try to convince the Arabs that maintaining an artificial no-war, no-peace atmosphere, which occasionally erupts into full-scale war, holds back progress rather than stimulating it; that cooperation would liberate forces and mutual interests which now go merely to neutralize one another. Israel should act decisively to meet the Arabs, to change the present tense and enforced coexistence in the Middle East into peaceful coexistence, and then into cooperation. Israel should seek to be *of* the Middle East, not merely *in* it.

Unless Israel acts to change the present situation, it will continue to be surrounded by a desert of hostility. Despite the stunning military victory in the third Israeli-Arab war, the great ideals and hopes of Zionism will trickle into the sands. Israel will survive; but it will survive as a model, progressive ghetto, turning inward in despair away from its neighbors and unable to discover the deepest secrets of its rebirth. This is the greatest and most crucial test of Israel's statehood.

2 The Arabs: Prisoners of a Dream

ISRAEL "constitutes a virtual touchstone of Arab capacities for self-preservation and self-determination."[1] It is a living monument to the Arabs' humiliation; a symbol of their inability to work together for a common objective; a twentieth century non-Moslem stronghold in the Moslem world. As such, it is an affront to their pride, a threat to their feeling that the Middle East is their unchallenged corner of the globe, their territorial home. The Arabs have an image of "the almost superhumanly clever and able Jew"[2]; and they are afraid of losing out in direct contact with what they consider a ruthless, dedicated, hard-bitten nation, interested in surviving at any cost and heavily backed by World Jewry and the Western Powers.

The Arab picture of the typical Israeli is not of a hard-working kibbutz member or a skullcapped devotee of the Talmud, but of the tough security agents who tracked down Adolf Eichmann or carried out the Kibya reprisal operation, in which sixty Arabs—men, women, and children—were killed in a Jordanian village in 1953 by Israeli troops. This image is distorted by the lack of direct contact with the everyday life of Israel and the atmosphere of heightened propaganda, which poisons even sincere contacts between men of goodwill on both sides.

One Arab who talked with an Israeli correspondent in Europe

1. Dr. Charles Malik, "The Near East: The Search for Truth," *Foreign Affairs*, January 1952, quoted by Sylvia G. Haim, *Arab Nationalism* (Berkeley and Los Angeles: University of California Press, 1962), p. 200.
2. Charles D. Cremeans, *The Arabs and the World* (New York: Frederick A. Praeger, 1963), p. 182.

later summed up his impressions to friends in his home country, in the following generalization: "Israelis are blond and usually blue-eyed." (What about the Oriental inhabitants, who make up more than half of Israel's population?) "They are sociable types, but fanatical in their Zionist views, and somewhat limited in outlook."[3]

An Arab friend of mine told me: "We think of the Israelis as the Japanese of the Middle East—and we fear them as the Asians feared the Japanese in World War II."

This image of the Israeli as an aggressive, uncompromising guerrilla fighter is a powerful deterrent to understanding. Yet this is the only image which has been projected since the drastic break in direct contact since 1948. From the first Israeli-Arab war after Israel's establishment until today the only Israelis most Egyptians, Jordanians, and Syrians have met have been soldiers. Even at the height of the Cold War the United States and the Soviet Union maintained cultural and scientific contacts, with normal travel facilities between the two countries. But nothing like this breaks through the pattern of hermetically sealed barriers in the Middle East, unrelieved by any civilian contacts whatsoever.

For the Arabs 1948 was a psychological watershed. Following the United Nations partition decision of November 29, 1947, the Arabs had the choice of two possible paths. One was what I would call the path of history—adding another bloodstained entry to the record of war, violence, and slaughter which has written the story of man on this planet. The other was the path of cooperation—accepting the decision of the highest international tribunal, conceding the Jewish people's right to their own small strip of territory, and admitting this state to the community of Middle East lands.

The Arabs rejected the path of cooperation and chose once again the path of history. This was scarcely a conscious, free decision. It was in line with their own traditions, with the way social change has always been effected in the Arab world. The Arabs knew only the path of history, of sporadic violence. They had never experienced the path of cooperation—the Western road

3. Noted by Amnon Kapeliuk, in article "The Key: Patience or Action," *New Outlook*, July–August 1964, p. 23.

of democracy, gradual progress, and unviolent political change. They simply could not conceive any other way of settling a dispute, and even if this had actually been suggested as a theoretical possibility, it could never have become policy. They saw the Palestine issue as a straight clash between Arabs and Jews, and felt the two combatants should be left alone to fight it out.

This pugilistic view of history was succinctly expressed by Auni Abdul Hadi, of the Arab Higher Committee, when he told the 1946 Anglo-American Commission:

"If your commission, for instance, says to the two parties this problem will not be solved unless we get out of Palestine, it may happen, it has happened all over the world, that people have come into clashes and they have solved their difficulties by their fists. Is that not the case in history?"[4]

Or as another prominent Arab wrote, after Israel's establishment:

"The purification of Palestine depends upon strength alone. Such a thing is not difficult for the Arabs, even though the Jews and the West support each other."[5]

The Arabs decided to solve their difficulties with the Jews with their fists. On the eve of the Arab invasion of Palestine Azzam Pasha, the Secretary General of the Arab League, declared:

"This will be a war of extermination and a momentous massacre which will be spoken of like the Mongolian massacre and the Crusades."[6]

But their attempt to write another bloodstained entry in the ledger of history failed. Today we can see more clearly that the Arabs' attack on the State of Israel was a tragic error which demonstrated their inability to understand the new forces at work in the world after World War II. Sick of the horror and slaughter which had turned Europe into a charnel house and the globe into one immense battlefield, the nations were making naïve but

4. Proceedings of the Anglo-American Commission on Palestine, 1946, stencilled and unpaginated, Central Zionist Archives, Jerusalem.

5. Muhammad Jamil Baihum, *Arabism and Jewry in Syria*: quoted by Sylvia G. Haim, *Arab Nationalism* (Berkeley and Los Angeles: University of California Press, 1962), p. 146.

6. Quoted by Joseph B. Schechtman, *The Arab Refugee Problem* (New York: Philosophical Library, 1952), p. 6.

sincere efforts to turn away from the path of history and to seek the path of cooperation and partnership. The Arabs' reversal to the path of blood ran counter to this new international mood and engendered sympathy for the besieged Jewish state and antagonism to the Arab attempt to wipe it out at birth. The Arab dilemma in 1948—as seen by Count Folke Bernadotte, the United Nations mediator for Palestine—was that "the Jewish State, established under the cloak of United Nations authority, can be eliminated only by force. The United Nations, however, has decreed that force must not be employed. Therefore the Arab states must resign themselves to the presence of the Jewish State or pursue the reckless course of defying the United Nations and thereby incurring liabilities the full burden and danger of which cannot be calculated in advance."[7]

We cannot predict today what would have happened if the Arabs had accepted the partition resolution and not attempted to violate it by force. But almost certainly the Arabs would have been today in a stronger objective political position vis-à-vis Israel. The Jewish State would have had a smaller area and a higher percentage of Arab citizens. It would have found it much more difficult—and perhaps impossible—to absorb the mass immigration of the late 1940s and early 1950s. It is doubtful whether Israel would have reached its present population of 2.4 million Jews, or whether its economic and social development would have been so striking. The Arab attack and the constant pressure from outside created internal cohesion in Israel and forged the Jewish Israelis into a highly motivated community with a will to survive which sparked the remarkable achievements of the last twenty years.

A leading Israeli paper underlined this when it remarked:

"But for this *period of encapsulation* [emphasis added] in which we find ourselves the embryo Israel of 1948 might not have become consolidated so quickly, or the population have established itself in that time."[8]

Many thoughtful and responsible Arabs—who are as yet in-

7. Progress report of the United Nations Mediator on Palestine, General Assembly Supplement No. 11 (A/648), Paris, 1948, p. 6.
8. *Jerusalem Post*, May 13, 1965.

articulate, at least in public—have come to feel that the 1948 attack on Israel was a mistake. They know perfectly well in their heart of hearts—particularly after the shattering Arab defeat in the third war against Israel—that Israel cannot be eradicated; that it is a permanent feature of the Middle East scene and will remain so for as long as anyone can look ahead in human affairs; and that some form of political settlement will eventually have to be arrived at. But they are unable to face up to the implications of this growing realization. As one Westerner who knows the Arab mind well has put it:

"There is a very real psychological block, an involuntary shrinking from the idea, an unwillingness to accept the fact, and a sometimes shamefaced realization that many Arabs prefer delusion to the humiliating and, as they believe, unjust reality. Some serious-minded and responsible Arabs, when asked if the Arabs can forever refuse to settle with Israel, answer that they cannot bind their sons or their sons' sons. The next generation can possibly take a fresh look at the problem of Israel, but they acknowledge that they are simply incapable of doing so."[9]

Unable to contemplate the thought of recognizing Israel's presence—much less entering into actual trade and cultural relations with it—most Arabs react by circumventing the need to confront reality and setting up defense mechanisms designed to avoid the need for any immediate decision.

These defense mechanisms take various forms. The most common—so common that they have lost most of their impact—are bloodcurdling but imprecise threats. These satisfy the emotional need for revenge against the intruding Jews, without committing those who utter them to any specific course of action. Thus virtually every Arab leader has at some time told his people that "the sole solution is the disappearance of Israel." President Nasser of Egypt has spoken about "entering Palestine on a carpet of blood." On another occasion he declared:

"The road to the liberation of Palestine is strewn not with roses but with blood. Palestine was taken by force. It will be restored by

9. Charles D. Cremeans, *op. cit.*, p. 194.

force when we decide, when we are ready with two, three or four million soldiers from this (Arab) nation of 100 million."[10]

One of the most belligerent Arab spokesmen has been the Syrian General Amin Hafez, chairman of the Syrian Revolutionary Council in 1965. Here is a typically vainglorious statement:

"The Arab nation will not yield to threats and will accept no substitute for the liberation of Palestine and its return to its people as a purely Arab land."

Hafez told a press conference in Damascus that Syria was not afraid of the U.S. Sixth Fleet (which is stationed in the Mediterranean) or atomic bombs, as long as she believed in the justice of the Palestine case. He added:

"We are 100 million and the Israelis are only two and yet Arab rulers still unfortunately talk about the Sixth, Seventh, and Ninth Fleets."[11]

Perhaps the most hysterical of all Arab spokesmen is Achmed Shukairy, a refugee from Acre who headed the Palestine Liberation Organization until December 1967. Shukairy's speeches are virulent, xenophobic, and feverishly unreal. They are the best possible propaganda for Israel. Shukairy's speeches have done so much harm to the Arab cause that some Arabs have suspected him of being in the pay of the Israeli intelligence. This irresponsible demagogue is one of a number of prominent Arabs who are unfortunately still active, at the same low and vicious level, and who continue to feed on the fears and ignorance of the Arab masses through such radio stations as *Saut el Arab* (the Voice of the Arabs) in Cairo.

The frequency, vehemence, and wild nature of these threats have reduced their credibility to the point of disbelief. They no longer make much impact on world opinion, and the usual reaction in Israel to one of these belligerent speeches is a shrug of the shoulders. This tendency to resort to threats unbacked by concrete action is doubly unfortunate because, in addition to misleading the Arab masses, it reinforces the Israelis' conviction that "the Arabs are all talk"; this distorts the mutually erroneous image both sides have of one another even further.

10. *Jerusalem Post*, June 1, 1965.
11. *Ibid.*, July 23, 1965.

Since the six-day war even the ordinary Arab has stopped believing in his leaders' militant anti-Israel statements. And some perceptive Arabs have warned that the hysterical tone and inflamed rhetoric of their information media put world opinion on Israel's side during the tense days before June 5.

This subject was discussed by the thirteen-nation Arab Information Ministers Conference in Bizerte, Tunisia, after the war. Chadli Klibi, the Tunisian Secretary of State, told the opening session of this conference that "verbal excess" in Arab information media had become so great that "no one any longer pays more than relative attention to what we have to say."

Klibi said the emotional oratory beamed to the Arabs has "led our peoples so far astray that they cannot conceive of reality and its problems except through a veil of passion concealing a truth which can no longer be grasped."[12]

Another device the Arabs use, consciously or unconsciously, is postponing action on Palestine until some unspecified future date, and relying on time and their own monumental capacity for patience to solve the problem somehow. This approach can be summed up in the Arab proverb: "If you have a bad neighbor, be patient; either he'll move, or some calamity will force him to move."

Exponents of this line of thought frequently refer to the Crusader period and to the eventual expulsion of the invading Westerners in 1291, after two hundred years of siege. Nasser often makes references to the struggle against the Crusaders, who held the hills and the plain, then lost first the hills and then the plain, and then were forced out of the country altogether.

In July 1965 Nasser was interviewed by a team of Columbia Broadcasting System correspondents at his home in Alexandria. He observed that there was no opportunity for a peaceful settlement with Israel, because "whatever the Israelis say it is only propaganda."[13] This led to the following exchange:

CBS correspondent Winston Burdett: "Does this mean a peaceful settlement or peaceful negotiations are not possible? Does this mean that, in your view, war is inevitable?"

12. London *Times*, September 29, 1967: AFP dispatch from Tunis.
13. CBS: verbatim transcript of program, July 11, 1965, p. 12.

President Nasser: "Yes. It may not be today. It may be five years after, ten years, but the Arabs during the time of the days when they occupied a part of the Arab countries, they waited for seventy years."[14]

This clear hint at a parallel with the Crusader period has cropped up in other statements by Nasser. It was in a similar spirit that King Hussein of Jordan and President Shukri el Kuwatli of Syria met in 1956 at the tomb of Saladin the Great, "who defended the Holy Land and purged it of intruders."[15]

This analogy with the Crusader era is a typical and favorite Arab evasive tactic. It is apparently so emotionally satisfying because it combines wishful thinking with memories of one of the most glorious eras in Arab history.

Running through many of these attempts to cope with the tangible presence of Israel is a curious wistfulness, a deeply felt vision of a day in the future when Israel would collapse, be abandoned by its Jewish settlers, or disappear in some mysterious way. Thus in the same CBS interview Nasser made this significant comment about the dream of Arab unity in pursuit of a common objective:

"People sometimes live on dreams, and people (who come) after that can fulfil these dreams. If we cannot fulfil the dreams of unity because of the complications which we face, . . . those who will come after us will fulfil them."[16]

And on July 23, 1966, the First Vice President of Egypt, the late Field Marshal Abdel Hakim Amer, told the annual military parade in Cairo that "the armed forces must be ready at all times to deter Israeli aggression and then advance to liquidate it in the battle that every Arab dreams of."[17]

Humiliated by the constant reminder of Israel's existence and growing strength, yet impotent to remove it, the Arabs comforted themselves with the distant vision of its vanishing in a manner that history would decide. They have paid the price for this

14. *Ibid.*
15. Walter Zander, "Arab Nationalism and Israel," *Commentary*, July 1956.
16. CBS: verbatim transcript of program, July 11, 1965, p. 16.
17. *The New York Times*, July 24, 1966.

chronic inability to face reality. The Arabs have become prisoners of a dream. In refusing to modify or abandon it in the light of experience, they have placed their faith in fantasies meant to exorcise the demon of Israel. These neurotic figments of the imagination are now being passed to the younger generation by the generation which suffered on the rack of the Palestine tragedy.

A Jordanian Arabic textbook for the fourth to sixth grades, found on the West Bank after the Israeli troops captured the area, contained these model sentences used in teaching grammar:

"The homeland has been stolen."
"The Arabs will not rest until their Paradise is returned to them."
"Holy war is a duty."
"The enemy was routed."
"Our army has torn the enemy apart."
"The number of survivors is very small."[18]

In another Jordanian school textbook the sentence *al hisan jamil* ("The horse is beautiful") was followed by *al Yahoud a'ada lil Arab* ("The Jews are the enemies of the Arabs").[19]

Before the school day in a Palestinian refugee camp opened, all pupils stood at attention turning their faces towards Palestine and chanting an oath in which they pledged:

"Palestine is our country,
Our aim is to return.
Death does not frighten us,
Palestine is ours.
We will never forget her.
Another homeland we will never accept!
Our Palestine, witness, O God and History:
We promise to shed our blood for you!"[20]

So the dream is passed on to another generation, which is imprisoned by it in turn.

The Arab states have made various attempts to implement their vision of Israel as a passing phase. But these programs have been

18. *Jerusalem Post*, August 15, 1967.
19. Verbal communication to the author, July 1967.
20. A. L. Tibawi, "Visions of the Return: The Palestine Arab Refugees in Arabic Poetry and Art," *Middle East Journal*, late autumn 1963, p. 523.

pursued with diminishing vigor over the years, as it became evident that they were failing to have any effect on Israel's viability and progress.

One of these concerted efforts was the boycott campaign, aimed at companies and countries trading with Israel. But this campaign has only underlined the Arabs' genius for political masochism. The legalistic application of the boycott often hurt the Arabs more than Israel. An American ship which brought a cargo of wheat to Beirut several years ago, after a stop at Haifa, was forced to travel to Cyprus to purge itself. Only then was it permitted to take on the wheat again and deliver it to Beirut.

Two years ago the Lebanese boycott office refused to allow Walt Disney's "Sleeping Beauty" to be shown because the horse in the movie had an Old Testament name—Samson. The Lebanese boycott director demanded that it should be changed to the Arab equivalent of Simson. But this would have required a new soundtrack. So "Sleeping Beauty" was not shown in Lebanon.

Sal Mineo, the American movie actor, was once blacklisted for having played a Zionist fanatic in "Exodus." But the ban was lifted after he portrayed an Arab nationalist in another movie, "Escape From Bahrein."

After twenty years of threatening to boycott any company that does business with Israel, the Arab campaign has been breached all along the line. The Hilton International Corporation, for example, has hotels in Cairo, Morocco, Tunis—and Tel Aviv. The Sheraton Corporation of America, which has a hotel in Israel, signed a contract in the summer of 1967 to run a hotel in Cairo. Several major airlines fly to Israel and the Arab states. And if the Arabs were to implement the boycott consistently, they would cut themselves off from international trade, commerce, and cultural contacts.[21]

To understand the way the Arabs approach what they consider a threat from Israel, it is instructive to study their reaction to the construction of Israel's National Water Carrier, which became a focal point of tension in 1965. This pipeline, carrying water from the Jordan River and the Sea of Galilee to the south and the

21. *The New York Times*, October 17, 1966.

Negev, was constructed under the plan drawn up in 1955 by President Dwight D. Eisenhower's envoy to the Middle East, the late Eric Johnston. This plan was accepted by the Arab countries involved, but rejected by the Arab League on purely political grounds. Israel proceeded to carry out its part of the project alone, with the moral and financial backing of the United States, and on the understanding that it would keep to the framework of the original Johnston plan and not exceed the quantity of water allocated to it under that plan.

When Israel's pipeline was almost completed and nearing the testing stage, the Arab countries threatened to divert the sources of the Jordan in Lebanon and Syria if Israel used the waters of what was "an Arab river." Several top-level Arab summit conferences were held to plan and execute this diversion project.

Meanwhile Israel began operating the pipeline without fanfare on May 26, 1964.[22] Small-scale work on the Syrian and Lebanese diversion was started, but this was halted after several border incidents in which Israeli guns and planes destroyed Syrian bulldozers and other earthmoving equipment. The grandiose scheme for setting up a United Arab Command, under the Egyptian General Ali Ali Amer, did not blossom into a military force capable of protecting the Syrian and Lebanese diversions. And neither of these two countries was prepared to face Israel alone.

While Jordan—the third country directly concerned—claimed to be proceeding with its diversion project, and even insisted that this would reduce the amount of water available for use by Israel, the fact of the matter was that the East Ghor Canal was financed by the United States, which was also financing the Israeli pipeline. Clearly Washington was not going to sink money into any water project designed to offset another scheme paid for by the United States Government.

In September 1965 the Arab monarchs and presidents met once more at Casablanca. There they heard a pessimistic report by United Arab Command head General Amer. It would take at least four years of intensive preparation, he told the conference,

22. Article by Mila Ohel on Jordan-Negev pipeline, *Maariv*, May 26, 1965.

before the Arab armies would be in a position to challenge Israel. And his forces would need men and equipment costing $420 million. Meanwhile the water of the Jordan went on flowing to Israel's arid south, unhindered.[23]

The Arabs themselves had tried to turn this constructive Israeli project into the most decisive trial of strength since the Sinai campaign. Now it became instead a test of the credibility of their threats. The inevitable setback led to feelings of deep dejection. This was accompanied by second thoughts which placed the entire campaign against Israel in a more realistic light. Eric Rouleau, the well-informed *Le Monde* correspondent at the Casablanca conference, quoted an unidentified Maghreb delegate as saying: "Our problem at present is less to destroy Israel than to contain her in her frontiers and to dissuade her from pursuing her aggression on the Arab world."[24]

The Syrian Ba'ath leader, Michel Aflek, declared that Israel's existence was "unacceptable." However, he went in a more sober vein, "we don't think armed conflict with Israel in the near future is possible or desirable. For the rest, we don't know what the future holds in store for us and whether the Palestine problem will be resolved by force or not, taking into account changes which will occur in the world and in Israel itself."[25]

Another Ba'ath leader, Dr. Mounif al Razzaz, told *Le Monde*: "We moved too late to prevent Israel appropriating the waters of the Jordan River. The Zionist state is busy fertilizing the Negev, while our own water schemes won't be finished for three or four years. Even if completed our diversion would only slightly reduce the flow in Israel, although salinity would of course be increased. Frankly, we don't think the game worth the candle."[26]

The growing Arab realization that Israel was there to stay, and the frustration this engendered, was intensified by President Lyndon B. Johnson's announcement in February 1964 that the United States and Israel would cooperate in the desalting of sea water. The joint desalting project was a political master stroke. It

23. London *Observer*, September 19, 1965.
24. *Le Monde*, September 16, 1965.
25. *Ibid.*
26. *Ibid.*

demonstrated to the Arabs that even if they succeeded in diverting or salting some of Israel's water in several years' time—after spending some $400 million on the United Arab Command and at least another $30 million on the diversion itself—Israel would more than make up this loss from the water desalted from the Mediterranean.

While the Arabs could perhaps make out a thin case for the Jordan being "an Arab river," no Arab spokesman would venture to claim that the Mediterranean was an Arab sea. The water of the Mediterranean was there for the taking, and if any country had the energy, skill, and know-how to turn it into fresh water, world opinion would only stand on the sidelines and applaud. The desalting decision emphasized Israel's positive approach to its problems—and the Arabs' negative approach to theirs.

Washington's emphatic and enthusiastic support for the joint desalting program aggravated the gnawing feeling among some Arab circles that Israel could no longer be removed from the Middle East scene without a regional upheaval. Time seemed to be on Israel's side. This feeling was expressed by one of the most respected papers in the Arab world, the Beirut *Al Khayat*, when it wrote:

"In another seven years at most Israel will drink the water of the sea—but not as the result of an Arab action which will throw its inhabitants into the sea and subject them to thirst and certain death, but in the positive sense of this term: through desalting, drinking the fresh water and irrigating fields, as the result of Israeli-U.S. cooperation."[27]

Here we see the entire tragedy of the Arab attempt to respond to Israel's existence, step by step: the initial emotional, irrational threat; then the slow awareness of what this entails in practical terms; the growing realization that the threat does not constitute a realistic course of political action; and the lurking setback, the humiliation, the feeling of impotence and inferiority. This has been the pattern of every Arab confrontation with Israel since 1948. And the same inexorable process was repeated almost mechanically during the summer of 1967.

27. *Al Khayat*, August 12, 1965.

Some Arab writers have tried courageously to analyze this self-destructive urge in the Arab makeup. One of them, Cecil Hourani, a former adviser to President Habib Bourguiba of Tunisia, claimed that the Arabs suffered from a profound psychological weakness: *"that which we do not like we pretend does not exist."* Because of this unwillingness to accept as real what is disliked, *"when reality catches up with us, it is always too late.* At every debacle we regret that we did not accept a situation which no longer exists. In 1948 we regretted that we had not accepted the 1947 UN plea for partition. In May 1967 we were trying to go back to pre-Suez. Today we would be happy—and are actually demanding the UN—to go back to things as they were before June 5, 1967. From every defeat we reap a new regret and a new nostalgia, but never seem to learn a new lesson."[28]

Throughout the last twenty years the Arab world has confronted the same basic dilemma it faced in 1948: whether to follow the path of history or the path of cooperation in its attitude toward Israel. Throughout this period no Arab more personified this dilemma, more expressed the vagaries and hesitations of Arab policy, than Gamal Abdel Nasser, President of the United Arab Republic. In a very real sense, the fluctuations in Nasser's fortunes and his present tragedy have paralleled the ebb and flow of Arab policies during the last two decades.

28. Cecil Hourani, "The Moment of Truth," *Encounter*, November 1967, pp. 4–5.

3 *Nasser's Dilemma*

GAMAL ABDEL NASSER has been personally involved in all three Arab-Israeli wars to date. During the first one in 1948 he was an officer in the Egyptian army trapped in the Faluja plains, in southern Israel. During the second war in 1956 and the third in 1967 he was President of Egypt.

No comparable Western statesman could have survived the military defeats of 1956 and 1967. Yet Nasser did. When he announced on Cairo Radio after the six-day war that he was resigning as President, the announcer came on the air immediately afterward, but broke down. People cried in the studio. Thousands of Egyptians blocked the streets of Cairo calling upon Nasser to stay. Messages poured in from all over the country. And of course Nasser stayed on, despite his staggering "setback"—the official Egyptian euphemism—in the long-awaited confrontation with Israel. He is the rubber man of Middle East politics, gifted with an astonishing resilience which enables him to turn his moments of most profound humiliation into triumphant recoveries.

This is partly a tribute to his *baraka*—a potent Arab concept signifying grace, charisma, unique personal authority amounting almost to the prophetic. He is a tribal leader, a master of radio and television oratory who understands the power of these media in the predominantly oral Arab culture. Nasser's critics often claim that the Arabs cling to him out of weakness, a sort of masochistic longing for strong leadership. Yet the outstanding fact about Nasser is that he is still there: after Suez, after the debacle of June 1967, after so many other Arab leaders have been assassinated or overthrown. He is worshiped by millions, hated by millions.

He cannot be ignored. No full peace in the Middle East will be possible until Israel and Egypt can find a way to live together.

Nasser's policies toward Israel often seem haphazard, the product of momentary whims and aberrations. But viewed in perspective since he took office in 1954 his approach will be seen to have an underlying consistency completely in line with his own concept of Egypt's role in the Arab world and his role at the head of Egypt.

Nasser's aims towards Israel have always been twofold:

1. To restore the land bridge to Jordan, Syria, and Iraq which Cairo lost in 1948 after Israel's establishment and to attain this either by eliminating Israel or reaching a settlement which would contain Israel, remove its potential threat to Arab sovereignty, and open up the routes to Beirut, Damascus, and Baghdad.

2. To use Israel as a lever for social reform inside Egypt, revolts against the existing regimes in the rich oil-producing countries of the Arab East, and eventually the hegemony of Cairo over the entire Arab world, under his own leadership.

In order to attain these aims Nasser could not afford to appear willing to come to terms with Israel. He had at all times to be in the forefront of the campaign against the Jewish state. At the same time, he knew that the Egyptian army was no match for Israel's taut, highly organized fighting force. So he decided on a policy of no-peace, no-war with Israel: a verbal aggression backed up by a worldwide political offensive, but without actual physical confrontation unless this could be carried out in an undercover manner, without risking large numbers of men or any fatal loss of prestige.

During the 1954–1956 period—Nasser's first two years in office as the open leader of the revolt against Farouk—this led to the guerrilla war directed against Israel from the Gaza Strip and exploiting the Palestinian refugees whom Nasser kept there as pawns and saboteurs. Israel used its momentary union of interests with the Britain of Anthony Eden and the France of Guy Mollet to break this ring of active enmity and halt the fedayeen attacks upon its southern flanks. After the 1956 fighting the United Nations Emergency Force patrolled the border between Israel and Egypt, which became nearly as quiet as Israel's border with Lebanon.

The UNEF protected Nasser as much as it did Israel. Behind it he could fulminate, threaten, call for Arab unity and convince most Arabs that he was their main hope of conquering Israel, without having to produce results on the ground. There were hundreds of minor and major border incidents on the Israeli-Syrian and Israeli-Jordan borders after 1957, but almost none along the border with Egypt and the Gaza Strip.

From time to time Nasser changed his tactics. When he needed wheat from the United States, he made pro-Western gestures. When he required Soviet arms, he offered Moscow naval facilities in the Mediterranean. At certain periods he emphasized Egypt's ties with the emerging African nations; at others he claimed the leadership of the neutralist bloc along with Yugoslavia's Tito and India's Nehru. Many Western statesmen or journalists who met him came away soothed by his apparent moderation and convinced he was not a hard-liner toward Israel. Yet a few days later he could deliver a tirade to a cheering, hysterical Cairo crowd almost as virulent and fanatical as Shukairy at his worst.

This chameleon performance was designed to do one thing and one thing only: to keep Nasser and his revolutionary Cairo regime in the van of Arab politics; to allow no one to usurp the ascendancy he claimed and jealously guarded; to seek constantly for chinks both in Israel's defenses and the armor of his Arab rivals; to exploit every nuance of regional intrigue and global tension in order to further his own position and win gains from his real or imaginary opponents. There are many parallels between Nasser's Egypt and de Gaulle's France. And the role Nasser has played in the Middle East has been remarkably similar to the role de Gaulle has played in Western Europe: the same seemingly broad view of history, which turns out to be based on a selfish, narrow nationalism; the same outwardly liberal and progressive stance, concealing a ruthless and arrogant dictatorship. Even their press conference styles are similar, and their curious blend of charm and malice.

This drive to dominate not only Egypt, but the Middle East— perhaps ultimately North Africa and the northeast corner of Africa—led Nasser into several costly blunders. The 1958 union with Syria proved abortive and broke up in 1961, when Syria withdrew. (Egypt still calls itself the United Arab Republic—the only relic of this fiasco.) 1962 saw the beginning of the long-drawn-out war in the Yemen, which sapped Egypt of more money and energy than it could afford and at one time saw 50,000 Egyptian troops—a quarter of Nasser's army—stuck down in the sands and grim mountains of southern Arabia. At home too he faced discontent from Communists on the left and the Moslem Brotherhood on the right. In Saudi Arabia King Faisal ousted his arch-reactionary brother Saud and formed a monarchic focal point of resistance to the waves of Arab socialism emanating from Cairo.

In 1963 the Ba'ath Party staged a successful coup in Syria and seized power. This party, which had branches in several Arab capitals, held progressive ideas about the need for reforms. For a time it seemed that Damascus might draw closer to Cairo again and concentrate upon domestic problems, with Israel slipping into the background.

But Syria is an unpredictable country, the odd man out in the Arab East. It lacks a clear identity or national purpose. Its people are volatile, fanatical, xenophobic, suspicious of outsiders. It has always been more vehemently anti-Israel than any Arab country, although it has less Palestinian refugees than Jordan or Egypt. Now, under the Ba'ath, and torn by rival factions who blocked any real progress at home, Syria turned its pent-up energies toward Israel and demanded that the struggle against the Zionist state be stepped up.

In 1964 Syria sparked the Arab attempt to divert the waters of the Jordan away from the pipeline which would carry them through Israel to the Negev. Damascus accused Nasser of soft-pedaling the campaign against Israel and hinted that he was doing this to qualify for wheat shipments from the United States. Guerrilla activity on the Syrian border was stepped up sharply. These actions were small-scale and caused little damage. But Syria used them to claim that it was pursuing the battle against Israel, and Cairo was not.

Nasser could not allow himself to play second fiddle to Syria in anti-Israel saber-rattling. He called several summit conferences and proposed the formation of a United Arab Command, with the aim of ending any separate action by the Ba'ath militants and regaining control of all armed forces along Israel's borders.

But the United Arab Command never got off the ground. Israel's pipeline began working ahead of schedule. And Syria increased its harassing tactics in the Jordan Valley and around the Sea of Galilee. Israel retaliated and blew up equipment used in Syria's "diversion scheme"—which was really nothing more than a shallow excavation that never looked like robbing Israel of any quantity of water.

In the summer of 1965 the Middle East seemed to be heading for one of the periodic bouts of senseless violence which attack it like a contagious disease. Nasser was seriously concerned about the danger that Syria would involve him in another war. With his best units stalemated in the Yemen and Egypt's economy in serious trouble, this was the last thing he wanted. Nasser suspected that the Ba'ath leaders were laying a trap for him which could lead to his being overthrown, either as the result of another defeat by Israel or because the Arab masses might lose faith in his leadership. He decided to avoid this trap.

On June 30, 1965, four hundred delegates to the second annual conference of the Palestine Liberation Movement assembled at Cairo University for the opening address by President Nasser. This would normally have been one of those rabble-rousing occasions so regretted by the Jews and Arabs who favor a new moderation in the exchanges between the two peoples. But instead the stunned delegates heard the frankest speech Nasser had ever made to a public Arab rally.

In his two-hour speech Nasser admitted: "We are at present still unable to protect diversion works." He proposed that the Arabs should hold up the diversion projects "until we are strong enough to protect them."

He took issue with the Syrians and others who were demanding immediate action against Israel:

"Let us face reality and stop deluding ourselves. We must face facts today and not close our eyes. Today each Arab state is afraid of the others. We are beset by suspicions, contradictions, and mistrust. Some countries demand that we immediately open war on Israel on several fronts. But how can we go to war when we are in such a state of disunity and lack of mutual confidence?

"Our Syrian brothers say, 'Let us attack Israel tomorrow or the day after.' Israel has attacked Syria's diversion projects. But if Israel attacks Syria, do I attack Israel? That means letting Israel set the time for the battle. But is this the wise course? Is it logical that I attack Israel when there are 50,000 Egyptian soldiers in Yemen? I say: let us postpone the diversion. We must provide for Arab defense before we can carry out our ultimate goal and liberate Palestine."[1]

Probably no other Arab leader could have told his people such home truths without being branded as a traitor to the cause of Palestine. The fact that Nasser chose a Palestinian Arab audience for this speech shows that he was motivated by more than just a desire to hit back at Syria. He was also trying to extricate himself from an impossible situation in which he would have had to stake all his personal prestige on a vigorous move against Israel.

By refusing to be pressured into a war with Israel over the waters of the Jordan, Nasser adopted a posture aptly described by a Western journalist in mid-1965:

"The Arab states bordering on Israel want neither to wage a war which they suspect they cannot win or to negotiate a peace from which they at present have little to gain. They are conducting a holding operation. They feel that the status quo—however baffling, intractable, and seemingly hopeless—is as fair a position as any."[2]

But Nasser was careful to avoid giving the Syrians a chance to accuse him of selling out to Israel. He continued his propaganda offensive against the Jewish state, insisting that he stood by his commitment to destroy it at some future date, when "the international circumstances are propitious."[3]

In July 1965 he told a team of American television interviewers that he could never accept the existence of Israel or coexistence with Israel. "The only solution is force," he declared emphatically.

CBS correspondent Frank Kearns: "Normally you have always

1. *Jewish Observer and Middle East Review*, June 4, 1965.
2. Patrick Seale, dispatch to London *Observer* from Beirut, May 2, 1965.
3. London *Jewish Chronicle*, September 3, 1965.

been a champion of peaceful settlements. Now, here is a case where you said a peaceful settlement is impossible."

President Nasser: "Peace needs two parts to agree. And if they want to agree about peace they must be logical.

"Suppose someone occupied California and expelled the people of California from California—brought other people from abroad to settle. Are you ready to negotiate peace with him and leave California to him? It is simply a question like that."[4]

On the thirteenth anniversary of the revolt against Farouk, Nasser spoke to a mass rally in Cairo. He told the crowd: "The Palestine people must recover their usurped country. The war between us and Israel is imperative. We must be the ones to decide its time."[5]

Nasser took Shukairy under his wing and set up the Palestine Liberation Army, as a counter to the Syrian guerrillas and proof that he was determined to wage active war against Israel, when he judged the time right. This was another example of Nasser's ability to oscillate between moderate and extreme policies according to the needs of the moment. Through the summer of 1965 and the dying crisis over the Jordan waters Nasser maneuvered between the extremist Syrians and Shukairy's supporters in Cairo; between the Saudi Arabian and Yemeni royalists he was fighting and the Abdullah al Salal puppet regime in Yemen; between attempts to impress Western public opinion with his reasonableness and efforts to obtain further massive aid from the Soviet Union.

But, although Nasser managed to perform this masterly tight-rope act, he could not conceal the fundamental difficulties facing him at home, where his position was not one of commanding strength. After thirteen years under a revolutionary government, Egypt's economy was in bad shape. Six out of every ten loaves of bread baked in Egypt that year were made from American wheat, and only the large shipments of grain supplied by Washington prevented a food shortage. In 1965 the Egyptians consumed 3.7 million tons of wheat, of which only 1.5 million tons were homegrown. The balance of 2.2 million tons was imported, mainly from the United States. In 1966 imports rose to 2.4 million tons,

4. CBS: verbatim transcript of program, July 11, 1965, p. 15.
5. *Jewish Observer and Middle East Review,* July 30, 1965.

and the United States Government was asked to supply about 2 million tons. But in June 1966 the Johnson Administration discontinued grain shipments to Egypt.

Egypt's basic economic problem is its phenomenal population growth rate of 2.7 per cent—one of the highest in the world. This adds 800,000 people a year to the 31 million population. The population of Egypt as a whole has doubled since 1930, and the number of people living in Cairo has quadrupled.[6]

Although Egypt covers an area of 385,000 square miles, it has only 6 million acres of arable land for its 31 million people. Former Premier Zakaria Mohieddin has pointed out that the completion of the Aswan High Dam, which will add another million acres of fertile soil, will not solve this problem.[7] By the time the dam is completed, several million more Egyptians will be born, and the million extra acres will be needed to grow food for them, instead of being used to improve the living standards of the existing population.

A birth control program has been launched. But President Nasser took a long time to commit himself to birth control. He did not publicly endorse the principle until 1962, and the Supreme Council for Family Planning was created only in November 1965.[8]

There was some religious opposition to birth control, although the Al Azhar Moslem authorities accepted the principle. Some members of the Arab Socialist Union still hint that population control is a Zionist-imperialist plot. But the program has gone ahead, although far too slowly; only 750,000 women have joined the scheme. And the population continues to rise inexorably.

Egypt's economic situation is gloomy. During the early 1960s the growth rate was between 6 and 7 per cent. Now it has slipped to between 2 and 4 per cent—barely enough to keep pace with the 2.7 per cent annual increase in population. Inflation has been reaching 15 per cent a year. The government deficit was $275 million in 1965. The national debt is estimated at $1.5–2 billion—

6. Neville Brown, "Birth Control in Egypt," New Statesman, February 3, 1967.
7. Hedrick Smith in The New York Times, November 28, 1966.
8. Neville Brown, op. cit.

more than $100 million of it overdue to Western sources alone.[9]

Part of the difficulties undoubtedly spring from the enormous sums Egypt spends on defense. The official budget for defense in 1966 was $400 million.[10] But in actual fact Cairo spends roughly $650 million a year—or almost 30 per cent of its annual expenditure—on military and security services. Since Nasser signed the first arms deal with the Soviet Union in 1955 over $1 billion has been diverted from development to pay for Russian weapons, homemade jets and rockets, and the war of attrition in Yemen.[11]

Small wonder then that Nasser was reluctant to enter into a full-scale war with Israel over the Jordan waters. Throughout 1965 it seemed that he was being forced to turn his attention to Egypt's pressing domestic problems, while reducing his involvement—or what his opponents consider his interference—in inter-Arab politics.

In short, Nasser's central role in the Arab world and the non-aligned bloc was being cut down to the size of his ability to handle problems at home. This did not diminish the Egyptian President's standing as the most prominent Arab leader, a man who had to be reckoned with by anyone who sought a way to the Arab world. But as one of the most intuitive Western observers of the Middle East put it in July 1965:

"The conclusion seems inescapable that this summer has seen the end of President Nasser's ten-year attempt to browbeat the Arabs into a united front under his direction."[12]

In the same year a former United States Ambassador to the United Arab Republic and a friend of the Arabs, Dr. John Badeau (now Director of the Near and Middle East Institute at Columbia University) offered Nasser some public advice:

"The sound development of the Valley of the Nile economy," he wrote, "with resulting success in raising living standards will do much more to win Egypt a good reputation in the Middle East and abroad than strident and vicious radio broadcasts. The real measure of the Egyptian revolution's place in history will not be

9. Hedrick Smith, *loc. cit.*
10. Middle East survey, *Atlantic Monthly*, September 1966.
11. Hedrick Smith, *loc. cit.*
12. Patrick Seale in dispatch to London *Observer*, July 18, 1965.

the extent to which it can outdo other Arabs in invective, but the degree to which it can stand upon its actual accomplishments of a better society."[13]

Thirteen years after his revolution Nasser was finding out how sound this advice was. He was also discovering that no statesman can long indulge in adventures abroad unless his base at home is solid, that strength abroad cannot be founded on weakness at home.

If this had led Nasser to follow a path of genuine moderation in his attitude to Israel, the region as a whole would not have suffered from such chronic tension. The trouble was that Nasser sought moderation in the privacy of Arab conferences, but preached extremism in public because he did not want to be outdone by other Arab leaders. The tragedy of Nasser is that he became a captive of Arab public opinion, which itself was imprisoned by an impossible dream. Instead of leading, of revealing the courage to be authentically moderate, Nasser allowed himself to sink to the level of the mob. He would have done better to heed the words of Dr. Badeau:

"The Egyptian policy toward Israel over the past few years has been encouragingly moderate. Nasser's public eschewal of aggressive military action as an answer to the current Israel utilization of Jordan waters is a case in point. The trouble is that Presidential speeches often outrun Presidential policies. The Israel dispute is unnecessarily dragged in on every occasion." Dr. Badeau pointed out that "vague verbal attacks on Israel," made by Nasser for domestic consumption, were taken at their face value by world public opinion.[14]

While Nasser wove his tortuous path between the rival camps in the Arab world, alternately breathing fire and pleading restraint, the most vehement anti-Israel line was being taken in another Arab country. In 1965 Syria replaced Egypt as the Arab country most active against Israel, both on the air and in actual guerrilla warfare. This was mainly because of its open sponsorship of the Fatah group.

13. Dr. John Badeau, "The U.S.A. and the U.A.R.: A Crisis in Confidence," *Foreign Affairs*, January 1965.
14. *Ibid.*

The word *El Fatah* means "The Phantom." It is the name of a small extremist group formed and trained in Syria. Its military arm is called El Asifa—"The Storm." Most of these guerrilla fighters are former Palestinians, recruited from the refugee camps in Jordan or Syria. But their motivation is as much mercenary as ideological. They are paid for their raids on a fee basis: the equivalent of $10 to $15 for every incursion into Israeli territory.

Since January 1965 these marauders have been sent into Israel to blow up houses, bomb pipelines, or mine roads along the frontiers. Most of these raids were planned in Syria, but the saboteurs crossed into Israel from Jordan or Lebanon, with the transparent purpose of embroiling Israel in armed combat with these two countries. The tracks found after one of these actions usually led to the Jordanian or Lebanese borders and showed no signs of any effort to obliterate them.

El Asifa is not a large organization. Informed sources estimate that there are only several hundred "storm troopers." Many of their sabotage attempts have been amateurish, and the damage done largely insignificant. Often they seemed like the actions of men who were doing the least possible to earn their payments from Damascus. But these deeds have been inflated and glorified out of all proportion by the Fatah communiques, intended to bolster the shaky Syrian regime and demonstrate that it alone was carrying on the struggle for "the liberation of Palestine," despite Cairo's comparative inactivity. On August 17, 1966, Damascus Radio—an official information medium—declared:

"Syria has initiated the slogan of the War of Liberation as an effective method: the only way of bringing our masses to victory in the battle against Zionism."

And on October 27, 1966, the same broadcasting station asserted that "the main factor upsetting the enemy's self-confidence is the acts of the fedayeen (literally, suicide squads), which will make it easier for the Arabs to liquidate Israel. It is armed operations that have shaken the very existence of Israel and will cause Israel great anxiety."

During 1965 and 1966 there were over seventy such raids inside Israel, conducted by Syrian-backed agents working together with Achmed Shukairy's Palestine Liberation Organization, which received money and arms from Cairo. The Jordanian and Lebanese governments realized perfectly well that the same people who infiltrated into Israel from villages along the border could one day turn against the elected regimes in Amman and Beirut. With this danger in mind, King Hussein in particular clamped down on the Fatah cells operating inside Jordan. After some of the gravest incidents the Jordanian press reported the arrest of saboteurs on their way to the Israeli border, and some of these men were jailed.

In the beginning the Fatah activities aroused little concern in Israel, which did not want to dignify this body by giving it free publicity and the heroic status it was seeking. But gradually the penetrations of the border became deeper, and the guerrillas' methods more professional. These clandestine operations seemed to be setting a pattern for a growing guerrilla war against Israel, in which the Arab governments would not be officially involved. The use of hit-and-run methods sidestepped the need for conventional army methods and neutralized Israel's superior military techniques and training.

Another disturbing development was that the PLO began playing a more active role and using refugees living in Jordan for attacks on Israel. Shukairy boasted openly, in an address at a PLO camp in Syria on June 7, 1966, that his officers and men were being trained "in the weapons of liberation and the experience of the Chinese People's Republic" and that arms were being received from Peking. According to sources in Cairo, rifles, pistols, grenades, and bazookas were being supplied, and PLO units which were training in China were expected to be sent to North Vietnam.[15]

The links between Damascus and Peking were further evidenced when the director of the PLO office in Damascus wrote in the official organ, Al Ba'ath, that "Chairman Mao's thesis of people's war was the only way to liberate Palestine." This statement was quoted with approval by Peking.[16]

15. *The New York Times*, June 10, 1966.
16. New China News Agency (NCNA), August 21, 1966: quoted by W. A. C. Adie, "China's Middle East Strategy," *The World Today* (London), August 1967.

All these indications naturally increased concern in Israel. This deepening anxiety came to a head in October 1966, when four Israeli border guards were killed near the Sea of Galilee, close to the Syrian frontier. Instead of retaliating, the Israeli Government acted on Washington's advice and took the issue to the Security Council.

On October 14 Israeli Foreign Minister Abba Eban told the Council that Israel requested its "assistance in restoring peace and security on Israel's borders." He described how the border police jeep had been blown up by a mine laid fifteen hundred yards inside Israeli territory and added: "The tracks of three men wearing rubber-soled boots led toward Syrian territory."

Surveying the "single organized system of violence," directed from Syria, Eban asked "whether it is legitimate for a neighboring state to fight against Israel by guerrilla war when it recoils from a confrontation of regular forces."

He called upon the Security Council "to express itself in clear condemnation of a concerted, organized, and proclaimed policy of aggression." Israel, he said, was ready "to discuss with Syrian representatives the methods and measures to be adopted in order to make the frontier utterly secure against all military actions, infiltrations, and guerrilla war."

But Israel's hopes were dashed. Its action in accordance with international law produced nothing more effective, after a protracted debate, than a mild resolution deploring the incidents and the loss of life and "inviting" the Government of Syria "to strengthen its measures for preventing incidents that constitute a violation of the general armistice agreement." The Council called upon the Syrian and Israeli Governments "to facilitate the work of the UN Truce Supervision Organization" and "to refrain from any action that might increase the tension in the area."

The United States, the United Kingdom, France, New Zealand, Holland, Nigeria, Uganda, Japan, Uruguay, and Argentina voted for this resolution. But it was vetoed by the Soviet Union, in its by now almost automatic defense of any Arab state in any dispute with Israel. In this case Moscow had another motive for applying the veto. It was engaged in a struggle with Peking for influence in Damascus. Using the veto could show the Ba'ath leaders who their true friends were. And Peking is not represented on the Security Council.

This ineffectual action by the world's highest international tribunal built up a feeling of frustration and resentment within Israel. Public opinion was not reassured by the United States claim—in private talks with Israeli officials—that Israel had won "a moral victory." Almost to a man Israelis argued that the Security Council debates were completely futile; that the proceedings were one-sided, because the Arabs could always rely on the Soviet veto in a pinch, whereas the United States had never vetoed an anti-Israel resolution; and that when the next serious incident took place, the Israeli Government should take action itself and not make a further complaint to the Council.

Even while the Security Council was meeting in New York, fresh incidents were taking place along Israel's borders. On October 14 a military vehicle was attacked by a group of saboteurs at Nehusha, south of Jerusalem. Mines were laid near the Syrian border and on the shores of the Dead Sea. On October 27 the main railroad line between Tel Aviv and Jerusalem was sabotaged. A water pipeline near Masada was cut three days later. The situation was becoming intolerable. Clearly the UN's impotence had encouraged the diehards of Fatah and the PLO and led them to believe they could shelter behind the Soviet veto.

There had to be a showdown sooner or later. It did not take long. On November 12 an Israeli command car patrolling a border road north of Arad, in the northern Negev, detonated a mine planted by infiltrators near the Jordanian border. Three soldiers were killed and five wounded.

The following morning at 6 A.M. Israeli troops in jeeps, personnel carriers, and tanks entered the village of Es Samu, south of Hebron, which had been harboring terrorists operating in Israel, only three miles away. The Israeli action was deliberately taken in broad daylight, so that the Jordanian villagers could be evacuated from their homes. Forty empty houses were demolished by sappers.

While this was being done, twenty truckloads of Arab Legionnaires were rushed to the scene and clashed with Israeli soldiers, while Jordanian Hawker Hunter jets fought Israeli Mirages over-head. Fifteen Jordanian soldiers and three civilians were killed, and one Hawker Hunter plane was shot down. At 10 A.M.—four hours after the operation began—the Israeli troops withdrew, leaving most of Es Samu in rubble as a warning against cooperat-ing with the Fatah and PLO saboteurs.

The day after the Es-Samu operation Prime Minister Levi Eshkol told the Israeli Knesset:

"No country where the saboteurs find shelter and through whose territory they pass on their way to Israel can be exempt from re-sponsibility for their actions."

The attack on Jordan led to rioting against King Hussein in such Palestinian Arab centers as Hebron, Ramallah, and Nablus. The Es Samu retaliation caused dismay in Washington, where it was felt Israel's action helped the militant Arab left and lessened U.S. influence with such relatively moderate Arab leaders as Hussein. No one had any illusions about what would happen if Hussein was toppled because of his failure to respond to the attack on Es Samu. This would almost certainly have led to the formation of a pro-Nasser government on Israel's eastern flank and the threat of an Israeli thrust against the West Bank of the Jordan.

There was an urgent need to bolster King Hussein and prevent any loss of internal stability in Jordan. The United States issued a strong statement regretting both "the large-scale retaliatory raid" on Es Samu and "the terrorist incidents in Israel which preceded this raid." During the subsequent Security Council session the United States supported the resolution which was approved by 14–0, with New Zealand abstaining. The Security Council cen-sured Israel and clearly implied that it would face possible sanc-tions if it conducted further reprisal operations.

The severe Council resolution mollified public opinion in Jordan and helped to end the rioting against King Hussein. But—as so often happens with Security Council resolutions—it ignored more questions than it answered. It left Israeli public opinion angry and frustrated. It seemed to establish a double standard under which Arab guerrillas could operate under a cover of anonymity—although covertly backed by recognizable governments—while if Israel launched an overt, official action it would automatically be condemned.

Most important of all, the Security Council gave no clearcut answer to the question worrying everyone concerned with Middle East peace: what should Israel do the next time Arab marauders crossed its borders to harass, pillage, and kill?

As Israeli UN Ambassador Michael Comay told the Council directly after the voting:

"The fundamental cause of Arab-Israel tension lies in Arab belligerence and military threats against Israel, in standing violation of the Charter and the armistice agreements."

And he added:

"I must record my government's disbelief that the resolution just adopted will resolve any of the problems the Council has already debated three times in the last few months. These problems cannot be resolved as long as the people of Israel are not permitted to lead peaceful and secure lives within their own borders, and as long as the international community does not insist on neighboring states conducting themselves toward Israel in accordance with Charter principles, armistice commitments, and the concept of peaceful coexistence."

Perhaps the seeds of the 1967 war were sown then, in Israel's feeling of despair and isolation, in the knowledge that the Soviet veto shielded the Arabs from any similar censure and the awareness that the United States was almost totally preoccupied with Vietnam and was not seeking actively to resolve the Middle East deadlock. Looking back, it seems clear that the Syrian guerrilla tactics during 1966 escalated tension in the region and brought it to boiling point the following year, in the absence of any concerted attempt to forestall a collision by the only two countries that could have done so—the Soviet Union and the United States. Things were allowed to drift, with the results we have seen.

Throughout this period President Nasser was following his usual tactic of being all things to all men: extreme when talking about the probability of a long war against Israel, moderate in conversation with visiting diplomats or newspapermen. He continued his support of Shukairy, who was given a powerful radio transmitter in Cairo from which to broadcast his attacks on Israel and Jordan.

A week before the Es Samu incident Nasser had signed a joint defense pact with Syria in which both sides agreed to coordinate political and military action.

Nasser seemed to be moving into another phase of cautious militancy against Israel, while still avoiding any open physical confrontation and the accompanying risk of a defeat on the battle-field. Israel appeared to be the calculated target of another Algerian campaign: a long-drawn-out, abrasive guerrilla war intended to fray the nerves of its inhabitants and drive them into acts of retaliation which would create an adverse climate to Israel at the United Nations. It was not a cheerful prospect. And Nasser said or did nothing to disassociate himself from this forecast or the announced Syrian intentions. This impression, which grew in force on the Israeli side of the border at the end of 1966, created the mood which led to the 1967 war.

While Nasser was maneuvering between his desire not to lose face because of his hesitancy over Palestine and his unwillingness to meet Israel face to face, other Arab countries were resisting Cairo's hegemony. Some were even beginning to question the order of priorities which placed the destruction of Israel above all other objectives. And for the first time an Arab leader of standing openly advocated a policy of cooperation with Israel and called for negotiations with it. This was the President of Tunisia, Habib Bourguiba.

4 Bourguiba: Beginning of a Breakthrough

AT THE BEGINNING of March 1965 Habib Bourguiba, the President of Tunisia, began a round of visits to various Arab capitals. The doughty 61-year-old fighter for Tunisia's freedom from French control was respected all over the Arab world, and his official calls on leaders in Cairo, Beirut, and elsewhere aroused no particular prior anticipation. Few people outside Bourguiba's immediate circle suspected that this visit would inaugurate a new phase in Arab-Israeli relations.

Bourguiba's first visit was to the Hashemite Kingdom of Jordan. He was received by King Hussein and toured the Israeli frontier and the refugee camps. On March 6 he held a press conference in the Old City of Jerusalem. What was scheduled as a routine exchange of views between local journalists and a visiting Arab dignitary turned into an impassioned appeal for a new approach to the Palestine question by an Arab leader of undoubted authority and standing.

The Arabs, Bourguiba said, should learn a lesson from past tragedies. "The rulers should not deceive their people, but should be frank with them and should refrain from being driven by sheer sentiments.

"We have not persecuted the Jews," he added, "and we can still cooperate with them on the basis of mutual respect. I saw Christians, laymen, and clergymen, living in peace and brotherhood with Moslems here in Jordan. This proves that when the inferiority complex and lust for control disappear there will be enough room for all sects to live together. Cooperation and understanding can serve as a strong basis for a real peace.

"Blood and war solve no problems," Bourguiba went on. "We want a true peace based on love and brotherhood. All I hope is that we can learn a lesson from the tragedies of the past and return to common sense. Islam does not differentiate between Moslems and non-Moslems. Had the Arabs accepted previous solutions and continued to demand their implementation, this tragedy would not have come about."

In his opinion, the Palestine tragedy had been caused by "international circumstances, the world wars, the Jews' efforts, and the mistakes the Arabs had made during the past twenty-three years." The time had now come, he concluded, to find a way to attain peaceful coexistence in the Middle East.

Bourguiba may have been thinking of the fate of the late King Abdullah—King Hussein's grandfather, and the last prominent Arab statesman to urge a reconciliation with Israel—when he added pointedly:

"These are my views and policies, for which I should not necessarily be charged with treason and exposed to assassination."[1]

Bourguiba's remarks were broadcast virtually in full over the Jordanian radio and published in all the leading Jordanian papers. They caused an immediate sensation in the Arab world and in Israel. Seldom had any Arab leader stirred up such a storm by a few remarks to journalists. Most Arab and Israeli commentators pointed out that Bourguiba had made his forthright statements after seeing King Hussein. Coupled with the fact that the press conference was broadcast over the state-controlled radio, this implied that Hussein knew in advance what Bourguiba intended to say and did not disagree with his approach, although he did not announce publicly that he supported it.

The choice of the Old City of Jerusalem was also considered significant. If Bourguiba really intended taking the initiative in seeking a more constructive line on Arab-Israeli relations, no venue could have been more suitable than this city, which housed the largest single concentration of former Palestinians in all the Arab world.

Some observers recalled that a few days before his remarks in

1. The English-language *Jerusalem Times* (published in the Old City of Jerusalem), March 7, 1965.

Jerusalem President Bourguiba had spoken more frankly to Palestinian refugees than any other Arab leader ever had. He told a rally of refugees in Akbat Jaber camp, near Jericho:

"Emotion is not enough: neither is readiness for sacrifice. . . . Nothing is easier than to compete in speechmaking and stirring up the masses. But no battle has ever been won in this way. What is important is loyalty in labor, truth in speech, straightforwardness in action, and winning the hearts of the people."[2]

The day after his Jerusalem press conference the Tunisian President flew on to Lebanon for a five-day visit. Here and in Turkey—a Moslem, but non-Arab, country—he followed up his line of thinking, extending it slightly and going into further details with every fresh statement during the rest of his fifty-day trip. In Beirut and Istanbul he called for a step-by-step approach towards Israel and opposed the idea of armed hostilities or other extreme positions.

But the full details of his proposals only appeared when he returned to Tunisia and was given an enthusiastic welcome by a large crowd. Shortly after he arrived back he addressed Tunisian students and members of the ruling Socialist Destour Party. He proposed that Israel and the "Palestine Arabs" open negotiations in a neutral capital, on the basis of the 1947 partition scheme. The Arabs, he said, should recognize Israel within the frontiers fixed by the United Nations in 1947, in exchange for Israel's repatriation of Palestinian refugees. He called for goodwill and readiness to accept a compromise solution of the Palestine question. Later, he indicated, further defreezing in relations would become possible; this would enable the Arabs and the Jews to coexist peacefully, to establish economic relations and to cooperate.

He had not embarked on his Middle East trip in order to solve the problem of Palestine, he said. "But once I was there I met some people whose destiny afflicted me. I am a serious and forthright man, and I saw for myself how these people were being made to live on illusions. For twenty years they have been living in immobility. I told them that when one understands he has made

2. *Falastin*, March 4, 1965.

a mistake, he has to find another solution instead of doing nothing. Each of them tried to find excuses. When I spoke to them about methods they talked about principles and justice."

Drawing a parallel with the French presence in Tunisia, Bourguiba recalled that he had begun negotiating with the French at a time when Tunisia was still under French protection. This approach had eventually led to full independence for Tunisia. And today France and Tunisia were cooperating with one another. If he had been a Palestinian Arab, he would have accepted a dialogue with Israel, in the same way that he had proposed talks with the French. He made it quite clear that he considered the settlement of the Palestinian issue a matter between the Palestinians and the Israelis, and that it was not primarily the concern of all the Arab countries: "if Israel accepts our proposals and shows readiness for negotiations, the partners will of course be the Palestinians and the Jews." "It is now up to Israel," he added.[3]

This was the furthest Bourguiba had yet gone. And it provoked the most vehement reaction from Egypt and other Arab countries. The Cairo newspaper *Al Akhbar* printed his statements under red banner headlines proclaiming: "Bourguiba Has Gone Raving Mad." Several papers accused Bourguiba of "high treason" for proposing talks with Israel. Faud al Rekabi, the Iraqi Minister of Municipal and Rural Affairs, said President Bourguiba's statement was "one of the cruellest stabs the Palestine case has ever received, either from imperialist forces or reactionary Arab circles."[4] Demonstrations took place outside the Tunisian embassies in Cairo, Damascus, and other Arab capitals.

Meanwhile favorable international reactions were coming back to Tunisia from various parts of the globe. The day after President Bourguiba made his statement to the Destour Party, the U.S. State Department spokesman said some of his suggestions could form the substance for negotiations. "We welcome wholeheartedly any initiative designed to bring about a permanent and peaceful solution of the Arab-Israel dispute," the spokesman said. "The forthright way in which President Bourguiba has approached

3. *Jerusalem Post*, April 25, 1965.
4. *Ibid.*

this subject offers hope that fresh approaches may be made to this difficult problem."[5]

Some of the world's most influential newspapers applauded Bourguiba's courage and initiative. In an editorial the *New York Herald Tribune* hailed his "wisdom and statesmanship." The paper added:

"It is profoundly disappointing, if not altogether surprising, that the first clear voice of sanity from the Arab side in the long Arab-Israel dispute has been greeted with a shower of abuse from the Arab press, ranging from allegations of madness to charges of treason."[6]

Le Monde remarked that by declaring that war with Israel was impossible and other solutions must be found, "President Bourguiba was only stating openly what many other Arab politicians said under their breath."[7]

The London *Observer* lauded Bourguiba's courage in becoming the first Arab leader of stature to advocate publicly terms by which Israel might be accepted as a Jewish state in the Arab world. "Even though his terms are unacceptable to both sides, he has broken the ice on the Arab side," the paper pointed out. The *Observer* suggested that "the score or so of African states which have cordial relations with both Israel and the Arabs" should make a new effort to end the quarrel between them, "which affects Africa as much as the Middle East."[8]

There was considerable speculation about Bourguiba's motives in launching his peace campaign. Some political commentators, particularly in Israel, suggested that he wanted to restore his standing in the eyes of President de Gaulle, with whom he had clashed on various issues. Some circles went so far as to suggest that Paris was behind the new peace feelers. Others linked Bourguiba's initiative to a United States drive to relax tensions in the Middle East and reduce Nasser's prestige.

However, it is unlikely that Bourguiba was inspired by an external factor. Almost certainly the peace drive sprang from his own

5. Reuters dispatch from Washington: *Jerusalem Post*, April 25, 1965.
6. *New York Herald Tribune*, April 24, 1965.
7. *Le Monde*, April 24, 1965.
8. London *Observer*, April 25, 1965.

feeling in 1965 that tension over the Jordan waters was building up to a danger point; that any clash over this issue would be both artificial and unwise; and that the Israeli-Arab dispute could be resolved through peaceful negotiations, like any other international disagreement.

Bourguiba is a pragmatic leader who has strong intellectual and cultural ties with Western thinking. In line with these ideas, he believes each Arab country should first try to solve its own domestic problems and should not dissipate its resources on barren disputes grounded as much in emotional nationalism as in logical grievances. As one Western correspondent explained:

"President Bourguiba is a statesman who likes to place himself in a liberal international tradition. . . . He believes the Arabs should seek to become part of a world civilization—that is to say a Western civilization—rather than withdraw into a narrow, sterile nationalism."[9]

Bourguiba's frank stand in favor of negotiations focused world interest on Israel and the Eshkol Government's reaction to his initiative. Many Israelis expressed admiration for his courage. It was noted that he was the first Moslem Arab leader to openly criticize the belligerent atmosphere built up over Israel's Jordan project. Several Israeli circles began urging the Eshkol Government to welcome Bourguiba's initiative and to make a gesture of good-will which would constitute a parallel indication of Israel's readiness to break the ice.

Few Israelis seriously thought that the 1947 partition plan, which had been rejected at the time by the Arabs, could serve as the starting point for fresh talks eighteen years later. But a growing number of thoughtful citizens felt that Bourguiba's proposal was only the opening bid in a move for a solution, and that what he really hoped to elicit was an Israeli counter-offer which could start the ball rolling and perhaps lead to direct peace talks or talks through a third party. Whether Israel should respond in kind or await further developments became the subject of a heated public debate.

A former Foreign Ministry official, Shlomo Ginnosar, declared

9. Patrick Seale in London *Observer*, May 2, 1965.

in a radio discussion that "the status quo between us and the Arabs is not the Ten Commandments." In his opinion, Israel should find "unofficial" ways of reacting to Bourguiba's statements and of bringing about talks with the Arabs. "The Israeli public should be accustomed to the idea of a compromise, and a compromise is impossible without mutual concessions."[10]

The public debate over Bourguiba's declarations uncovered a fascinating series of letters about the Tunisian leader, written in 1952 by the Speaker of the Knesset, the late Yosef Sprinzak, one of the most distinguished and respected figures in Israeli political life at that time. Sprinzak was convalescing in a Swiss sanatorium when he wrote these letters to his friend Marc Yarblum, a French Zionist leader who later settled in Israel.

Sprinzak began with a blunt observation:

"The fact is that in regard to the relationships between us and the Arabs we have reached a dead end."

He was concerned with finding ways of bridging "the tragic chasm that has come to exist between the two nations." During his period of convalescence he came to the conclusion that "if a leading Arab personality were to appear on the humanitarian or cultural level of Nehru, he would be able to grasp the universal basis of the reconciliation and brotherhood of the two peoples— the Arab and Hebrew."

It seemed to Sprinzak that Habib Bourguiba—then the leader of the Tunisian people's struggle for freedom from France—was a personality of the nature of Nehru. This led to the thought that Bourguiba might perhaps be able to carry out the great historic mission of bringing about a reconciliation between Arabs and Jews. If the Tunisian people attained its independence, Bourguiba would become an authoritative personality in the Arab world. This was one of the two conditions Sprinzak thought would have to be fulfilled if Bourguiba was to be in a position to undertake this mission. The other was that "there must be a Jewish contribution to the success of Habib Bourguiba. . . . The Jewish contribution can pave the way and serve as the moral justification for Bourguiba's proper attitude to us and for the idea of his mission."

10. *Haaretz*, April 29, 1965.

Although, as Speaker of the Knesset, Sprinzak was one of the most influential people in Israel, he admitted to Yarblum: "I do not have the courage to discuss this matter with our 'diplomats'." He asked his old friend to explore the ground with French socialists and such prominent French Jewish statesmen as Jules Moch and Daniel Mayer.[11]

These letters were first published by Yarblum in 1965. In a radio interview shortly afterward he recalled meeting Bourguiba about ten years earlier. During their private conversation Bourguiba had argued—as he was to do ten years later in public—that the Arab leaders were mistaken not to recognize Israel. He suggested that Israel should be accepted as an accomplished fact, no matter how painful this might be to the Arabs, and that peace talks should be initiated. He added that he himself could not undertake any such initiative as long as Tunisia remained under French domination.

As international appreciation of Bourguiba's stand heightened, increasing attention was directed to the Eshkol Government's reaction to his statements. For several weeks there was no public comment at all by official Israeli spokesmen. One observer in Jerusalem explained to me at about this time that "to praise Bourguiba now would be the kiss of death."

At the end of April 1965 the Israeli Cabinet discussed Bourguiba's declarations and decided to view them as part of an inter-Arab debate, rather than as concrete proposals for a settlement. At the same time, it welcomed this innovation as a welcome, refreshing break after ten years of immobility. Deputy Prime Minister Abba Eban commented indirectly at this time on the call for a return to the 1947 boundaries, when he asserted: "An egg broken eighteen years ago cannot be put together."[12]

On May 5 Prime Minister Levi Eshkol made the first detailed high-level Israeli statement on Bourguiba's proposals. He told *Davar* that "Bourguiba's new approach is a positive phenomenon in itself, and perhaps he is not speaking only on his own behalf." However, Eshkol made it clear that no official Israeli reaction would be forthcoming. "The intention is to wait and see how

11. *Jewish Frontier*, Summer 1965, p. 28.
12. *Jerusalem Post, loc. cit.*

things turn out"—in other words, whether any other Arab leaders would follow Bourguiba's lead.

On the specific proposal that talks with Israel should be made conditional on a return to the 1947 partition borders, Eshkol added:

"I think that someone should sit with a map in his hand and explain to Bourguiba that this is not realistic. I am happy that there is a readiness for peace in principle. But in addition to explaining matters to the world, the Arabs must be educated to know what is possible and what is impossible."

For Israel any territorial concessions are out of the question, Mr. Eshkol declared in plain terms. He also rejected the possibility that any Arab refugees might be returned. But, he went on, "we have something to propose in return for peace, and this will have more concrete value for the Arabs than concessions on the borders or the refugees."

What did Israel propose?

Eshkol indicated that this could be the payment of compensation to the refugees and assistance in rehabilitation and development. He also hinted that there was room for "a framework of cooperation with Jordan; there's the question of ports and common plants." But he made no concrete proposals and announced no steps which could have been construed in the Arab world as an indirect answer to Bourguiba's proposals.[13]

At the end of May Prime Minister Eshkol spoke in the same general manner to the twenty-fourth annual B'nai B'rith assembly in Caesarea:

"When an outstanding Arab leader finally states in public that it is time to end the threats, and that there is no basis or hope for the Arab plans to wipe Israel off the map, this is a significant development. Though it is not the generally accepted Arab view, I tend to believe that this leader is not alone or isolated in his attitude. At any rate, a significant debate has started on the other side, with the very idea of coexistence no longer pilloried by all as anathema."[14]

Meanwhile President Bourguiba was continuing to follow up his

13. *Davar*, May 5, 1965.
14. Official text of address, pp. 2 and 10.

line of reasoning. In an interview with Jean Daniel, chief editor of the Paris *Le Nouvel Observateur*, Bourguiba spoke perhaps more frankly than ever before about his peace initiative. He noted that when he had visited President Tito of Yugoslavia, they had agreed "to denounce colonial oppression wherever it still scourges the world." But the Yugoslavs firmly refused to include Israel among the colonial countries. This attitude of Tito's confirmed a long-standing impression of Bourguiba's: namely, "that as far as the Israel question is concerned, their best friends don't support the Arabs. . . . Either Arab propaganda is clumsy or there is something, some aspect of Israeli colonialism, which must be taken into account and given careful consideration."

He had told President Nasser in Cairo that many friends of the Arabs were embarrassed by their inability to solve the Palestine problem. "Everyone knows that a war is impossible, that it would be stopped after a few hours by the Great Powers, that the United States is committed to intervene with equal firmness against aggression either by Israel or against Israel."

Analyzing the shortcomings of the Arab hatred for Israel, Bourguiba added:

"If hatred makes me uncomfortable, it is not only because I despise this emotion, but also because, among us Arabs, it obstructs intelligent action; it is an excuse for inertia. We Arabs shout, we hurl insults, we indulge in abuse, we curse, and we feel that in so doing we have discharged our responsibilities, done our duty and can now live at peace with our conscience. Behind this is an inferiority complex; we overestimate our adversary.

"I think"—Bourguiba went on—"the time was ripe for saying publicly what leaders in the Middle East think privately. . . . Anything is better than the present state of affairs. Things must move. There must be proposals, counter-proposals, action on the international level. A situation must be created which will make new appraisals necessary. I say that no one must talk about pushing the Jews into the sea unless he is able to do so. And even to refrain from talking this way may promote coexistence between Arabs and Jews."[15]

15. *Le Nouvel Observateur*, April 14, 1965: quoted in *Atlas*, June 1965.

In May three CBS correspondents—George Herman, Martin Agronsky, and Winston Burdett—went to Tunis to interview Bourguiba for the *Face the Nation* program. He told them that "many countries" in the Middle East supported his proposals for a relaxation of tension between Israel and the Arab states. He had assumed the burden of outlining a compromise solution because he believed a path had to be opened to enable Israel and the Arabs to exist side by side. Bourguiba insisted that he was only stating publicly what many Arab diplomats and other informed people had been saying in private. "What I consider as my real ally is common sense. Reason will prevail."[16]

Throughout the entire period of Bourguiba's peace initiative, he enjoyed the full backing of his own administration and public opinion in Tunisia. Shortly after the Old City press conference, for example, the Tunisian Ambassador in Paris, Muhammad Masmoudi, told foreign correspondents that Israel's existence was a fact. "Israel," he added, "has solved the problem of the victims of Nazism—a problem which has been understood everywhere, including the Arab world." In his opinion, Bourguiba's campaign had planted seeds "which would germinate sooner or later."[17]

The organ of Bourguiba's Neo-Destour Party, *Al Amal*, consistently supported its leader's approach all through the controversy. In one editorial the paper declared: "There is room for peaceful coexistence between the Arabs and the Jews in the liberated homeland. We should try to reach a situation in which there will be neither victors nor vanquished."[18]

An important role was played by the French-language weekly *Jeune Afrique*, published in Paris by a group of Tunisian intellectuals who have close ties with Bourguiba. This weekly brought the Tunisian views to the French-speaking public. This led to a debate on the future of Israeli-Arab relations, in which Arab and Israeli articles were published.

Throughout the summer of 1965 the inter-Arab discussion over Bourguiba's Palestine proposals continued. In Israeli and Jewish circles too there were differences of opinion. Such groups as

16. UPI dispatch from Washington: *Jerusalem Post*, May 24, 1965.
17. *Hatzofeh*, March 24, 1965.
18. *Al Hamishmar*, April 6, 1965.

Mapam (the United Workers Party) and the circles close to the English-language monthly *New Outlook* argued that Israel was missing a historic opportunity by failing to make a concrete response to the Tunisian move. Attempts were made to contact Tunisian circles in Paris and elsewhere in Europe, in order to find out what Israeli response would be acceptable and how the dialogue could be continued.

Other Israeli circles—particularly the Ben-Gurion-Dayan activist school of thought—warned that there was no basis for negotiations on the 1947 partition resolution and claimed that Bourguiba was simply setting a trap. The editor of the London *Jewish Observer and Middle East Review*, Jon Kimche, who was close to these circles, expressed their viewpoint when he wrote: "One can only wonder that anyone should be so naive as to expect Israel, or any other country for that matter, to enter into negotiations on the basis of a prefabricated 'Munich'," which would lead to Israel having to give up "an area which houses a quarter of her Jewish population, over half a million, and which has over three hundred settlements, in addition to the towns of Acre, Lydda, Ramle, Jerusalem, Beersheba, and Ashqelon. Does anyone expect the Israelis seriously to negotiate the surrender of these areas?"[19]

Meanwhile Bourguiba himself was becoming increasingly discouraged. He was fighting a lone campaign against the bulk of Arab opinion. While other Arab leaders in such countries as Jordan, Lebanon, and Saudi Arabia—and in the Maghreb itself—unquestionably agreed with him, no other prominent Arab openly supported him in word or deed.

Reluctantly he decided at the beginning of July to drop his campaign for a negotiated settlement of the Palestine problem. He told the London *Observer* correspondent Patrick Seale, who visited him at Carthage:

"My compromise plan has failed. Neither the Arabs nor Israel want anything to do with it. I do not intend to take the leadership of a movement to press for a settlement. I have neither the inclination nor the means. The problem must be left to time."

Bourguiba emphasized that the situation in the Arab East—i.e., the countries bordering immediately on Israel—was fluid and

19. *Jewish Observer and Middle East Review*, April 30, 1965.

would change further. The words he used most frequently were "realistic" and "pragmatic." He was certain that one day his advice would be accepted, and that his ideas had already had an impact on the younger Arab generation.

He also made this interesting revelation about his private talk with President Nasser in Cairo, before proceeding to the Old City of Jerusalem in March:

"I put the matter very frankly to Nasser. I said that if we could only invoke all the United Nations resolutions—those dealing with partition as well as with the return of refugees—this would be a compromise position which would open the way to a peace settlement or at least to a less explosive situation than we now have.

"I added that we had neither the strength nor the will to fight. A readiness to compromise would bring over to our side all the peace-loving members of the UN.

"Nasser replied that he had said much the same thing at the Bandung conference of 1955, and that the Afro-Asian countries had welcomed his statement.

"I then said this was fine and that we should make our views public. I pressed him particularly on the question of the UN resolution which created Israel. Would he agree to this one too? He said he would. But he added that the Arab public could not accept anything which might seem like a recognition of Israel.

"So I decided to make no public statement about it. But then I saw Nasser's interview with the French magazine *Réalités*. He there made it quite clear that if all the UN resolutions were applied, something called Israel would continue to exist.

"What separates us then? It is that which separates an honest man from one who conceals his views."

Bourguiba pointed out that the Arabs were not ready to fight Israel in order to destroy it in one single step. He felt therefore that the UN resolutions should be accepted by the Arabs. This meant "agreeing to coexist. It meant coexisting with an injustice—but only as a preliminary to improving one's position." Clearly Bourguiba felt that "the tide of Arab politics was running in his favor." But for the moment he was dropping his one-man campaign.[20]

20. London *Observer*, July 11, 1965.

From then on Bourguiba made no more statements calling for a Middle East reconciliation. But there was one further attempt to initiate a dialogue between Israel and at least some of the Arab countries.

In August 1965 Pierre Mendès-France went to Israel, ostensibly to attend an international monetary conference in Rehovot. Mendès-France, a French Jew, had been Prime Minister in 1954 and had proclaimed Tunisia's independence. He had released Bourguiba from jail so that he could become the first President of the country for whose liberation he had fought so gallantly and so long.

Before traveling to Israel Mendès-France went to Tunisia and was given a hero's welcome. Then he went to Rehovot and devoted himself to fiscal policy, refraining from meeting the press or making statements on Israeli-Arab relations. But he did have a long tête-à-tête with Prime Minister Levi Eshkol. Mendès-France brought Eshkol a verbal message from Bourguiba and urged the Israeli Premier to make a concrete gesture which would reinforce the moderate Tunisian position and show that Israel too was ready to work for a compromise solution through diplomatic contacts.

But Eshkol was fighting a desperate battle against his former mentor, David Ben-Gurion, who was trying to oust him by dragging up the eleven-year-old security scandal which has become notorious as the Lavon Affair. The Israeli Prime Minister was struggling for his political life and was trying to shake off charges of being weak and vacillating. He did not want to risk any move which would lay him open to renewed claims that he was soft towards the Arabs. Eshkol told Mendès-France he was interested in Bourguiba's statements and had followed them closely, but the time had not yet come for any Israeli gesture. Perhaps later on something could be done.

Mendès-France conveyed this reply to Bourguiba. And with this final attempt Bourguiba's initiative came to an end. During the next two years he occasionally demonstrated that he had not wholly abandoned his deep interest in a peace settlement. On July 11, 1966, for example, the Harry Truman Center for the Advancement of Peace was dedicated at the Hebrew University of

Jerusalem. Bourguiba created a sensation by sending ex-President Truman a cable regretting that he could not attend the ceremony because of "prior obligations." He added: "I wish full success to this daring venture of yours." This cable was read at the Jerusalem ceremony by Truman's representative.

But Bourguiba made no more public attempts to express his conviction that the Arabs were sinking deeper and deeper into a morass of their own creation, apparently powerless to extricate themselves. Yet, although this particular chapter of Middle East history produced no immediate practical results, I believe it might one day be seen to have had a considerable long-term impact. The very fact that Bourguiba spoke in matter-of-fact terms about accepting Israel and eventually cooperating with it brought this devastating possibility down to the level of reality, instead of making it seem a highly colored Oriental fantasy.

This was the Tunisian President's greatest achievement, and in it lies the real hope for the future. Once a shocking political sentiment is uttered aloud, it loses much of its shock effect. The next generation is able to assess the once-shockable proposition at its face value, free of the emotional overtones which once made it absolutely inacceptable. By uttering aloud these heretical ideas about the inevitability of Israel being accepted, Bourguiba prepared the ground for this reassessment. And he made it easier for such relatively moderate Arabs as King Hussein to talk about finding a *modus vivendi* with Israel after the June 1967 war, instead of seeking another military confrontation.

The best way of summing up what will probably go down in history as "the Bourguiba affair" is to recount a conversation I had in the summer of 1965 with a leading European statesman. He had just come from Tunisia, where he had seen Bourguiba and discussed his peace proposals. But he would not discuss these in detail. Instead, my informant—who is renowned for his skill in conducting delicate negotiations—chose to speak about the way these high-level diplomatic talks are conducted and the need to respond to an opening bid with a counter-proposal, if only to demonstrate willingness to bargain on terms.

Drawing the moral of this abstract dissertation for the Arab-Israeli conflict, the distinguished statesman added:

"What Israel should do now, in my opinion, is to work out what it feels it can offer the Arabs as an initial move in a possible dialogue, without endangering its national security. I know that public opinion in Israel is opposed to territorial concessions. And I understand this. No one expects Israel to harm its own vital interests. But a carefully considered concession on the refugees, for example, could lead to negotiations and bring peace closer. This is certainly in your interests. Only when Israel has made a real counter-offer can the Arabs weigh this up and decide whether it can form a basis for discussion."

I asked him whether any significant Israeli gesture or proposal would evoke a response in the Arab world.

He replied:

"It is like a letter thrown into the sea in a bottle. Someone always picks it up. It always comes to shore somewhere."

As we said good-bye he added:

"Remember that in the Arab world there is always someone listening. You might not know who it is. You might even be surprised to know who is listening. But if you speak they will hear, as you listened when Bourguiba spoke."

5 *The Jews: Strangers or Partners?*

IN OCTOBER 1964 the Histadrut daily *Davar* published a remarkable letter by the highly respected former Prime Minister, Moshe Sharett.

Sharett, who spoke Arabic fluently, had listened to King Hussein's speech from the throne to the Jordanian Parliament. He then compared what he had heard in Arabic with what was reported afterwards in Hebrew by Kol Yisrael radio and by the Israeli press.

Sharett was shocked by the way Hussein's speech had been covered. He did not want to comment on the political section of the speech.

But, he noted, "the speech concluded with a survey of economic and cultural achievements. Facts and figures were given about the allocation of state-owned land to farmers, progress in irrigation, industrial development, plans for exploiting phosphate deposits and prospecting for oil, the construction of hospitals, the building of more roads, advances in vocational education, the over-all growth in the number of schools, teachers and pupils, and so on."

This survey had been completely omitted by Kol Yisrael and the next day's newspapers.

"In my opinion," Sharett wrote, "this is a shortcoming which we would do well to redress. Most of the Israeli public does not read the Arab press and does not listen to the broadcasts from the Arab capitals. The impression created by the Israeli press and Kol Yisrael's broadcasts is that the only things taking place in the neighboring countries are the hatching of plots, internecine strife, and mutual subversion. About positive activities and processes of development the average Israeli reads and hears next to nothing."

True, "the scope of Israel's development cannot be compared with what is being done in any of the Arab countries. . . . But the picture painted at present should certainly be corrected by presenting the positive aspects, limited as they might be, together with the negative ones, for the sake of the public's education and the sake of the truth. Our information must be balanced, particularly if this balancing is so instructive."[1]

Another leading Israeli statesman who is an Arabist in his own right—Foreign Minister Abba Eban—has also pointed out that "the Arab-Israel dialogue is not distorted on one side alone. Hostility usually evokes an attitude in its own image. The Israeli vision of Arab life and culture is being eroded by years of conflict and separation."[2]

Sharett and Eban have pinpointed one of the gravest problems facing Israel today: its lack of direct contact with the peoples of the neighboring lands. The borders to the north, east, and south have been sealed and are crossed only by the invisible radio and television waves, which do not respect man-made frontiers. Many Israelis derive their main knowledge of the Arab world from the flickering images on their television screens. But they cannot travel to Lebanon, Syria, the East Bank of the Jordan, or Egypt. There is no contact with flesh-and-blood Arabs across the border and little real contact with Arabs living in Israel itself or in the West Bank of the Jordan.

A whole generation of young Israelis has grown up without any understanding of Arab history and culture. For these young people the Arabs are simply *ha'oyev*—"the enemy." This ingrained attitude has led to a decline in the study of Arabic in Israeli schools. Out of 10,000 Jewish pupils who took matriculation examinations in 1965, only 370 were examined in Arabic. Twenty-four thousand high school pupils are studying French, while only 7,000 are taking Arabic. The Committee of Arabic Teachers has suggested that Arabic should be made a compulsory subject in the schools, on

1. *Davar*, October 5, 1964.
2. Article in *Jewish Observer and Middle East Review*, September 11, 1964 (written when Eban was Deputy Prime Minister).

the grounds that every educated Israeli should know Arabic—
Israel's second official language.[3] Yet from year to year the study
of Arabic declines. Where Arabic or the Arab way of life is
studied, this is often more out of the desire to "know the enemy"
than for objective scientific reasons or intellectual curiosity.

How can Israel break this ring of hostility? How can it gain the
confidence of the surrounding peoples? This is the major task of
the second stage of Israel's national rebirth. Since winning its
statehood in 1948 Israel has become an accepted factor on the
international scene. It is self-governing, sovereign, and independent. It has established diplomatic relations with virtually
every member of the United Nations, apart from the Arab bloc.
Its economic and scientific achievements have earned worldwide
respect. Israel has shown that, although it is a small country, it
can make a unique, specific contribution to human civilization.
But Israel has not yet come to grips with the next stage of its
renaissance: forming stable and peaceful relations with its geopolitical neighbors.

As an Arab historian, Dr. Charles Malik, has observed, Israel's
fundamental problem is not how to establish herself, but "how to
integrate herself, economically, politically, spiritually, in the life
of the Near East; how to promote friendly, creative, sustained and
sustaining, trustful, peaceful, internal relations with the Arab
and Moslem worlds. Self-establishment by force is fairly easy—at
least it is possible; but self-perpetuation by force is, in the nature
of the case, absolutely impossible. At least history has not known
an instance of a nation at permanent enmity with its immediate
world."

According to Malik, the question is whether the "exceedingly
potent" Zionist idea, "in the next crucial stage of its development,"
will be "resourceful and resilient and humble enough to create
genuine, internal relations of confidence and cooperation between
itself and the Moslem-Arab world in which it has chosen to plant
itself."[4]

3. Education section of *Jerusalem Post*, July 8, 1965.
4. Dr. Charles Malik, "The Near East: The Search for Truth," *Foreign
Affairs*, January 1952: quoted by Sylvia G. Haim, *Arab Nationalism* (Berkeley
and Los Angeles: University of California Press, 1962), p. 202.

At the very core of this issue lies another fundamental question: How does Israel conceive its identity and destiny? Is it an extension of European civilization into Asia Minor, or an organic part of the Middle East? Is Israel a Western bridgehead in an Oriental environment, or an ancient Semitic community returning to the land which gave it form and birth? Is Israel a stranger, an intruder, or a potential partner?

Too often in the past, unfortunately, Zionist leaders have conveyed the impression that Israel is the cultural heir of Europe and that it is inherently alien to the indigenous peoples of the Near East.

In 1961 David Ben-Gurion—then Prime Minister—was interviewed by the Indian poet and journalist, Dom Moraes. A talk with an Asian journalist could have been an opportunity to point out that the Jewish people were seeking to recover their roots in the region and that they sought an affiliation with its peoples. Yet when Moraes asked Ben-Gurion: "How do you see Israel developing? Do you think of it as primarily a Middle East country?" the Israeli Prime Minister replied:

"No. It is not a Middle Eastern country. It can never be a Middle Eastern country. We have cultural roots in Europe for the most part."[5]

This Europe-centered view is held, consciously or unconsciously, by many Israeli leaders of Polish or Russian origin. Such an influential member of the Eshkol Administration as Finance Minister Pinchas Sapir has insisted that "Israel belongs to Europe culturally, politically, and economically, despite her being situated in the Middle East geographically."[6]

Statements like these sound irritatingly superior. They can only support the Arabs in their claim that Israel is a foreign element in the Middle East. And they should be deplored by anyone who thinks Israel should stress that the Jewish people are returning today to the land in which they once lived and the Western Asian environment from which they sprang as a people.

It was a Christian friend of the Jewish people who pointed out that "the majority of the inhabitants of Israel have never, in the

5. *Jerusalem Post*, August 18, 1961.
6. *Le Monde*, March 9, 1966.

more than three thousand years of their recorded history, lived in any other continent or among any other nations. Israel is today a Middle Eastern country, the majority of whose inhabitants are descendants of the oldest identifiable group of Semitic-speaking peoples in the Middle East, a group which left the Semitic heartlands in the Arabian Peninsula two millennia before their cousins who are now identified as Arabs, but which went no further afield than the Mesopotomian empires in the East and the North African people in the West."[7]

The conflict between Europe-centered and Middle East-centered schools of thought can be traced throughout the ideological history of the Zionist movement. The "Europeans" saw themselves as settlers who would bring a high level of civilization to a backward area. They were generally insensitive to the feelings of the indigenous population, and considered that they should be grateful for the benefits they would receive as a result of the Jewish settlement. The "Middle Easterners"—not all of whose members were Oriental Jews—insisted that the Zionist movement should try to win the goodwill of the Arabs living in Palestine, and should emphasize the kinship between the two peoples and their mutually beneficial relations in the past. These conflicting trends have always coexisted side by side in the Zionist movement, each gaining power in turn according to the changing circumstances in Palestine and the decline or ascendancy of various key Jewish leaders. These divergent views can still be easily detected today, in the great debate inside Israel over the future of the territories occupied during the June 1967 war.

Already in Theodor Herzl's famous slogan, "A people without a land—to a land without a people," we can discern an attitude which virtually ignored the fact that Palestine was not by any means "a land without a people" but had a resident population.

Before Herzl visited Palestine himself he knew little about the realities of life in that country and the national and political implications of the fact that it was not an empty land. Professor A. S. Yehuda, a distinguished Oriental Jew, has recorded the re-

7. Dr. James Parkes, *The New Face of Israel*, Sixth Brodetsky lecture at Leeds University, 1964, pp. 1–2.

sults of his attempts to convince Herzl to approach the Palestinian Arabs. He wrote:

"I met Herzl in London in July 1896, after his first public address on the idea of a Jewish state. . . . As a delegate to the Congress, I was asked to represent the Hebrew-speaking Society I had founded among the university students. I was the youngest delegate to the Congress. My main purpose in attending the Congress was to continue my conversation with Herzl about the Arabs of Palestine.

"I tried to prove to Herzl that the Arabs of Palestine should be won over to our cause, so that they should realize the benefits which would accrue to them and to the country as a whole from the idea of the Return to Zion. I urged him to establish friendly relations with the Arab notables and to create ties of mutual understanding. But Herzl's intimate advisers scoffed at my views.

"Time has shown that I was right. We neglected the task of informing our neighbors about our aims, leaving their hearts open to the seeds of hatred, sown by troublemakers and agitators."[8]

Max Nordau was another of the early Zionist leaders who was concerned about resistance to Jewish aims by the Arabs. Martin Buber has related: "When Max Nordau, Herzl's right-hand man, learned for the first time full details about the presence of Arabs in Palestine, he was greatly concerned. He came to see Herzl and called out: 'I didn't know about this. We are doing an injustice!' "[9]

In 1920 Nordau wrote to Dr. Chaim Weizmann about this question:

"Although not officially connected with the Zionist organization of which you are the head, you will surely find it natural that I am greatly concerned with all the political doings of our organization, which have a bearing on the affairs of the Jewish people. For the last year I have not ceased to follow with growing anxiety the new currents which are taking visible possession of the Arab

8. Professor A. S. Yahuda, *Hadoar*, New York, 1947, No. 25, p. 1,037: quoted by Aharon Cohen, *Israel and the Arab World* (published in Hebrew by Sifriat Ha'poalim, Tel Aviv, 1965).

9. Martin Buber, in anthology *At the Crossroads*: quoted by Aharon Cohen, *op. cit.*

mind. I have not ceased to utter warnings. I spoke to you about it in February. I urged taking measures, establishing a line of conduct. Nobody paid the slightest attention. Things have been allowed to drift, with the results we see—the Jerusalem pogrom, the unrest among the Arabs.

"My conscience does not allow me to remain silent. If we continue to treat our relations with the Arabs as in the past, it may mean the end of Zionism. No British Government would be willing to incur the active hostility of the Arabs to please the Jews. We must therefore come to a peaceful and friendly understanding with the Arabs."

Nordau proposed appointing "men speaking perfect Arabic to establish personal relations with Arab notables, to mix with the Arab populations, and to enlighten them about our peaceful and friendly intentions."[10]

While Nordau was expressing these views and calling for an information campaign aimed at the Arab masses, another Eastern European Zionist leader, Vladimir Jabotinsky, was voicing the "European" approach. When Nordau and Jabotinsky met in Spain the former recalled how he had pleaded for an attempt to reach an agreement with the Arabs, in an address to the 1909 Congress. "To this day I cannot forget the trouble I had afterward with our sentimental idiots," he said. "They shouted to me that I must leave Uncle Ishmael alone."

Jabotinsky told Nordau: "That is only a legend. Ishmael is not our uncle. We, thank God, belong to Europe. We are going to Palestine to extend the boundaries of Europe there."[11]

Dr. Weizmann was a dedicated Middle Easterner during the early period of his Presidency of the Zionist Congress. He took the initiative in meeting the Emir Feisal, and they wrote a famous letter affirming that Zionist aspirations were not against the genuine interests of the Arabs.

Today this meeting might seem naive, romantic, far removed from the violent realities of the 1930s and 1940s in Palestine, with its riots, massacres, and terrorism, or the three bloody wars fought

10. Joseph Leftwich, "The Noble Arab," *South African Jewish Times,* March 6, 1964.
11. *Ibid.*

since 1948. And cynics could argue convincingly that with the British Mandate walking the tightrope between the two sides and struggling to preserve British interests, a clash was unavoidable. Others could correctly date the deterioration in Arab-Jewish relations from the coming of Hitler and the mass flight of Jews from Germany to Palestine.

But in the days after World War I relations between Jews and Arabs in Palestine had not yet been embittered. Zionist thinkers like Achad Ha'am believed that Palestine should be a spiritual center, a focal joint of Jewish life throughout the world. If this center was to have real force, the Jewish community in Palestine had to be established in a truly Jewish way, according to the ethical and moral principles of Judaism. The way the Jews attained their spiritual home among its future Arab neighbors, he felt, would dictate the inner value of that home.

But Achad Ha'am's high-minded vision was not realized in the everyday pattern of Jewish settlement. Surveying his life's work in 1920, he declared that "from the beginning of the Palestinian colonization we have always considered the Arab people as nonexistent."[12] And after one visit to Palestine he cried out in despair:

"Is this the dream of a return to Zion which our people have dreamt for centuries: that we now come to Zion to stain its soil with innocent blood? . . . Are we really doing it to add in an Oriental corner a small people of new Levantines who vie with other Levantines in shedding blood, in desire for vengeance, and in angry violence? If this be the 'Messiah,' then I do not wish to see his coming."[13]

For Achad Ha'am the Jewish ethic was not a bloodless and abstract moral imperative, but a living commandment which should be expressed in political action. As one of Achad Ha'am's spiritual heirs, Dr. Judah L. Magnes, put it:

"It is one of the great civilizing tasks before the Jewish people to try to enter the Promised Land, not in the Joshua way, but bringing peace and culture, hard work and sacrifice, and a deter-

12. Quoted by Aharon Cohen, *op. cit.*
13. Quoted by Hans Kohn, *Reflections on Modern History* (Princeton, N.J.: Van Nostrand, 1963), pp. 203–204.

mination to do nothing that cannot be justified before the conscience of the world."[14]

Magnes and his followers banded themselves together into the *Brith Shalom* (Covenant of Peace) group and then into the *Ihud* (Union) Movement for Jewish-Arab Rapprochement. Among the leading members of this group were Henrietta Szold, founder of Youth Aliyah; Professors Martin Buber and Ernst Simon; Dr. Werner Senator and the writer Rabbi Benyamin. During the tense years of the 1930s and 1940s this group tried vainly to find allies among moderate Arab circles, while opposing violent acts by Jewish extremists.

An example will illustrate the idealistic approach of the group. Dr. Magnes was chairman of the Middle East Committee of the Joint Distribution Committee, which looked after the needs of Jewish refugees from Hitler's persecution. In the fall of 1948 Magnes suggested that the JDC should also aid the Arab refugees who had become the victims of the fighting in Palestine. The JDC did not reply to this proposal, thus in effect rejecting it.

Magnes felt a principle was involved. He resigned as chairman of the Middle East Committee because he felt "the Joint has failed to avail itself of an opportunity to become a factor of the first magnitude in bringing peace to the war-torn Holy Land." He declared that he could not continue to be officially connected with an organization that could so easily dismiss "such a great and urgent welfare problem."

"Peace can only come if Israel and Ishmael feel they are brothers," Magnes wrote to the chairman of the JDC. A few days later he was dead, his heart broken by the fighting between the two peoples whom he had sought to bring together.[15]

The lofty ideals of Magnes and his followers were doomed to failure. The issues at stake at the end of World War II were too vital and passions too high for either side to heed them. *Ihud* was unable to influence either the Jews or the Arabs, or even to apply an effective corrective to the acts of violence on both sides. The

14. Quoted by Norman Bentwich, *For Zion's Sake*, a biography of Judah L. Magnes (Philadelphia: Jewish Publication Society of America, 1954), p. 178.
15. *Ibid.*, p. 302.

extremists took control, and the voices of reason were drowned by the sound of cannons. An Arab proverb puts this succinctly: "The peacemaker shall not profit save in the rending of his garment."

Even before Israel's establishment the moderate "Middle Easterner," Dr. Weizmann, had been replaced at the head of the Zionist movement by David Ben-Gurion. Ben-Gurion was an out-and-out "European." His attitude toward the Arabs was shaped by his experiences at Sedjera, the Galilee farm where he had worked after arriving in Palestine in 1904. There the Jewish pioneers had competed with the Arab laborers for a few Turkish coins a day. In April 1909 two of his comrades were murdered in front of his eyes by two Arabs, in a blood feud meant to avenge another Arab, killed during an attack on the Jewish farm.[16]

Ben-Gurion had little time for the Arabs. He felt scarcely any compassion for the suffering of the fellaheen who were forced to leave Palestine during the 1948 war. He despised the Arab way of life and warned publicly against the danger that Israel would become another Levantine country "like Saudi Arabia or Iraq." He did not seem to appreciate that the Arabs too sought technological development; that no one in the Middle East sought to return to the nomadic and pastoral concepts of traditional Arab life. Ben-Gurion was congenitally incapable of showing any response to hopeful signs of Arab concentration on economic and social development. Quite simply, he had a blind spot about anything connected with the Arabs. It is significant that during his thirteen years as Prime Minister of Israel he did not pay a single official visit to the city of Nazareth, the largest Arab center in Israel. True, he was in Nazareth, but only to inspect progress on the Jewish town he was building as a watchdog for the Arab town across the valley. But he did not call on any Arab dignitaries, as custom and respect demanded of a Prime Minister. Nazareth received its first official visit from Prime Minister Levi Eshkol— sixteen years after Israel's establishment.

During Ben-Gurion's period of office Israel adopted an increasingly "European" posture. A stringent military administration was imposed on the Arabs living in Israel. Israel adopted positions

16. Speech by Ben-Gurion to National Bible Conference, Jerusalem, reported in *Yediot Aharonot*, April 8, 1965.

hostile to the Arabs on several issues between 1948 and 1963, when Ben-Gurion resigned for the last time. Thus Israel helped France during the 1954–1958 struggle in Algeria; the 1956 Suez campaign was only one episode in this continued cooperation. The cable of congratulation that Foreign Minister Golda Meir sent the Algerian Government after de Gaulle had proclaimed independence counted for little against the years of anti-Algerian effort by Israel and was inevitably regarded as hypocritical by the Arabs.

Volumes could be written about the Ben-Gurion era and the path along which it took Israel, in opposition to what some circles consider the state's real long-term interests. But one example must suffice here.

In 1946, while the Anglo-American Committee of Inquiry into Palestine was sitting, the Maronite Archbishop of Beirut, Monsignor Ignaz Moubarak, issued a statement which represented an act of real courage in the political climate of that time. Addressing the people of Palestine and the world, Archbishop Moubarak declared:

"The development of the Lebanon is tied up with that of Palestine. We Christian Lebanese know that. We realize that Zionism is bringing civilization to Palestine and to the entire Middle East. I am very much in favor of Zionism because I have the good of Palestine at heart. . . . In the Jews who are rebuilding Palestine there burns a very pure flame. We must not extinguish it. The Jews in Palestine and the Christians in Palestine can work together. If the Arab Moslems would wish to assist, it would be magnificent. . . . I have been in Palestine thirty years ago. It was an arid forgotten land. I have seen it since. I tell you: We Lebanese are jealous of the good fortune Palestine has had."

Archbishop Moubarak made it clear that his views represented also those of His Beatitude the Maronite Patriarch, the spiritual head of the Maronites everywhere in the world, "who has often expressed his sympathy with Judaism and Zionism."[17]

The Maronites are a small community, in world terms. But they form the majority of the people in Lebanon and have many

17. *Palestine Post*, March 21, 1946.

adherents in Galilee. The 1946 statement reached world public opinion and was used by Israel to show that peace and cooperation in the Middle East was possible.

How did Israel reward the members of the Maronite community?

There is a village in Israel called Bar'am. In 1948 it was taken by the Israeli army. The six hundred Maronite villagers were ordered to move to the nearby Moslem village of Jish for a fortnight. The fortnight passed, but the villagers were not allowed back. Nineteen years have passed, and they have not been given back their homes or lands. In 1953 the villagers obtained a Supreme Court order allowing them to return. But before this could be carried out the Ben-Gurion Government ordered that the deserted village be blown up by the army.

Bar'am was only one of the many opportunities Israel has lost in the last two decades. The Arabs living in Israel could have been offered a fair deal which would have given them a strong stake in the country's future. Instead they were treated with suspicion and denied full civil liberties, largely because of the authorities' "European" bias.

Many groups and individuals tried to convince Ben-Gurion to make a gesture toward Israel's Arab neighbors and the Arab citizens within its borders. One of these was Martin Buber, the great philosopher. He has recorded a conversation with Ben-Gurion at a particularly important moment in Middle East history, shortly after the end of the 1948 war:

"In political history the time and the tempo are almost decisive factors. . . . In 1949 Prime Minister Ben-Gurion invited several other people and myself to a talk, the subject of which was how to shape the image of the nation. . . . I said then, *inter alia*: in my opinion, a government can exert a certain spiritual and moral influence on world opinion. For example, when, at a certain time, in a given situation, the government takes a step which, at least outwardly, appears opposed to all national reasoning and logic, the man in the street is liable to ask: Why was this done? What benefit will it bring to the state? And then the government comes and explains: this certain step has latent in it a reason which transcends the purpose of the hour, and it is intended for the hours to come, for future generations, for the long range. This is how it is possible to try to shape a nation's image.

"And at the same meeting I spoke very clearly and said: gentlemen, the Palestine Conciliation Commission is to meet in the next few days. Let us invite representatives of nations, even of churches, and say to them: we are ready to aid the solution of the Arab refugee problem. We bring this matter before you, so that we shall find a way out together, and Israel will play an active part in implementing the solution.

"There was a discussion, and before we parted beside the door, Ben-Gurion said to me: 'Mr. Buber, don't think that I am opposed to what you said. But you forget that in history there is something called early—and something called late.' I thought for a moment, and then replied: 'Yes! That is exactly what I meant.' . . . That was in 1949."[18]

We have traced the development of a "Middle Eastern" trend in the Zionist movement from Yahuda and Nordau through Achad Ha'am and Weizmann to Magnes and Buber. Now for the first time a confirmed "Middle Easterner" took office as Prime Minister of Israel. This was Moshe Sharett, who replaced Ben-Gurion in 1953.

Sharett's parents came from Russia. He himself had spent his childhood in Palestine and spoke Arabic fluently. Sharett understood the Arabs and knew how to talk to them. He did not believe that their enmity was based on misunderstanding or evilness. Instead he tried to discover the deeper source of the Arab hostility, in order to overcome it.

In a striking lecture given to a closed group of Mapai members in November 1957—a year after the Sinai campaign—and published for the first time ten years later, Sharett offered "Some Reflections on the Years 1947–1957." He began by sharply criticizing two fundamental errors prevalent in Israel: the first concerning the sources of Arab enmity, and the second concerning the way to combat this enmity and attain the essential permanent peace.

18. *Maariv*, January 27, 1961.

Sharett pointed out that the Arabs had always considered Palestine part of their national patrimony. They found it difficult to accept the establishment of a Jewish state, with a Jewish majority, in this territory. Further, the Arabs were shocked to discover in 1948 and 1956 that the Jews were well rooted in their country and could not easily be dislodged. Because of this state of psychological shock, the process of losing the current enmity and acquiescing in the new situation that had been created would be one "not of years but of decades."

Although he felt that the road to Jewish-Arab peace would be long and arduous, Sharett disagreed completely with the view so widely held in Israel, that—as he put it—"there was nothing that could be done, or that it didn't matter what we did." "I claim," he said, "that there is importance, both positive and negative, in what we do, from the viewpoint both of bringing peace closer or of pushing it further away."

Sharett summed up the "European" or Ben-Gurionist hard line approach, with which he disagreed, as follows:

"The Arabs only understand the language of force. The State of Israel must from time to time demonstrate clearly that it is strong and able and ready to use force in the most emphatic and efficient manner.

"As for peace, in any case it is doubtful or at least very far away. . . . There is more chance of it coming by the conviction of force than by talk of Israel's honest and true desire for peace. The question of peace therefore does not have to be considered when we are discussing some large-scale demonstration of strength in order to solve a problem of current security. If such actions or retaliations or new campaigns feed the fires of hatred, that shouldn't frighten us; the fire is being fed in any case. On the other hand, if we avoid a sharp reply for fear of aggravating the situation, we'll end up the loser. . . . If we add to these arguments the human inclination to retaliate, the Jews' special sensitivity to being suspected of weakness, and the proximity in time to the glorious era of the victorious (1948) war, we can understand the factors which have created the atmosphere supporting this attitude, in addition to the political and military considerations which are themselves quite weighty."

The approach Sharett himself favored, which I term "Middle Eastern," was described by him as follows:

"We must not stop thinking of peace, not for one moment. This is not only a political consideration, but also a long-range security one. Without detracting from the importance of current security factors, we always have to include the matter of peace among the elements to be considered. We must restrain our retaliations. The question remains whether it has actually been proven that acts of retaliation solve the security problems for which they are intended."[19]

During Sharett's period of office as Prime Minister there were several attempts to reach a *modus vivendi* with the Arabs, and particularly with Egypt. This was a period of great tension in the Middle East: border incidents, fedayeen raids, and reprisal operations. Yet 1954–1956 saw at least four high-level attempts to bridge the chasm.

In 1954 a direct Israeli initiative, prompted by Sharett, led to talks between top Arab and Israeli representatives in Paris and other European capitals. During these undercover negotiations the Egyptian spokesmen showed readiness to reach a secret agreement on normalizing relations and maintaining a tranquil border, without a formal peace treaty. Egypt was to agree to the passage of Israeli cargo through the Suez Canal, though not under the Israeli flag.

"The Egyptian representatives explained that their country had no evil intentions toward Israel, but because of Egypt's status among the Arab countries the military junta then just beginning its rule could not reach an open normalization of relations with her. The top Israeli Foreign Office people, headed by Sharett, who either took part in or knew about the negotiations, appreciated their value and considered this the beginning of a quiet normalization with other Arab countries and a chance to break the ring of hostility against Israel." It was suggested that Israel and Cairo should maintain direct contact in a European capital, as a means of settling controversial current matters.[20]

19. Mordehai Nahumi, "Ten Years After Suez," *New Outlook*, December 1966.
20. Uri Dan in *Maariv*, May 25, 1961.

But in the summer of 1954 the Egyptians arrested a group of Jews in Cairo and Alexandria on charges of trying to blow up the United States Embassy and Information Services. The talks in Paris were broken off and not resumed.

At the end of 1954 the British Labor Member of Parliament, Maurice Orbach, flew to Cairo to intercede on behalf of these Jews, two of whom had been sentenced to death. Orbach saw Nasser, who sent a letter to "my brother Sharett" through Orbach. At Nasser's initiative, Orbach and Ali Sabry—then Nasser's chief aide—worked out a *modus vivendi* under which both sides would halt belligerent threats and border incidents. Israel would help Egypt to develop its industry and technology.

In the middle of these negotiations the Baghdad Pact was signed. Nasser considered this an anti-Egyptian move, and suspected Orbach of setting up a smoke screen to conceal the talks on the pact. The talks between Egypt and Israel broke down. Shortly afterward the death sentences against the two Egyptian Jews were carried out.

In February 1955 Ben-Gurion returned to the government as Defense Minister, following the ousting of Pinchas Lavon in the aftermath of the Cairo sabotage trial. Sharett continued as Prime Minister until the 1955 elections, won by Ben-Gurion. The next government saw Ben-Gurion as Prime Minister and Sharett as Foreign Minister. But in June 1956 Sharett was forced to resign so that he would not prove an embarrassment when the Suez campaign was carried out. Since that time he was out of the Cabinet and on the sidelines of politics.

Another influential Zionist leader who has called for a more active Israeli policy toward the Arabs is Dr. Nahum Goldmann, president of the World Zionist Organization and the World Jewish Congress. He has criticized those Israeli leaders "who foster a do-nothing policy toward the Arabs."[21] While everything possible should be done to strengthen Israel's security against Arab attack, no effort should be spared, he believes, to create a climate in which peace negotiations could become possible.

Dr. Goldmann has suggested that Jews living abroad could play

21. Press conference in Tel Aviv: *Jerusalem Post*, May 4, 1965.

an important role in improving relations with the Arabs. He told a press conference in New York on June 13, 1965:

"The time has come to begin to create the atmosphere for Arab-Israel talks which may have to follow later. Just to sit and wait till a new generation of Arabs grow up who may be ready to accept Israel is not enough and nobody knows if time, in this respect, works for a peaceful solution.

"Israel should get Jewish communities outside Israel interested in this problem, especially in countries where there is a large Arab diaspora, which for many years lived in good relations with the Jewish communities, primarily in South America.

"It would be a denial of the past, and a violation of the tradition of Arab-Jewish relations for many centuries, if a violent conflict would develop between the Arabs and the Jewish people, with the Arabs becoming the forefront of neo-Nazi movements.

"Naturally, the Jews outside Israel cannot negotiate on behalf of Israel. The concrete problems will have to be discussed directly between Israel and the Arabs when the time comes. But the Jewish people, with the help of many non-Jewish liberals of good-will, could help create an atmosphere which would facilitate and create a psychological basis for direct Israel-Arab contacts."[22]

Dr. Goldmann has spoken about Israel's future as part of a Middle East federation with the Arab states. He has urged Israel to follow a policy of neutrality and non-identification in the Cold War, pointing out that because there are Jews in the United States, the Soviet Union, and most countries of the West and Eastern Europe, Israel should not align itself with any side involved in the global struggle.

Similiar views have been expressed consistently over the years by various groups and parties in Israel. These include Mapam (the United Workers Party), *Ihud*, the *New Outlook* group centering around the English-language magazine of that name and the Semitic Action group linked with the Hebrew weekly *Ha'olam Hazeh*.

While these groups held differing views and each had its own particular nuance, they all had several things in common. They

22. *Jewish Observer and Middle East Review*, July 2, 1965.

all felt strongly that Israel should accept its role as part of the Middle East, as a future partner of the Arabs in bringing technological and economic progress to the region. They all urged the Israeli Government to recognize that the Arabs living in Israel could be the bridge to peace; that a genuine attempt to solve the Palestinian refugee problem could change the atmosphere in the region; and that Israel should try to understand the Arab national liberation movement and express its readiness to help it free the Arab people from the shackles of poverty, illiteracy, and disease.

All these groups wanted Israel to take the initiative toward the Arabs—to act first without waiting for social and demographic changes in the Arab world to produce their results. This meant concessions by Israel, significant gestures which would symbolize boldly its determination to talk and act as an integral part of the Middle East.

But most Israelis feared the idea of concessions to the Arabs. They thought this would only open the door to further Arab demand and indicate that the Israelis were weak and could therefore be pressed. As a senior government official in Jerusalem told me: "If we are weak, we cannot afford to make concessions. And if we are strong, why should we?"

Or, as a writer on Israeli strategy has remarked:

"By the nature of her position, Israel has no choice but to prefer endangered existence to concessions incurring the greater danger of nonexistence. Any concession which may weaken Israel is too big for her; yet any concession that leaves the existence of Israel intact is considered by the Arabs as too small."[23]

The peace groups inside Israel argued, on the other hand, that an imaginative Israeli gesture would be a sign of strength, not of weakness. It would have a tremendous impact on world opinion. It would strengthen the moderates who were beginning to emerge in the Arab world, as shown by President Bourguiba's statements. Israel's action would be on record, in the eyes of the world. The Arabs would not be able to ignore it. And, most important of

---

23. Yehoshafat Harkavi, "The Arab-Israel Confrontation," *Midstream*, March 1966, p. 12.

all, it would emphasize the constructive nature of Israel and the negative enmity of those who deny it the right to exist.

Prime Minister Eshkol has said that "in several of the Arab-states secret groups have been formed who hope for peace with Israel. They are to be found here and there, among young students, intellectual circles, teachers and professors who have different views about Israel. With a little more patience—and you know that our people is endowed with patience—the influence of these peace-seeking groups could spread through the whole Arab world."[24]

This was precisely the issue raised by the peace groups within Israel: whether the country should wait patiently with folded hands for an Arab change of heart or take action to accelerate the awareness that Israel stood ready to play its legitimate and positive role in the region.

Prime Minister Eshkol himself aroused the hopes of the peace groups when he took office after Ben-Gurion resigned in June 1963. His first official statements were conciliatory and underlined Israel's desire for peace and progress. And his Foreign Minister, Abba Eban, was the most ardent "Middle Easterner" in the Cabinet since the days of Sharett.

But Eshkol's first years in office were dogged by a constant struggle with Ben-Gurion, who was trying to unseat him in favor of Moshe Dayan, Shimon Peres and the other Young Turks of his Rafi Party. On the external front, Eshkol had to confront the Arabs' attempt to divert the waters of the Jordan. From being a mild "Middle Easterner" Eshkol became more of a "European," his usual posture being somewhere between the two.

After a year or two of moderation, which saw Bourguiba's abortive peace campaign fail, Israel's foreign and security policy drifted once more into the pattern of Arab border raid and Israeli massive response so sadly familiar from the Ben-Gurion era. Tension along the Syrian border increased throughout 1966, and the arms race intensified. Slowly, with mounting pressure from extremists on both sides, the Middle East moved toward its rendezvous with war on June 5, 1967.

24. Television interview in New York: reported by *Davar*, June 8, 1964.

6 *The Third Round*

AT THE BEGINNING of April 1967 some Israeli farm workers began plowing in the demilitarized zone southeast of the Sea of Galilee. They were unarmed and had a long-standing legal right to work this piece of land. But for years the spring and fall sowings in the demilitarized zones had been the subject of bitter disputes which often resulted in violence. On this occasion too the Syrians opened fire with artillery.

As a reprisal, Israel decided to knock out the Syrian guns. This was done on April 7, using tanks, mortars, and heavy cannon. An aerial battle broke out, and seven of Syria's Russian-built MiG fighters were shot down.

The Damascus regime, headed by Nureddin Atassi, called upon Cairo to support it and attack Israel, in accordance with the mutual defense pact the two countries had signed in November 1966. But Nasser was not ready for a military clash with Israel. He did not intend to let Syria drag him into a war he did not want, at a time and place he could not choose. He made no move in response to the Syrian request.

Tension grew along the Syrian border following the Israeli punitive action. During the next thirty days there were fourteen incidents in this sector. On May 10 Israel's Chief of Staff, Yitzhak Rabin, warned that if the provocations continued, Israel would consider attacking Damascus and eliminating the threats to the Jewish settlements in Galilee.

From Cairo the situation was beginning to look alarming. It seemed as if Israel was preparing the ground for a full-scale attack on Syria aimed at gaining control of the heights overlooking the kibbutzim at the foothills of Mount Hermon. Nasser was not equipped logistically or politically for a war on Syria's southern border. Yet he knew that if war broke out and he declined to go to Syria's assistance, this would be used against him by the Ba'ath in Damascus—and his arch-conservative "Islamic alliance" rivals in Saudi Arabia and Jordan—as a sign that he was abdicating his leadership of the Arab world. He set out to seek a way of recapturing the initiative and restoring his hero image, without committing himself to an open combat with Israel.

The Soviet Union also was concerned about the way things were moving. Syria had become a useful springboard for Soviet influence in the region. Russian arms, advisers, and propaganda flowed through Damascus in increasing quantities. Supplying land mines and bazookas to the Syrian El Fatah guerrillas was a cheap and easy way of making things difficult for the United States and its friends in the region. But Moscow did not want a shooting war between Israel and Syria, in which Syria would ask for Russian assistance. This did not form part of the Kremlin's plan for this part of the globe.

Soviet policy in the Middle East aimed at the following objectives:

¶ Establishing footholds in such "progressive" Arab countries as Egypt, Syria, and Iraq and trying to persuade these countries to work together against Western influence.

¶ Embarrassing the United States and Britain by stressing their support for Israel. This enabled Moscow to claim that it was the friend of the Arabs against "the Western imperialists and colonialists," who were in league with Israel.

¶ Exploiting the vacuum left in the Middle East by the American preoccupation with Vietnam to nibble away at the edges of the U.S. presence in such countries as Jordan and Lebanon. The Soviet leaders were convinced that the Johnson Administration was far too deeply involved in Vietnam to do much more than talk about the Middle East. This gave Moscow the opportunity to show that it considered the Middle East one of its spheres of influence and that no settlement in this region could be reached without Washington's acknowledging Soviet influence in the Eastern Mediterranean.

A state of ferment and instability in the Middle East suited the Soviet Union. But the threat of an open war alarmed it. Moscow had long been urging Egypt and Syria to work together more closely and perhaps to return to the period of union in 1958–1961, which had ended in such vehement mutual recrimination. This was probably one of the reasons for Soviet Foreign Minister Andrei Gromyko's hush-hush visit to Cairo at the end of March. Now the Russians decided to use the crisis and the danger of an Israeli move against Damascus to press the "progressive" Arab countries to unite and stop their incessant internecine quarrelling.

At the beginning of May the Soviet Government informed Egypt and Syria that Israel was calling up troops and planned to attack Syria between May 17 and May 27. They produced intelligence reports claiming that Israel was massing at least eleven brigades on the Syrian border.

After the June war, in a speech in Cairo on July 23, Nasser revealed that Syria had at first referred to eighteen Israeli brigades. The Egyptian Government checked these reports and was "wrongly informed" that there were thirteen brigades.

It is now known that these reports were deliberately blown up by Moscow in order to press Nasser to act. At that time Israel had less than two hundred men in the area, on the lookout for Fatah saboteurs. The United Nations Truce Supervision Organization itself reported on May 19 an "absence of troop concentrations and significant troop movements on both sides of the line."

Some observers believe that if the guerrilla raids had continued for another few weeks, Israel would have carried out a reprisal action against Syria along the lines of the November 1966 Es Samu action. It is true that Eshkol and Rabin had come to the conclusion that another reprisal against Jordan could not be launched, both because of the strain it imposed on relations with the United States and because Es Samu had shown that Hussein was weaker than Israel had thought and could be toppled by another blow to his prestige. But they were fully conscious of the risk that an Israeli punitive action against Syria would push the Ba'ath even further into Moscow's hands and enable the Russians to push Nasser and the Syrians closer together—something which was not in Israel's interests. Israel's leaders decided to step up surveillance techniques on the border instead of becoming embroiled in another Security Council debate so soon after the Es Samu censure. In the middle of May there was no plan for direct action against the Damascus regime.

But the Arabs took the doctored Soviet reports seriously. They confirmed their own misgivings. Moscow urged Nasser to divert Israel's attention by staging troop movements on its southern flank. They pointed out that this would protect the Syrians, warn the Israelis, and increase Nasser's own prestige in the eyes of the Arab masses.

However, the Kremlin leaders made two colossal miscalculations. They assumed their arms shipments, technical aid, and political support gave them sufficient control over the Arabs. And, by the same logic, they took it for granted that the United States could control Israel equally firmly and that Israel would not dare to launch a war without the agreement of Washington. Both these assumptions were wrong. The Soviet policy makers did not reckon with the volatile Arab temperament or the mood of the Arab masses. And they did not appreciate the feeling of isolation and growing encirclement within Israel. The Russians were to learn to their cost that the Middle East does not respond logically to political planning and follows its own volcanic rules.

Nasser listened to the Soviet advice, but as always he remained his own man. He decided to act before May 15, when Israel would celebrate its nineteenth Independence Day with a military parade in Jerusalem.

The parade through the streets of Israel's capital was kept small in accordance with the 1949 armistice agreement, which banned heavy weapons and planes. Prime Minister Eshkol told the nation that day:

"It is quite clear to the Israeli Government that the focal point of the terrorists is in Syria. But we have laid down the principle that we shall choose the time, the place, and the means to counter the aggressor. . . . Syria has apparently assumed the role of spearhead in the Arab campaign against Israel. But the Syrians realize their limited strength, and it is not without reason that Syria seeks the patronage of bigger countries. But this does not alarm us."

During the parade Eshkol asked Rabin to call at his house after the parade. The Prime Minister had been informed that an Egyptian division was marching through the streets of Cairo before leaving for the Sinai Peninsula. During the whole of Israel's Independence Day the Egyptian radio and television gave these troop movements massive publicity.

On May 16 the Israeli Cabinet met in Jerusalem to discuss the situation. It was decided to call up some of the country's 250,000 reservists in order to strengthen the forces in the Negev facing the Sinai Peninsula.

At 10 P.M. that night the Egyptian Chief of Staff, General Mohammed Fawzi, sent a telegram to the commander of the United Nations Emergency Force in the Gaza Strip, General Indar Jit Rikhye, requesting the withdrawal of the force from Egypt's eastern borders. The telegram was vague; UN Secretary General U Thant later termed it "cryptic" in an official report.

But the next day, May 17, Egypt spelled out its intentions more clearly in a letter to U Thant himself from Nasser's Foreign Minister. This remarkable communication read as follows:

> United Arab Republic
> Ministry of Foreign Affairs
> El'Nil Street
> Giza, Cairo
> 17 May 1967

"Dear U Thant,

The UAR Government has the honor to inform you that it has decided to end the presence of the UN Emergency Force in the UAR's territory and in the Gaza Strip. Please take the necessary measures for the departure of these forces as soon as possible.

I take this opportunity to express to you my profound gratitude and respect.

> The Foreign Minister
> Mahmoud Riyad"

Nasser almost certainly thought this demand would lead to a Security Council debate at which Egypt would explain that it wanted to remove the UNEF from the area so that it would not be harmed if hostilities broke out. The debate would have given Moscow the opportunity to accuse Israel of planning an attack on Syria. The Eshkol Administration could have come under the same kind of pressure it had faced after the Es Samu incident the previous November.

Few people—least of all Nasser himself—thought that Thant would order the UN troops to leave the area at once without even consulting the General Assembly or the Security Council. Yet that is what happened. U Thant later tried to justify his decision on legal grounds, in a memorandum published on June 26. He argued that the UNEF could not remain in Egypt when its presence was undesirable to the Cairo authorities. But his action was widely criticized as an incredible blunder, the worst ever made by a UN Secretary General. Most commentators agreed with the senior foreign correspondent of *The New York Times*, C. L. Sulzberger, when he wrote:

"U Thant used his international prestige with the objectivity of a spurned lover and the dynamism of a noodle, thereby encouraging a storm that seems fated, sooner or later, to end in war."

Already on the morning of May 17 Egyptian troops began replacing Yugoslavians along the border of the Gaza Strip. By May 19 the world's first international peacekeeping force, which had kept the peace between Israel and Egypt for nearly eleven years, had been disbanded. And Israel watched in dismay as the Egyptian army once more occupied Sharm el Sheikh, the strategic outpost which controlled the Straits of Tiran and the entrance to the southern Israeli port of Eilat.

On May 22 Nasser struck a dramatic blow. He told his pilots at Advanced Air Headquarters in the Sinai Desert:

"The armed forces yesterday occupied Sharm el Sheikh. What does this mean? It is affirmation of our rights and our sovereignty over the Gulf of Aqaba, which constitutes Egyptian territorial waters. Under no circumstances will we allow the Israeli flag to pass through the Gulf of Aqaba."

And Nasser added:

"The Jews threaten war. We tell them: you are welcome. We are ready for war."

Nasser had played the ace in his dangerous game of poker. The cards were on the table. He had made a direct challenge to Israel which the latter could not ignore. The day after Nasser's announcement Prime Minister Eshkol told the Israeli Knesset in

Jerusalem:

"We are facing a crucial hour, crucial not only for Israel but for the entire world. In view of this situation I again call on the Great Powers to act without delay to maintain the right of free access for shipping to our southern port, a right that is reserved to every state without distinction."

On the same day President Johnson declared that the Egyptian blockade of Israeli shipping was illegal. He noted that four Presidents of the United States—Truman, Eisenhower, Kennedy, and himself—had strongly opposed aggression by anyone in the Middle East, "in any form, overt or clandestine."

"The United States," he stated, "considers the gulf to be an international waterway and feels that a blockade of Israeli shipping is illegal and disastrous to the cause of peace. The right of free, innocent passage of the international waterway is a vital interest of the entire international community."

Britain also criticized the closing of the gulf to Israeli shipping. The Foreign Office said:

"If it appeared that any attempt to interfere with ships going through the waterway was likely to be made, we should support international action through the United Nations to secure free passage."

The Soviet Government also issued a statement which noted that leading Israeli statesmen had called for a decisive blow against Syria. "It is quite clear that Israel could not act in this way were it not for the direct and indirect encouragement it has had from certain imperialist circles which would like to bring colonial oppression back to Arab lands."

Moscow issued a warning to those circles in Israel who were urging an immediate strike against the Egyptian positions in Sharm el Sheikh:

"Let no one have any doubts about the fact that should anyone try to unleash aggression in the Near East he would be met not only by the united strength of Arab countries but also by strong opposition to aggression from the Soviet Union and all peace-loving states."

The Cabinet met in a tense atmosphere. Some Ministers favored prompt action to open the strait. But Foreign Minister Abba

Eban urged the Cabinet to delay any military moves until the United States and the other powers were told that Israel would have no choice but to fight if the gulf was not opened. Eban was sent to Washington to remind Lyndon B. Johnson of the solemn U.S. promise in 1957 to guarantee the right of free passage for Israeli ships if Israel withdrew its troops from Sharm el Sheikh after the victorious Sinai campaign.

Eban flew to Paris, where General de Gaulle tried to persuade Israel not to fire the first shot in a Middle East war. In London the Israeli Foreign Minister discussed with Prime Minister Harold Wilson the formation of a permanent international naval force in the Gulf of Aqaba—a sort of UNEF at sea.

On May 26 Eban met President Johnson at the White House. During their ninety-minute talk Johnson outlined various proposals for an international maritime move to break the blockade. One of these called for an Israeli merchant ship flying the Israeli flag to pass through the strait escorted by U.S. and British vessels, ready to respond if the Israeli ship was stopped.

Eban was left with the impression that the United States would honor its commitment to free passage for Israeli ships. But Johnson told Eban he needed more time. He wanted to take the issue to the Security Council. If this failed, and if other maritime nations refused to cooperate, Washington would act alone to open the gulf, Johnson affirmed.

The President asked Eban to advise Israel to use restraint for another fortnight while these moves were being considered. Eban flew back to Israel on May 27 to report to the Cabinet. But even as he reported the American plan for what was termed Operation Regatta it ran into trouble. The British and Canadians had lost much of their initial enthusiasm; the French, Scandinavians, and Italians were not eager to join the scheme. Only the Dutch were ready to take part in the pro-Israel flotilla.

Later on, after the war had begun, Prime Minister Eshkol was to recall these promises with unaccustomed bitterness. He told a gathering of Mapai Party officials:

"President Johnson promised great things. They told us that forty to fifty maritime powers would sign a guarantee for free passage through the Tiran Strait. We examined the situation and found that it really came down to a dozen and finally to only two countries and then, perhaps, to only one—Israel."

Meanwhile, back in Cairo, Nasser was keeping the pot boiling and the lid tightly on. On May 26—while Eban and Johnson were meeting in Washington—he told the heads of the Pan-Arab Federation of Trade Unions in Cairo that if war came "it would be total and the objective will be to destroy Israel. We feel confident that we can win and are ready now for a war with Israel."

"This time," Nasser told the cheering trade union leaders, "it will not be like 1956, because we were not fighting Israel then, but Britain and France."

"Today the world must know the reality of the Arab world," he declared. "What is Israel? Israel today is the United States. The United States is the chief defender of Israel. As for Britain, I consider it America's lackey. . . . Wilson always follows in Johnson's footsteps and says what he wants him to say. All Western countries take Israel's view."

Was Nasser merely saber-rattling in the hope that the United States would offer him some concrete inducement—such as another wheat supply agreement—to call off his campaign? Or was he just blundering into a war because to backtrack then would have lost him too much face?

Perhaps he may simply have decided that, with the United States so deeply involved in Vietnam, it would not want to enter another war with the Soviet Union over Israel's shipping difficulties and hence would press Israel to remain moderate. The London *Times* was probably near the mark when it wrote in its May 23 editorial:

"It is puzzling why President Nasser should have pushed things so far and so hard. Has he himself been pushed? Is he relying on U Thant finding a rescue formula?

"Both these possibilities may be true.

"It may also be true that Nasser, who, though shrewder than most of the other Arab leaders, is no less convinced that a final round with Israel has to come eventually, may have calculated that on balance the present moment has a lot to be said for it. American attention is distracted; the Russians are friendly; his reputation has always grown in crises. His big gambles—the 1952 coup, Suez, the High Dam—have come off. Why not this one?"

One thing Nasser's speech to the trade unionists did accomplish: it alarmed both the United States and the Soviet Union and led to separate efforts that night to restrain him. Nasser himself told the story in his June 9 "resignation" speech:

"A message from the U.S. President Lyndon Johnson was handed to our Ambassador in Washington on May 26 asking us to show self-restraint and not to be the first to fire, or else we should have to face severe consequences.

"On the very same night, the Soviet Ambassador asked me to have an urgent meeting with him at 03:30 after midnight. He informed me of an urgent request from the Soviet Government not to be the first to open fire."

In this midnight confrontation the Soviet Ambassador to Cairo, Dmitri P. Pozhidayev, expressed his government's concern about Nasser's remarks the previous day. He made it clear that Egypt could not count on any direct Soviet support if it began a war in the Middle East.

Pozhidayev told the UAR President the Kremlin did not consider Israel strong enough to attack Egypt and believed Jerusalem would not act against Washington's known desire for restraint. He tried to persuade Nasser that he could attain his objectives most effectively through political and diplomatic pressure, and promised full Soviet support for this strategy.

The same day Soviet Premier Alexei Kosygin sent a letter to Israeli Prime Minister Eshkol. This was made public in Jerusalem eight days later. Kosygin appealed to Eshkol to "take all measures to prevent a military conflict." "We are confident," he added, "that—however complex the situation on the frontiers of Israel, Syria, and the UAR—measures ought to be found to settle the conflict by non-military means; because it is easy to start the fire, but to put the fire out may prove not as simple as those who are edging Israel on to the brink of a military abyss think."

Meanwhile the Israeli Cabinet held a crucial session on May 27, after a tense Saturday, the Israeli Sabbath. Eban arrived back in the evening, and met with the Cabinet at the Ministry of Defense in Tel Aviv's *Hakirya* government compound. Many of the Ministers were in an anxious mood. They felt Israel was marking time and allowing Nasser to take the initiative. But Eban felt President Johnson should be given the two weeks he had asked for. He argued that Israel's readiness to wait for the West to act was placing world public opinion on its side, and this would be vital if war did eventually break out.

Several Ministers insisted that the United States and Britain would not send ships to break the blockade of the gulf. Hence they wanted immediate Israeli action, without waiting any longer for Johnson and Wilson to form an international flotilla. A cargo ship was being prepared by Israel at the port of Massawa, in Ethiopia, ready to force the blockade at Sharm el Sheikh. The Ministers proposed that this ship should be sent into the Strait of Tiran. If Egypt stopped it, Israel should declare war at once.

No decision was reached that night. But public opinion was growing restive. Several right-wing papers were pressing for a wall-to-wall coalition government which would include strong military figures. The feeling was growing that Eshkol was not vigorous enough for the dangerous situation Israel faced.

The next day, Sunday, May 28, Nasser added further fuel to the fire. He gave his only full-scale press conference of the crisis, attended by two hundred reporters from most of the world press. The eighty-minute press conference at the Kubbah Palace at Heliopolis, just outside Cairo, was broadcast live by Cairo Radio.

Winston Burdett of CBS asked President Nasser: "Is your confidence due to your reading of the international political situation, or does it stem from your belief in the military supremacy of the UAR armed forces?"

"Today we are alone face to face with Israel," Nasser replied. "And if Israel wants to try war I would again say to it: welcome. As for the question of military supremacy, we believe of course that our armed forces are capable of carrying out their duty with honor, strength, and sincerity.

"We accept no kind of coexistence with Israel," Nasser declared. "The rights of Palestinians should be given back to them. Israel expelled the Palestinians from their country in 1948 and stole their property. Where are the rights of the Palestine people? We will remain patient, one, ten, or more years until we secure the rights of the people of Palestine. As I have said before, the Arab people are not a people who easily forget. They are a people who have a civilization and a history and they must achieve their aim."

The Tiran Strait, Nasser said, was Egyptian territorial water. "No power however strong it may be can touch Egypt's sovereign rights or circumvent them. Any such attempt will be aggression on the Egyptian people and all Arabs and will bring unimaginable harm to the aggressors."

If war broke out with Israel, he added, conditions in the Suez Canal would remain unchanged. But if other countries intervened on Israel's behalf, "there will be no Suez Canal."

This was interpreted in Israel as a warning that Nasser would block the canal to American and British ships if an international flotilla was formed. It was intended to deter any country which was thinking of joining the Johnson-Wilson project.

That night Prime Minister Eshkol met in Tel Aviv, at the Defense Ministry, to discuss the implications of Nasser's press conference. His military advisers now felt there was even less chance than before of the West making a really tough attempt to open the strait, following Nasser's warning. They also told Eshkol bluntly that every day of inaction could cost up to two hundred people killed in battle if a war did break out. They estimated that mobilizing the reserves and keeping them in the field was losing the country $20 million a day in crops that could not be harvested and goods that could not be produced.

Eshkol left the meeting in a depressed frame of mind. He drove to his official residence in Sderot Ben-Maimon, in the Rehavia quarter of Jerusalem, and went to bed.

At 2 A.M. he was awakened by the Soviet Ambassador, Dmitri Chuvakin, with a note from his government. This accused Israel of planning to attack Syria and Egypt, in collusion with the imperialists, and warned of the dire consequences which would face Israel unless it desisted. The two men spoke in Russian, Eshkol still half-dressed, with a jacket over his pajamas. The Israeli Prime Minister firmly denied the charges, accused Nasser in turn of building up tension along the Sinai frontier, and said there were no Israeli troops on the Syrian border. He was ready, he said, to send Chuvakin there for an on-the-spot inspection. Eshkol added that he was even ready to accompany him personally.

The portly Chuvakin was taken aback by this suggestion and by Eshkol's remark that he also would be ready to visit the Kremlin to explain Israel's attitude to the crisis, if he would be invited. Chuvakin refused to travel to the Syrian border and left after repeating the official Soviet warning. Eshkol went back to bed.

That was on the morning of Monday, May 29. Later that day President Nasser addressed the National Assembly in Cairo, which granted him emergency powers to rule by decree. Nasser focused his attack on the Western countries, which, he claimed, were slighting Egypt and denying it the rights it was entitled to. "We shall teach them how to respect us," he told the cheering delegates. "We are not facing Israel but those behind it. We are facing those who created Israel." And he concluded by telling the National Assembly: "The preparations by the United Arab Republic and its allies for the liberation of Palestine are complete." This boast was noted in Jerusalem and not taken idly. There were signs that Nasser was no longer in control of the situation and had carried the national mood in Egypt over the brink.

That night the UN Security Council held an emergency session in New York, to discuss a United States proposal that Egypt should return to the status quo which existed in the Strait of Tiran before Nasser's May 22 bombshell. The American delegate called for a breathing spell during which freedom of navigation in the gulf should continue, while the UN held talks on a lasting solution. The Egyptian spokesman rejected this and stated categorically that the strait was Arab territory and Israeli ships would no longer be allowed through. No vote was taken and the negative discussion petered out in a display of weakness that dealt the death blow to the position still held then by such moderate Israelis as Foreign Minister Eban.

The turning point—the swing of the balance from tension to war—came the next day, with the dramatic news that King Hussein of Jordan had flown to Cairo and signed a mutual defense pact with Nasser.

Hussein was the Arab ruler most hated by Nasser and the Syrians. Only a month earlier Nasser had dubbed him "an imperialist agent who wants to deceive the Arab people." The

Egyptian President delighted students at Cairo University by punning in classical Arabic, calling Hussein "the fornicator (*a'aher*) of the Hashemite royal family," instead of "the ruler (*a'ahel*)." A joint Egyptian-Syrian government statement, broadcast on May 2, said that "Hussein's country is becoming a garrison of imperialist weapons, a camp for training mercenary gangs." On the Voice of the Arabs radio from Cairo Achmed Sa'id had threatened Hussein with "the punishment of death" because of "his open collusion with Israel, the United States, and Britain." Cairo Radio itself often referred to him as "the Hashemite harlot" and "the hyena of Jordan."

Yet on that black Tuesday of May 30 Hussein paid a six-hour visit to Cairo to meet President Nasser, bury the hatchet, and agree that the Egyptian Chief of Staff would command both the Jordanian and the UAR armies if war broke out.

To the shocked Israelis watching Hussein and Nasser kiss at Cairo airport this could mean only one thing: the Arabs had decided to attack Israel, and Hussein did not want to be left out and isolated as the man who did not join in. He had jumped on the bandwagon to save his throne and had in effect placed Nasser on Israel's eastern border. There was now a hostile ring encircling Israel from Syria, on the north, through Jordan, on the east, to Egypt, in the south.

Two weeks earlier Amman Radio had attacked Nasser for "cooperating with Zionism and Marxism to cause chaos and further the cause of Socialism." Now it proclaimed:

"Blessed be Hussein and his brother President Nasser who have signed the joint defense agreement to establish Arab troops on the borders of the usurped homeland with power and might."

The Hussein-Nasser embrace settled the internal debate between hawks and doves in Israel. It made the Tiran shipping issue seem suddenly academic. The frantic efforts being made in Washington and London to find other countries willing to act for maritime freedom became irrelevant. This was the crunch, and everyone in Israel knew it at once, with the instinct and chill at the back of the neck that besieged people acquire. An Israeli officer told me: "When I saw Hussein and Nasser together I knew it was war. The war really began at that moment."

On the same day Abba Eban told a press conference in Jerusalem that Israel could not wait indefinitely for its friends to act. There must be a time limit of "weeks or days" for diplomatic moves, he said. "We will act alone if we must to break the blockade, but with others if we can." Even as he spoke his position was being eroded by the Cairo pact. The time for patience had gone. The nations of the world had been given their opportunity and had failed. From now on Israel was a fortress.

That night Eshkol went to a Mapai meeting. His own supporters told him the public mood was against him and calling for some decisive action. They warned him that unless he broadened his Cabinet and brought in a recognized military man as Defense Minister he would face public demonstrations and could come under pressure to resign.

Eshkol was taken aback. He had not expected this lack of confidence in his leadership. But his worst fears were confirmed a few hours later when he met with Moshe Haim Shapiro, the Minister of the Interior and leader of the National Religious Party. He went away from this meeting convinced that he should give up the Ministry of Defense, which he held in addition to the premiership, and appoint Labor Minister Yigal Allon to the post. Allon was a 1948 war hero, and his approach was close to Eshkol's own. His appointment would be popular and would end speculation about the inclusion of any of former Prime Minister Ben-Gurion's protégés in the government.

All next day—Wednesday, May 31—the discussions went on. Some right-wing circles wanted Ben-Gurion in the government. But Eshkol had been fighting a running battle with Ben-Gurion since the latter resigned in 1963. The two men could not sit around the same table, even in this moment of national crisis. Eshkol flatly refused to stand down for Ben-Gurion.

As for Ben-Gurion, he still hoped that the nation would call him back in its hour of danger. He had visions of ousting Eshkol and Eban and bringing his own Young Turks, Dayan and Peres, into a war Cabinet, which would repeat his 1956 military victory over Nasser.

But Dayan had other ideas. He felt his hour had come. And he did not feel bound to follow Ben-Gurion's personal vendetta against Eshkol. Dayan got Rafi—the splinter group Ben-Gurion had formed when he left Mapai—to propose him as its candidate for an enlarged Cabinet. Ben-Gurion was angry at Dayan's move and his readiness to serve as Defense Minister under Eshkol. He refused at first to agree to this.

By the evening of Wednesday, May 31, everyone in the government felt the main danger was the Egyptian troop buildup, no longer the naval blockade. It was becoming clear also that the United States was alone in proposing tough international action to open the strait. No leading Israeli felt President Johnson would act alone when the chips were down. Israel had to see it through alone or face the possibility that this time the Arabs were not bluffing. Even Eban told his colleagues that he would no longer insist on waiting for effective international action and exercising restraint. During the last two weeks Israel's patience had placed world public opinion on its side. But, Eban added, he would not oppose military action if there was a real danger that Nasser would strike first.

Eshkol still favored Allon as Defense Minister over Dayan. So did his closest supporters, who feared Dayan would receive the credit for the planning already put in by the Chief of Staff, Yitzhak Rabin, and his brilliant team of officers. But many of the Mapai rank and file preferred Dayan. On Thursday, June 1, the Mapai Secretariat met to decide the issue. Of the twenty-four speakers nineteen backed Dayan and only five Allon. And an alternative proposal by Eshkol, to appoint the noted archaeologist, Professor Yigael Yadin, who was a former Chief of Staff, was turned down by Yadin and Rafi.

That evening Eshkol agreed that Dayan should become Defense Minister. But it took Rafi two hours of stubborn argument with an enraged Ben-Gurion before the latter withdrew his opposition to Rafi joining a government led by his arch-enemy Eshkol. At 11 P.M. the Cabinet decided to coopt Dayan and two Gahal representatives, Menachem Beigin and Yosef Saphir.

Even before Dayan entered the Government war seemed inevitable. Now all that remained unclear was the timing. Even if Dayan had not joined the Cabinet, Israel probably still would have gone to war. But his inclusion symbolized the national realization that no external friend or ally would risk war with the Arabs or the Soviet Union on its behalf. His value was perhaps more psychological than technical. Now the Israelis knew there was no choice and the moment they had not thought would come again had come. They had to close their ranks or scatter them. From then on party differences were submerged, with survival the only political principle.

At the end of the week Israeli diplomats in Washington reported their conviction that if Israel attacked Egypt the United States would not intervene and would not call for an Israeli withdrawal as it had in 1956. This was what Jerusalem was waiting for, and it set the seal on the approaching decision.

Meanwhile the Arabs were engaged in feverish activity. President Abdel Rohman Aref of Iraq agreed to send troops and armored units into Jordan, at Hussein's personal request. In Amman Achmed Shukairy forecast that it was "possible and even most likely" that his Palestine Liberation Army would fire the first shot against Israel. If the Arabs took Israel, he declared confidently, the surviving Jews would be helped to return to their countries of origin. "But," he added, "I do not think any will survive."

And on Saturday, June 3, the Egyptian Commander in Chief, General Abdel Mohsen Mortagi, issued an order of the day to his soldiers in Sinai:

"The results of this unique moment are of historic importance for our Arab nation and for the *jihad* (holy war) through which you will restore the rights of the Arabs which have been stolen in Palestine and reconquer the plundered soil of Palestine."

That night the Israeli Cabinet held a secret meeting and decided to strike first. The preemptive attack was fixed for the morning of Monday, June 5. War was only thirty-six hours away.

The same evening Dayan drew a red herring across the trail. He held a press conference in Tel Aviv—his first public appearance as Defense Minister. One correspondent asked him whether Israel had lost its military advantage by waiting. He replied blandly:

"I would think just now it's too late and too early: too late to react right away against the blockade and too early to draw any conclusions on the diplomatic way of handling the matter." He added: "Before I became a member of the Government, it decided on diplomacy. We must give it a chance."

Several thousand Israeli soldiers were sent on leave that weekend, and the world press carried photographs of them basking in the sun on the beaches of Tel Aviv and Ashqelon. The mood in the country was relaxed, but not from complacency or overconfidence. Now that the decision had been taken, everyone was calm. It was better to know and to be prepared to act than to live in indecision. The last three weeks of strain had been too much. Nothing could be worse than waiting for others to save one, not knowing whether they could be relied upon. All Jewish experience, a worldly-wise and cynical discounting of Gentile promises, a tribal awareness of isolation, and a new irritation with passivity, a flint-hard impatience born of the difficult, unfamiliar land, a refusal to undergo another ritual slaughter, culminated in a moment of supreme anger in which individuals and nation dared, decided, and fused into one.

In Cairo there was uneasiness behind the boasting and militant talk over the air. On June 4 Cairo Radio proclaimed that the combined forces of the Arabs were poised "to wipe Israel off the map." But Nasser and his top advisers were concerned. Dayan's appointment had the same meaning for them that Hussein's reconciliation with Nasser had had for the Israelis.

Field Marshal Abdel Hakim Amer, Nasser's right-hand man and closest confidant, was particularly worried. At a meeting of the Supreme Command of the Egyptian General Staff on June 2 Amer warned of an Israeli attack within the next ten days and urged Nasser to strike first. He wanted a land invasion of Israel from the Sinai Peninsula and an air attack on the heavily populated coastal plain. But the Soviet Union was still pressing Nasser hard to avoid any military action and to rely on political and diplomatic moves. Nasser placed the one hundred thousand Egyptian soldiers in the Sinai on a general alert, but did not give in to Amer's repeated pleas for war on Israel.

On the morning of Monday, June 5, the entire Egyptian Supreme Command, headed by Amer, left Cairo by plane at 8

A.M. Egyptian time, heading for the Bir Thamada Airfield in Sinai. At 8:45 Egyptian time (7:45 Israeli time) the first wave of Israeli planes attacked ten Egyptian airfields in the Sinai and Egypt proper. The senior Egyptian officers were in the air when this devastating attack was launched. En route to Bir Thamada they were told the airfield had been raided. The pilot tried to find an undamaged airfield in Sinai, but failed. Amer and his officers finally returned to Cairo ninety minutes later. By then the damage had been done and it was too late to strike back.

The first news that war had broken out came over Kol Yisrael (the Voice of Israel) radio station in Hebrew, at 9:05 on the morning of June 5. It announced:

"Israeli forces are attacking an Egyptian armored column moving towards Israel."

This feeble fiction was soon abandoned, and after the second day Israel did not try to deny that it had attacked first. There was little need to explain the provocation to which it had been subject; this was the chief value of the two-week delay Eban had secured.

The aerial attack blasted the Arab air forces on their runways and caught Cairo on the wrong foot. The war was won in those first crushing 70 minutes. Cairo Radio announced at 10:30 A.M. that 23 Israeli aircraft had been shot down, and at 11:00 A.M. increased this figure to 42. Both these claims were false. And the Arab losses were so enormous that when the Israeli radio announced at 11:48 A.M. that 120 Egyptian planes had been destroyed, most foreign journalists did not believe it.

But that night Colonel Mordechai Hod, Commander of the Israeli Air Force, gave the full staggering details. Speaking over the Israeli radio at 2:15 A.M., he said:

"Today we had a showdown with the Air Forces of Egypt, Jordan, Syria, and Iraq. In today's battle we destroyed about 400 enemy aircraft. The following are details of the enemy aircraft destroyed:

"In Egypt about 300 planes were destroyed. These include 30 heavy bombers of the Tupolev-16 type, about 26 medium bombers of the Ilyushin-28 type, 12 fighter bombers of the Sf-7 type, which were received by Egypt only recently, about 90 MiG-21 aircraft, about 20 MiG-19s, 75 MiG-17s, and another 22 transport aircraft and helicopters. About 20 of these were destroyed in air battles.

"In Syria about 52 planes were destroyed. They include 30 MiG-21s, 20 MiG-17s, and 2 Ilyushin-28 aircraft.

"In Jordan 20 Hunter aircraft and 7 transport planes and helicopters were destroyed.

"When a group of Iraqi aircraft attacked Israeli settlements we attacked their H-3 base in Iraq and destroyed 6 MiG-21 planes and 3 Hunters."

The Israeli losses were 19 pilots and 15 planes.

In the same dramatic broadcast Major General Yitzhak Rabin, the Israeli Chief of Staff, summed up the first day's fighting in typically laconic language:

"In the northern Sinai sector our forces captured Rafah, Sheikh Zuair, and in the evening El Arish. Our forces captured Khan Yunis and Deir el Balah and are now fighting along the approaches to the town of Gaza." Rabin also announced Israeli victories in the Sinai and on the Jordanian front.

This was the beginning of six days which stunned the world and left even the most optimistic Israelis gasping and incredulous. The June 5 campaign already belongs to the history books. It will be studied by future soldiers and strategists as a model of swift, ruthless attack. It was like an operation by a skilled surgeon: deft, economical, clean. And it was fueled by an army of people who knew they could not afford to lose, who knew what they could expect if they fell into the hands of the Arabs. The power behind the Israeli planes and tanks was not fear, not desperation, just a fierce will to survive, a refusal to die.

To come from the terrible isolation and growing chill of the last few weeks to these almost incredible victories was an overwhelming experience. One of Israel's leading soldier-politicians told the *Observer* correspondent, Colin Legum, later:

"The only analogy I can think of is if Britain had found herself in occupation of Berlin just three days after Dunkirk. The suddenness of the transformation from a situation of acute danger to unparalleled victory is too much for any people to absorb. It will take time to get over it. Israel is still in a state of shock."

In the evening of that fantastic first day the BBC in London received a dispatch from its Jerusalem correspondent, Michael Elkins. It was broadcast on BBC-1 television at 8:50 P.M. that night. The BBC was so sceptical of the report's accuracy—and it is easy to see why—that it stressed it was "unconfirmed."

Elkins said:

"History has been repeating itself in the Middle East today—except that things are moving faster now than they did in 1956, when Israel took a hundred hours to smash the Egyptian army and conquer the Sinai Peninsula and Gaza Strip.

"Less than fifteen hours after the fighting began at dawn this morning, there was every evidence that, though fighting will continue, Israel has already won the war. . . . This time Israel has created the nearest thing to instant victory the modern world has seen."

Within 48 hours of the beginning of the war the first Israeli forces reached the Suez Canal—only to be ordered back 20 miles to the east, to avoid an international controversy over the canal, which they returned to the next day, Thursday, June 8. In less than four days the Israelis had smashed Nasser's 100,000-strong Sinai army. They had taken or destroyed over 700 up-to-date Russian tanks. Thousands of transport vehicles, troop carriers, and cars lay in the sand of the desert or were standing by the side of the road waiting to be taken back to Israel. Three MiG-21s—the most modern Soviet fighter planes—were captured intact. Six SAM ground-to-air missiles, together with their computers, guidance equipment, and fueling systems, fell into Israeli hands at an Egyptian base near the Suez Canal. One captured rifle—a 130-mm. M-63 capable of firing six 70-lb. shells per minute as far as 17 miles—was so new that it had not even been shown at a May Day parade in Moscow.

No wonder then that the Arab defeat led to such bitter recriminations between Nasser and the Kremlin, or that Moscow Radio gave this biting explanation of why the Arabs lost, in a commentary on June 13:

"The Israeli forces represented a well-trained army of educated men, equipped with modern weapons. . . .

"The Arab armies were also equipped with modern weapons.

They had hundreds of tanks, planes, and artillery pieces. Their commanders went to a school of modern warfare, learning from the experience of the most powerful army in the world, the Soviet Army.

"However, if we examine the ranks of the Arab armies we shall see that they are composed of peasants, most of them with a poor education, not always able to make the best of modern weapons. This was the big difference."

On Monday, the day war broke out, the Israeli Air Force smashed the air forces of Egypt, Syria, and Jordan. Tuesday and Wednesday saw the heaviest fighting in the Sinai and the West Bank of the Jordan. The Egyptian Government agreed to a cease-fire late on Thursday night, with Israel troops encamped on the eastern bank of the Suez Canal. Syria joined in the ground fighting on Tuesday. But the really heavy clash on the Syrian border—the grimmest and bloodiest of the entire lightning campaign—took place on Thursday, Friday, and Saturday.

At the end of the most astonishing week in Israel's modern history it had become the strongest country in the Middle East, with the exception of Turkey. Israel controlled the Gaza Strip; the whole of the Sinai Peninsula up to the Suez Canal, including Sharm el Sheikh, overlooking the Strait of Tiran; the Old City of Jerusalem; the West Bank of the Jordan; and the Syrian Heights around Kuneitra. Israeli troops were only eighty miles from Cairo and thirty miles from Damascus and Amman.

Israel also held, as a result of the war, the source of the Banias River, which Syria had threatened to divert in 1964 to stop water flowing into the Jordan and then to the Negev. The unfinished excavation of this abortive diversion scheme was also in Israel's hands. So was a ten-mile strategic position along the Yarmuk River, into which the diverted Banias was to have flowed.

There were other by-products of Israel's victory. The oil fields of Sinai, on the Gulf of Suez, which produced 150,000 barrels a day, made Israel self-sufficient in oil and in fact, together with its domestic production from the Heletz fields, enabled it to become an oil-exporting country instead of an oil-importing one. Thirty miles of the Trans-Arabian underground oil pipeline running from the Persian Gulf through Syrian territory to the Lebanese coast is now controlled by Israel, which could thus cut off the flow of

Middle East oil to Western Europe—at least theoretically. And the Syrian Heights contain good wheatland which could overcome Israel's need to import grain.

The Arabs learned the bitter facts of their colossal defeat only slowly over the next few months. Even in his phony resignation speech of June 9 President Nasser did not dare to reveal the whole truth. It was only much later, in a speech to the opening of the fifth session of the Egyptian National Assembly—made on November 23—that Nasser admitted the UAR's losses. He put these at 10,000 soldiers and 1,500 officers. Five thousand soldiers and 500 officers were prisoners of war. These casualties, Nasser said, did not include the Air Force.

"Eighty per cent of our equipment was lost in the first six days," Nasser told the hushed National Assembly. "Our forces were scattered. It was a complete panic. We had no defenses on the western bank of the Suez Canal. Not a single soldier stood between the enemy and the capital. The road to Cairo was open."

But although the people of Egypt were deprived of true information about the defeat for more than five months, the consciousness of Israel's victory could not be suppressed. Many Egyptians had kinfolk fighting in Sinai. The inhabitants of such towns as Ismailia and Suez could see the Israeli soldiers one hundred yards away, on the other side of the canal. Officers were spat on in the streets of Cairo. And whether Field Marshal Amer's sensational suicide in September was genuine or staged, it gave the people of Egypt a glimpse of the struggle behind the scenes after the reality of defeat sank in.

Visiting Cairo at the end of June, Anthony Nutting noted, in a report to the London *Sunday Times*:

"As the shock and humiliation of defeat takes hold, like the gradually mounting throb of a deep wound, so the sense of isolation grows and with it the inevitable search for scapegoats."

A very prominent Egyptian newspaper editor told the London *Times*:

"When we lost, the impossible happened; everything else since that only added to our hopelessness."

And an Egyptian civilian at the Khartoum summit conference of Arab leaders in September said bitterly:

"For fifteen years we've been asked to make sacrifices to build up an army which we thought would make us strong and safe. But when it came to the test it took Israel only a few hours to defeat us."

One of the best-known Lebanese writers, Leila Balabaki— sometimes called "the Lebanese Françoise Sagan"—expressed her feeling of shock in the Beirut weekly *Al Osavua al Arabi:*

"We are a deceived people. A defeated people. A people fed by false dreams and vain promises. A people that must gather its strength, unite, and awake from the memories of its past."

Some Arab papers accused the Soviet Union of backtracking on its promises of help and of letting the Arabs down when it came to the crunch. But some others were prepared to draw more realistic conclusions from Moscow's policy throughout the crisis. They knew now that the Kremlin was not ready for a global war with Washington over the Israeli-Arab dispute. And these feelings were strengthened when Soviet Premier Kosygin met President Johnson in Glassboro, New Jersey, for their summit conference, only three weeks after the war ended.

On June 16 *Time* magazine revealed that at 8 A.M. that fateful Monday, June 5, the hot-line link between Washington and Moscow was activated from Moscow. Since the "hot line" had been put into operation on August 30, 1963, it had mainly conveyed New Year's greetings and hourly routine testing messages. It had never before been used for communication between the U.S. and Soviet governments in time of crisis.

"Now, at the cable circuit's terminus in the Pentagon, lines of Cyrillic type sent from Soviet Premier Alexei Kosygin began clattering in at sixty-six words a minute on a teletype machine. . . .

"Concerned, President Johnson hurried to a mahogany conference table in the basement Situation Room of the White House. He was joined there by Defense Secretary Robert S. McNamara, Secretary of State Dean Rusk and Walt W. Rostow, the President's national security adviser.

"Kosygin's message was decoded and relayed instantly in Russian from the Pentagon to the Situation Room, where it was rendered into English within minutes. A glance at the rough translation told Johnson what he wanted to know: there would be no face-down between the Big Two. Russia, said Kosygin, did not plan to enter the conflict but would do so if the U.S. stepped in. Johnson and his aides drafted a reply on the spot, directly assuring Kosygin that the U.S. did not intend to intervene."

Time itself summed up the meaning of the mutual consultations between Johnson and Kosygin throughout the fighting:

"Though the Israelis and Arabs were able to launch a small but ferocious war on their own turf, the key to a big war remained in the hands of the U.S. and the U.S.S.R. Given prudence and restraint on both sides, the key will not be turned."

This lesson was not lost on President Bourguiba, who took the opportunity to remind the Arabs of his warnings only two years earlier. Speaking on August 24 at Kef, ninety miles southwest of Tunis, he pointed an accusing finger at some Arab leaders whom he blamed for the lightning Israeli victory.

"The State of Israel has been recognized by both the United States and Soviet Russia," Bourguiba declared. "It is a member of the United Nations, and its existence is challenged only by Arab countries.

"In these circumstances it is useless to continue ignoring this reality and to claim that Israel should be wiped off the map. In so doing one drives himself into near-total isolation."

In a clear reference to Nasser and the Syrian leaders, the Tunisian President castigated "mistakes which led to the June war":

"Because one expected the aggressor to come from the east and he came from the west, because one misjudged the relative balance of power, because one chose the wrong time for a blunt challenge to the adversary, the Arab states are now subjected to the worst humiliation of defeat and occupation.

"Israel was satisfied with its frontiers," Bourguiba added. "It did not ask for either the whole of the city of Jerusalem or for Cisjordan and the other territories in the north or east."

Yet, "deliberately and without weighing up the risks sufficiently, steps were taken to ban Israel from access to the Gulf of Aqaba in spite of international agreements and the prevailing situation."

Even in Cairo some people were ready to face up to the implications of the Arab defeat. Achmed Baha'eddin, editor of the mass-circulation paper *Al Mussawar*, pointed out that "the postulate that Israel must disappear is not accepted by all our friends and enemies, nor the neutrals, nor anybody else in the world, apart from ourselves." Baha'eddin argued that because the Arabs insisted they wanted to destroy Israel, they "made it possible for Israel to win the first round even before we had fired the first shot."

And Professor Arnold Toynbee—generally considered a friend of the Arabs, who had criticized Israel's *raison d'être* and policies —gave them some sound advice:

"The Arabs have to face the fact that Israel has come to stay; that a three-times-repeated experience has shown that they cannot defeat her; that the Soviet Union is not going to go to war with the United States for the Arabs' sake; and that, in the unlikely event of the Arabs becoming, one day, able to destroy Israel, the United States would not let this happen."

The saddest and wisest of the Arab leaders who fought Israel was King Hussein. He had patently backed the wrong horse. For years he had resisted Nasserist pressure at home and from abroad. Most Israelis had admired the young king's efforts to stay on his throne and had not considered him a deeply committed enemy. But when Hussein lost his nerve at the end of May and decided Nasser was going to attack Israel and he could not afford to stay out, he made a crucial decision which cost him more than he could possibly have foreseen.

Even after Hussein embraced Nasser at Cairo airport on May 30 he could have abstained from a direct confrontation with Israel. On June 5 the Chief of Staff of the United Nations Truce Supervision Organization, the Norwegian General Odd Bull, delivered to Hussein a message from Israeli Prime Minister Eshkol assuring him that Israel would not initiate any action against Jordan and appealing to him to desist from war.

But Hussein could not resist the pressure from Cairo, Syria, and Iraq, and from his own refugees from Palestine. Against his will, the king decided he could not remain passive as Jordan had in 1956. He did not feel he could remain on the sidelines this time, as Lebanon was to do, or Saudi Arabia, whose ruler, King Faisal— in Paris when war broke out—prudently stayed in Europe until

July 21. Hussein decided to fight, and to attack the Israeli positions facing Jordan, which were defensive and meant to hold the line while the main battle went on against Egypt. Some observers believe he took this step because if he had not joined the war with Israel, his army would have thrown off his authority and taken orders from Cairo.

In any event, shells began dropping on the Jewish side of Jerusalem at 8:30 A.M. on June 5, shortly after the first air raids and despite Eshkol's message to the King via Odd Bull. By noon that first day of the war fighting had broken out along the entire Jordanian sector, and Israel was facing a second front on its eastern border.

The Jordanian troops fought hard and well. But when the battle ended Jordan had been cut in two. Hussein had lost nearly half his country, including the fertile farm land of the West Bank and the Old City of Jerusalem, Bethlehem, and Hebron, with their tourist income. Seen on television in London and New York later in June, Hussein looked shattered, the bone-weary soldier ruler of a country whose economy had been destroyed and which had virtually nothing left except an empty piece of desert country which could not feed the refugees streaming in from Israeli-occupied territory. Hussein must bitterly regret the decision he made in the last week of May, to throw in his lot with Nasser and thus ultimately to share his debacle and humiliation.

As for Achmed Shukairy, who had boasted that no Israelis would be left alive to be shipped back to their "countries of origin," his heroic stance was soon punctured by reality. The Israeli radio gave the story on Tuesday, June 6—the second day of the war—when it told listeners in Arabic:

"Do you know that no one has heard Achmed Shukairy say anything since the beginning of the battles? Do you know that Shukairy, who last week said: 'We shall fight in the trenches and not in the hotels,' was in one of Amman's hotels all day yesterday and did not ask the Jordanian command to take him to one of the trenches to fight?

"Do you know that Shukairy became hysterical when he heard the news about the surrender of the Palestinian battalions? Do you know that Shukairy left secretly for Cairo early this morning wearing women's clothes and accompanied by a doctor friend, out of fear of the wrath of the Palestinians in Jordan?"

As the world reeled from the impact of the fifty scimitar hours which spun history like a top, the Arabs licked their wounds and the Israelis exulted like men reprieved from execution who had taken over the prison. And slowly men in the Middle East and the world began thinking about the shape of the future that could emerge from the savage six days in June, about solutions and possibilities which began dimly to present themselves, if anything had really changed in this part of the world.

The British journalist James Cameron, writing in the *Daily Express* only a few days after the war ended, caught this feeling of an opportunity arising out of violence, the anguish, blood, and hope, when he wrote:

"If war could ever solve anything, this war could have been the answer. It was terrible, unrelenting, pitiless, and cruel, but it was at least surgically brief. But, of course, the agony remains and will remain until what—with the most gruesome and awful irony—must be called the Final Solution, which is the recognition by fifty million Arabs that the Jews are here to stay, and the recognition by the three million Jews that they belong hereafter not to Zion but to the Middle East."

Sources

The BBC Monitoring Service
Kol Yisrael (the Israeli radio)
Cairo Radio
Haaretz, Davar, and *Maariv* (Tel Aviv)
The *Jerusalem Post* (Israel)
The *Jerusalem Times* (Jordan)
Al Ahram, Al Mussawar and the *Egyptian Gazette* (Cairo)
Al Khayat and *Al Nahar* (Beirut)
Le Monde and *Jeune Afrique* (Paris)
The Times, the *Guardian*, the *Financial Times*, and the *Daily Telegraph* (London)
The New York Times and *Time*

The *International Herald Tribune* (Paris)

Randolph S. and Winston S. Churchill, *The Six Day War*, (London: Heinemann, 1967)

War File, edited by Tim Hewat (London: Panther Books, 1967)

"The 5-Day War—And After," *Daily Express*, London, 1967

Robert J. Donovan, *Six Days in June* (London: Signet, 1967)

William Stevenson, *Israeli Victory* (London: Corgi, 1967)

Glubb Pasha, *The Middle East Crisis* (London: Hodder and Stoughton, 1967)

Professors Arnold J. Toynbee and J. L. Talmon, "Arabs and Jews: An Exchange of Letters," *Encounter*, October 1967

7 The Challenge to Israel

THE WAR ENDED officially at 7:30 P.M. on the evening of Saturday, June 10, when Syria and Israel accepted the Security Council's call for an end to hostilities.

The next morning the London *Sunday Times* published an interview with Prime Minister Eshkol—the first statement of Israel's intentions since the war.

"The time has come," he said, "for peace and cooperation in the Middle East in place of enmity, blockade, and boycott. New vistas open up for Arab-Jewish cooperation reminiscent of the Middle Ages—a cooperation which can assure our region's proper place in the mosaic of human progress."

Eshkol pointed out that since 1952 Egypt alone had spent $4 billion in developing its war machine. And the Arab peoples and Israel together had spent $10 billion on a futile arms race. "Had these vast sums been applied to economic and social needs, millions of human beings who are steeped in poverty could by today have enjoyed an appropriate standard of living."[1]

On the next day, June 12, Eshkol spoke to the Israeli Knesset (Parliament) and outlined the type of postwar settlement he wanted. He made it clear that Israel would never agree to revert to the situation which existed before the outbreak of war. Its objective was a lasting peace settlement which would enable the Middle East countries to live together and cooperate instead of fighting. And he added: "A new situation has been created that could lead to direct negotiations with the Arab countries."

1. London *Sunday Times*, July 11, 1967.

The Middle East, Eshkol declared, was now at a crossroads: "In one direction lie peace and true cooperation, resting upon the sincere desires of the peoples in the area and their true interests. In the other direction lie the danger of continued hostility and hatred because of the absence of stable peace."

The Prime Minister addressed part of his speech directly to the Arab people: "We did not go to war with rejoicing," he told them. "We did it only to protect our lives and our rights."

Eshkol called upon the world powers to contribute to Middle East peace by telling the Arab countries they were bound, under the United Nations Charter, to resolve conflicts by peaceful means.[2]

This was a statesmanlike speech, free of jubilation and saber-rattling. It indicated the line Israel would take in the months to come. It was conciliatory toward the Arabs and stressed the benefits they could derive from orderly relations with Israel. But it was vague and made no specific proposals.

This Israeli line was spelled out a little more clearly by Foreign Minister Abba Eban in the next few weeks. Speaking at Heathrow Airport, London, on his way back to Israel after the abortive UN General Assembly session in July, he promised that Israel would have "serious, viable, and honorable proposals to make" if its Arab neighbors would sit down at the conference table with it.[3]

Later in July Eban spoke again about "viable, honorable, and durable" proposals Israel would offer Egypt, Jordan, Syria, and Lebanon if they agreed to negotiate collectively or singly.

There were only two alternatives, the Foreign Minister said: a state of war and a state of real peace—for the twenty-year armistice had proved a "monstrosity" which had failed to prevent war.

The peace which Israel wanted would normalize relations with the Arab world. It would be a clear-cut juridical concept giving Israel the same relations with Arab countries that all members of the United Nations enjoyed with one another.[4]

It was clear from this that Israel intended holding out for direct talks with the Arab countries which would lead to full recognition;

2. London *Times*, June 13, 1967.
3. *Guardian*, July 8, 1967.
4. *Ibid.*, July 25, 1967.

that it would not accept any contrived arrangement which would enable the Arabs to regain their lost prestige while still refusing to acknowledge Israel's existence; and that it would use the occupied territories as its most powerful bargaining counter and would not evacuate them as easily as it had in 1957.

All this was eminently reasonable. And the statements made by Eshkol and Eban the first few weeks after the war were clear, sane, and utterly logical. They came from the leaders of a country which had been threatened with annihilation, had gone to war with those who threatened it, and had inflicted a staggering defeat upon them. Now it was offering to meet the Arab leaders for peace talks based on "honorable and durable" proposals.

Israel knew it was in a strong position. It held the upper hand in the Middle East and could expect to gain the maximum benefit from its victory on the battlefield. Certainly no other country in the world—least of all any of the Arab states—would have meekly withdrawn from its positions of strength without obtaining adequate political advantages. As Eban was to say later: "The idea that Israel should move from the cease-fire lines without a peace settlement, including demarcation of permanent frontiers, is so irrational that it is amazing to hear it put forward at all."[5]

And what was Israel demanding? Not the subjugation of the Arabs—not their political serfdom—not any loss of Arab sovereignty or independence, but simply the recognition that Israel was a state like all other Middle East states, a fact long accepted by the Soviet Union and reaffirmed by Premier Kosygin in his address to the UN General Assembly after the June war. By current international standards, this is a comparatively small price to demand from a defeated opponent. And Eban was surely right when he remarked, in a moment of understandable exasperation, that for the first time after a war "the victors had sued for peace and the vanquished called for unconditional surrender."[6]

Yet, sane, reasonable, and logical as the Israeli position undoubtedly was, there was one thing it failed to take into account: the psychological inability of the Arabs to make the excruciating

5. Speech at jubilee celebration of the Balfour Declaration in London: *Financial Times*, November 6, 1967.
6. *Guardian, loc. cit.*

transition from the vision of an Israel overthrown and weakened to the reality of having to bargain and plead with an Israel that held all the cards. A great national humiliation takes time to absorb. Twenty-two years after its defeat by the Allied Powers, West Germany is still unable to accept the loss of its eastern territories to East Germany and Poland. Japan is still trying to recover Okinawa from the United States. Why should we expect the Arabs to concede defeat so soon and to accept philosophically the loss of Jerusalem—which Israel has said is not negotiable—and perhaps other territory?

When Israel made its offer of direct peace talks, it was not thinking of any of the outer ring of Arab states in the Maghreb and Arabian Peninsula. A peace treaty with Tunisia would not have reduced tension on Israel's borders, even if President Bourguiba had been prepared to sign one. And even among these outer Arab states were some who were not ready to recognize Israel, such as Algeria. President Houari Boumédienne, who had not lost a single soldier or plane in the war, could afford to promise that the struggle would be continued.

Israel's leaders also knew perfectly well that the Syrian Ba'ath would not come to the conference table so soon after the war. They knew that Syria sought an open guerrilla offensive by El Fatah, the PLO, and saboteurs based in the occupied territory. As *Al Baath*, organ of the ruling party, wrote: "Popular revolutionary war is the only way to counter Zionist challenges. Traditional wars exhaust the material resources of the Arabs. Popular war exhausts the enemy."[7]

Israel also understood that Lebanon would not agree to independent peace talks unless other Arab countries joined in. As the only Arab state with a Christian majority, it could not afford to be seen making a deal with the Jews while the Moslems held back. The popular saying was that Lebanon would be the second country to make peace with Israel, and this quip exactly fitted the facts.

Clearly Israel was hoping that either Nasser or Hussein—or both —would be ready for a détente, and that this would pave the way for Lebanon and any of the outer ring states that wanted to con-

7. Gavin Young in London *Observer*, July 30, 1967.

cur. Hence the real question was whether the heavy losses sustained by both these countries would persuade them they could no longer afford to continue a state of belligerency with Israel.

For a month or two after the war it seemed as if Nasser was indeed taking a moderate line. With the Suez Canal closed and losing $250 million a year in dues; with over $800 million worth of planes and military equipment destroyed; with Egypt's tourist industry wrecked; with resentment at home rising as officers and men returned from the front bringing the truth, he could not allow himself to be as aggressive in public as those leaders who had come through unscathed.

Those following trends in Cairo detected strong signs of a split between hawks and doves in the Egyptian leadership. The editor of *Al Ahram*, Mohammad Hassanein Heikal, who is considered Nasser's closest journalistic confidant, wrote a series of articles probably designed as trial balloons to test the mood and predict the public's reaction if Nasser agreed to talk with Israel. He advocated the re-establishment of diplomatic relations with the United States and said "total victory" over Israel was no longer possible because of the international situation.

This led to a sharp attack upon Heikal by *Al Gomhouria*, the official organ of the Arab Socialist Union, which is the only political party permitted in Egypt. The paper called Heikal a "defeatist" who wanted reconciliation with Israel and "the liquidation of our battle." His views meant that "we have no alternative to submission." And *Al Gomhouria* added pointedly: "What the chief editor of a certain UAR newspaper writes expresses no more than his own view." In other words, the Arab Socialist Union was reminding Nasser that he was its President, and that progress toward Arab socialism was identified with extreme anti-Israel policies, while those who favored a moderate policy toward Israel were bourgeois and pro-American.[8]

Field Marshal Amer's arrest and subsequent "suicide" brought this internal rift out into the open. It also explained Nasser's incessant vacillation between hints of readiness to end his war with Israel and bellicose public harangues against the Zionists. Dictator as he was, he was not master of his own house. The

8. Victor Zorza in the *Guardian*, August 9, 1967.

defeat in the sand trap of Sinai had weakened his authority, and while his word was still law for the masses, the officers, civil service, and intellectuals were watchful. Nineteen years earlier Nasser and some brother officers, isolated in the Negev, had brooded on the reasons for their defeat and planned the coup which overthrew Farouk. Perhaps Nasser wondered if among the beaten officers in the Mitla Pass or Gaza there was one thinking the same thoughts and bent on the same destiny.

So Nasser followed his own highly individual zigzag strategy, throwing out hints of a more flexible approach to Israel, but without direct negotiations, while at the same time insisting for mass consumption that the UAR's armed forces were being reorganized to continue the fight against Israel. While drumming up support for Yugoslavian President Tito's peace feelers, he declared: "There is only one solution: we haven't given in and the struggle goes on. We are not the first to lose a battle."[9]

Hussein, who lost even more than Nasser from the war and did not have the Soviet Union to lean on, was more ready to come to terms with Israel. We shall see later that he was prepared to negotiate with Israel if Nasser did the same. But Hussein did not feel himself secure enough at home to sign a separate agreement with Israel unless at least one other Arab country joined him, and that meant Egypt, which was divided on this issue.

Hussein sent an exploratory message to Eshkol through Arab dignitaries living under Israeli occupation in the West Bank, who were able to travel between Amman and Jerusalem. He wanted to know whether Israel was ready to reach an agreement without direct, face-to-face talks. Israel rejected this proposal and insisted on direct and open negotiations.

Eshkol later revealed the tip of this iceberg when he told *The New York Times* correspondent in Jerusalem that in the weeks before the Arab summit conference at Khartoum in July Hussein had been ready to negotiate a settlement with Israel.

"We know he was preparing to negotiate," Eshkol said. "He'll deny it if he is asked, but we know it."[10]

9. *International Herald Tribune*, July 24, 1967.
10. Dispatch from Jerusalem: *International Herald Tribune*, October 13, 1967.

However, Hussein was not prepared to act completely on his own by becoming the first Arab ruler to meet Israel's leaders. And Nasser, facing heavy pressure from his militant socialist supporters and his humiliated officers, was not ready to risk their displeasure and a possible coup. Unable to act together and unwilling to act singly, they decided not to act at all. The brief moment of hope passed. The Arabs were still imprisoned by their hopeless dream, which was now compounded by even deeper feelings of frustration and inferiority. And no Arab leader, not even Nasser, had the courage or moral force to free them from this dream and replace it with another, grander vision.

The Arabs began building up their strength again and talking once more as they had in May. Since the war the Soviet Union has provided the UAR with over 200 jet planes, or roughly two-thirds of Cairo's losses. U.S. sources estimate that Moscow has also supplied about 200 tanks, or roughly one-third of the Egyptian war losses. It is true that a fair proportion of the Soviet replacements are used planes and older model MiG-15s and MiG-17s. The Kremlin has only replaced a handful of the 25 medium-range Tu-16 bombers Egypt lost in the war, and there is no evidence that Nasser now has more sophisticated equipment than he had before the war. Syria and Algeria also have received Russian planes, tanks, and guns.[11]

Prime Minister Eshkol claims that the Soviet Union has re-supplied Egypt with 80 per cent of the planes, tanks, and artillery it lost during the war. "This influx of Soviet weapons has again upset the balance of power in the Middle East," he warns. "It has made our position more precarious and made it all the more important that the Western Powers permit us to buy the weapons we need to defend ourselves."[12]

While Israel ran into difficulties in obtaining planes from France, because of de Gaulle's cynically pro-Arab stance aimed at ousting British and American oil interests from the region, it could count on direct arms supplies from other countries aware that Moscow was keeping the arms race alive. American officials con-

11. Hedrick Smith in *The New York Times*, October 13, 1967.
12. Dispatch from Jerusalem, *loc. cit.*

firmed in December that the first of 48 UE A-4 Skyhawk fighter planes sold to Israel since the war were being delivered. These are subsonic planes, and Israel did not consider them adequate replacements for the French-built supersonic jets it lost in June. For this Israel hoped to obtain 50 F-4 Phantom jets—one of the most advanced U.S. fighter-bombers, now being used for attacks against North Vietnam. But Washington was postponing a decision on the Israeli request for the Phantoms until it became clear whether Paris had definitely canceled Israel's order for 50 Mirages, two-thirds of which had been paid in advance before June 5.[13]

With the arms race starting up again, the war of words was not slow to follow. Both sides noticeably stiffened their political positions, after it began to seem unlikely that direct peace talks would be held soon.

In Jerusalem Foreign Minister Abba Eban delivered a blunt warning that Israel was perfectly prepared to remain indefinitely in its present positions unless the Arabs were willing to sit down and negotiate and embrace not only "non-belligerence" but a meaningful peace.

There were just two choices, he told a press conference: "A cease-fire map as of today or a new map of the Middle East which can be achieved only by a peace settlement. It is time to restrict the area of choice. If our neighboring governments are forced to face only two alternatives—the present situation or a negotiated peace—they might begin to change their minds about negotiations."

Eban placed no limit on how long Israel would wait for the Arabs to accept the principle of face-to-face talks. "Time is an important element in this diplomatic and intellectual revolution," he observed, and hence time could not be limited. "But there is no substitute for a directly negotiated peace settlement," he stated categorically. In other words, Israel would not accept a third-party mediator, such as President Tito, whose purpose was to avert the need for the Arabs to meet Israel around a conference table.[14]

On October 3 Eban told the UN General Assembly that Israel would not return to "the political and juridical anarchy or to the

13. *The New York Times*, December 20, 1967.
14. *Financial Times* and *International Herald Tribune*, August 15, 1967.

strategic vulnerability" from which it had emerged. He repudiated the 1949 armistice agreements and said his country had "no valid contractual engagements" with its neighbors, other than the June cease-fire agreements. Eban summed up Israel's position by saying: "We must now build not a ramshackle structure based on ambiguity and doubt, but a durable edifice of relations embodied in treaties of peace."[15]

Many Israelis had hoped that the war would jolt the Arabs into a more realistic attitude. But as this hope evaporated and the euphoria of victory wore off, public opinion began pressing Eshkol for the annexation of the Syrian Heights and the Gaza Strip and the establishment of Israeli agricultural settlements in the occupied territories. Israelis began saying that if the Arabs were not going to change, Israel must carve out its own future without continuing to plead for peace talks.

This tougher, more uncompromising line was summed up by Israel's Ambassador to France, Dr. Walter Eytan, in a speech to the Anglo-American Press Association in Paris. Eytan was blunt, firm, and cynical. He described his speech as an attempt "to explode a few legends current about the Middle East situation." One of these legends was that the Great Powers were sincerely interested in solving the Israeli-Arab dispute. "During the past nineteen years none of the Great Powers has shown the slightest interest in bringing about a permanent settlement," he said. The basic obstacle was the Arab refusal to recognize Israel's existence. "In all these years no one in the outside world has made any effort to uproot this notion that Israel did not exist from the Arab mind. Suppose Russia were really a peace-loving power. She would be in an ideal position to influence the Arabs on this score.

"Israel did not grab territory just for the sake of it, but to save our lives," Eytan said. "That territory did not belong to anyone else—save perhaps the Sinai Desert.

"The western part of Jordan never belonged to Jordan any more than it belongs to Israel today. It was annexed unilaterally by Jordan fifteen years ago and the other Arab countries refused to recognize the annexation at the time. The legal claim of Jordan is not better than Israel's. The same is true of the Gaza Strip."

15. *Guardian*, October 4, 1967.

Eytan saw no chance of the Arabs recognizing Israel. But the situation changed so rapidly in the Middle East, he would not like to predict anything. However, "if the Arabs do not get over this block in their minds, it is very difficult to see what the future holds, save a fourth war some time in 1976–1977."[16]

The Arabs too were talking about "continuing the struggle" and referring to the June war as a "setback," a temporary slip back on the long march against Israel. Incidents in the Suez Canal area became more frequent. Arab saboteurs began causing trouble in the West Bank and even near Nazareth, in the heart of Israel. Israeli troops found Fatah terrorists hiding in caves near Nablus with Syrian grenades and Chinese automatic weapons. Other infiltrators captured near Jenin had been trained in Algeria, where they had gone from West Germany during the June fighting.

In this atmosphere of gathering tension and Israel's disappointment with the lack of political movement after the war, a major clash occurred near the Suez Canal. On October 21 the 2,500-ton Israeli destroyer *Eilat* was patrolling in the Bay of Romani, at the Mediterranean entrance to the Suez Canal, just outside Egyptian territorial waters. On July 12—a month after the end of the third round—it had sunk two Egyptian torpedo boats in the same bay. Egyptian radarmen in Port Said tracked it and asked headquarters in Alexandria for instruction. On the direct orders of Nasser, two more torpedo boats left Port Said harbor to attack the *Eilat*. Each of these boats carried four Russian-made Styx self-guiding surface-to-surface missiles. Four of these hit the *Eilat*, which sank, with the loss of forty-nine lives.

Israel was stunned by this disaster, the loss of its best warship and the death of so many seamen only four months after the June war. No one in Israel doubted that its army would hit back.

Meanwhile crowds gathered at the docks in Port Said to cheer the returning torpedo boats, and Nasser ordered their crews decorated, while the Arab press crowed over "the victory over a cunning enemy." The Beirut paper *Al Moharrer* prophesied that "the Israeli army is going to suffer a defeat that will make the world forget the Arab defeat of last June."

But three days later, on October 24, Israeli guns set two Egyp-

16. London *Times*, July 19, 1967.

tian oil refineries at Suez on fire. The refineries had a total annual capacity of 5.5 million tons of refined products and provided five million tons of Egypt's annual consumption of 6.5 million tons. The flames from the exploding oil tanks could be seen twenty-five miles away. When Israel called off the shelling, after three hours and eleven minutes, 80 per cent of Egypt's oil capacity was destroyed and much of the city of Suez was in ruins.[17]

This savage encounter—the fiercest outbreak of violence since the end of the war—sent tension in the region soaring. The moderate politicians and journalists on both sides were silenced, while the extremists took over. Public opinion in both Israel and Egypt called for firm action. The Soviet Union sent seven warships on a so-called "courtesy visit" to Egyptian ports, presumably to prevent any further attacks by Israel. And the UN Security Council in New York displayed its usual impotence by arguing for thirty hours before passing a milk-and-water resolution calling for a cease-fire—long after all firing along the Suez Canal had stopped.

Five days later, on October 29, Prime Minister Eshkol reported to the Knesset on the Middle East situation. Eshkol was in a fighting mood, and his speech was the toughest and most sternly worded policy statement by Israel since the June war.

He warned the Powers and the UN that they should avoid "obscure and meaningless formulae like declarations of the cessation of belligerency without a real peace settlement." These could only have the "perilous" effect of "strengthening those who are bent on war."

"Only direct negotiations can bring a solution," Eshkol declared. "Only direct contact can open the way to mutual understanding." Those who wanted to resort to obscure formulae were "undertaking a grave responsibility for the deterioration of the position in the area."

The Prime Minister made it clear that Israel would not return to the June 4 frontiers. He recalled that "both the area under Jordanian occupation and the Gaza Strip which the Egyptians ruled were held by them not of right but of force as the result of military aggression and occupation.

17. *Ibid.*, October 21–25; *Time*, November 3, 1967.

"This occupation was recognized in the (1949) armistice agreements. But these agreements have been nullified by military provocation and aggression."

Eshkol noted further that the armistice lines were determined by purely military considerations and "do not have the character of frontiers. The Arab Governments have insisted on this principle throughout these years. For these reasons there is ample justification both from the legal and the political and security point of view for Israel's attitude that the aim should now be to determine agreed and secure national boundaries within the framework of peace treaties."

Eshkol added: "In the Golan (Syrian) Heights we shall not permit a restoration of the situation before June 5. Nor will the situation in Sinai, in the Gulf of Eilat, and in the Suez Canal be restored to what it was."

And he concluded by making another call for peace. "Peace," he said, "is the only solution that has not yet been tried, and the time has come to try it." But Eshkol stressed: "We shall continue to consolidate our strength and fortify our security, so long as the threat against us continues and we are in danger of destruction."[18]

Compared to Eshkol's statements immediately after the war, this speech was almost martial in tone. It reflected Israel's anger over the sinking of the *Eilat* and the growing irritation and impatience with the Arabs' inability to confront reality.

On the other side of the Suez Canal an extreme position was also hardening and intransigence becoming the normal posture. This was partly due to the coming UN Security Council debate and to both sides' desire not to make any concessions before the debate. But most of the mutual toughness sprang from the natural desire of politicians to satisfy public opinion at home and not to appear too pliant. It was obvious that time was not on the side of reconciliation and that the longer both sides moved from that seminal week in June the harder it would be to bring them together.

On November 22 the Security Council adopted a British resolution appointing a special representative as mediator between

18. *Guardian* and *Financial Times*, October 31, 1967.

Israel and the Arabs. Both Israel and Egypt agreed to the appointment of Dr. Gunnar Jarring, the Swedish Ambassador to Moscow, as UN representative for the Middle East.

But the next day, November 23, President Nasser addressed the opening of the fifth session of the Egyptian National Assembly. What he said sent the temperature of the Middle East up several degrees.

The British resolution had linked the withdrawal of Israeli troops from Arab territories with an end to the state of belligerency and Israel's right to use international waterways. Now Nasser seemed flatly to reject the Security Council's call for a détente when he vowed: "Whatever the price, we will not permit Israel to pass through the Suez Canal."

The National Assembly burst into thunderous applause when he said: "Israeli passage through the Suez Canal is an integral part of the Palestine issue, not part of the removal of consequences of the Israeli aggression. What has been taken by force cannot be recovered without force."

"No peace with Israel, no recognition of Israel," Nasser pledged. Egypt's defense forces were "stronger now than in June before the Israeli attack, and they are already capable of strong and impressive action."

He insisted that Egypt's pursuit of a political solution to the crisis did not denote weakness:

"We can undertake political action while preparing for military action, if the latter becomes necessary."

"Above all," Nasser told the Assembly, "we need time to complete our military preparedness. We can now defend ourselves. I tell you that if the time comes for military action we will not be on the defensive. We will attack to liberate our lands occupied by the enemy. This is our legitimate right. We cannot accept another setback. If we resort again to military action, our friends would understand and even support us."[19]

To Israeli observers this sounded like Nasser's old style, a sign that nothing had really changed in the Middle East. Even an indirect Soviet rebuke for Nasser and the Syrian leaders, who had

19. *Daily Telegraph* and *International Herald Tribune*, November 24, 1967.

also rejected the Security Council resolution, did not lighten the gloom.

The Soviet Union had accepted the Council resolution, which had been passed unanimously. Nasser's speech to the Egyptian National Assembly had not been reported in the Russian press. A few days later, on November 27, the Soviet Communist Party newspaper *Pravda* criticized unnamed "hotheads" in unnamed Arab capitals for rejecting the UN resolution. This was coupled with a much sharper attack on Israeli "extremists," and a flattering reference to Nasser's "moderation" in the face of Israeli provocation.[20]

At the end of 1967 the fluid situation of midsummer had jelled into the incendiary blend of threats and raw nerves the world knew so well. The shock of the war had not galvanized any Arab leader into fresh, courageous thinking, and Israel seemed to be accepting a new status quo without fully thinking out where this would lead it.

Has Israel lost the initiative? And what can it do to break the deadlock?

Before answering these questions, and outlining a policy which I believe Israel can and should follow, let us examine the situation inside the Arab lands occupied by Israel.

The numbers of Arabs in these areas are as follows:

In the Syrian Heights (mostly Druse):	6,400
In the West Bank of the Jordan::	600,000
In the Gaza Strip (120,000 in the city of Gaza and 175,000 in the refugee camps)	350,000
In the Old City of Jerusalem	70,000
In Sinai (mainly in El Arish)	33,000
TOTAL	1,059,400

With the addition of the 300,000 Arabs living in Israel before the war, we arrive at a figure of 1,359,400 Arabs under Israeli control, compared with 2,365,000 Jews.[21]

20. *International Herald Tribune,* November 28, 1967.
21. Hugh Thomas, "Why Israel Will Not Give Ground," London *Times,* October 24, 1967. However, Thomas adds up these figures and arrives at a figure of 1,385,000 Arabs.

These figures, based on an official Israeli census completed in October, were confirmed by Prime Minister Eshkol when he told the B'nai B'rith Israel Commission in Jerusalem:

"In Greater Israel today we have a population of 3.8 million souls. Of these, 2.4 million are Jews: 1.4 million are non-Jews. The percentage of Jews in the total population is 64 per cent; the non-Jews are 36 per cent."[22]

According to official Israeli statistics, the Arabs who lived in Israel before June 5 have a birth rate of 47.8 per thousand per year. The Jewish birth rate is 21.9 per thousand. Thus the Arab citizens of Israel are more fertile than in the rest of the Arab world and also exceed India's birthrate of 40.9 per 1,000.

This means that the Arabs in Israel multiply three and a half times in a generation, while the Jews multiply only one and a half times.[23]

In other words: if Israel remains in control of all the territories it now holds and if the Arabs living in them remain where they are the multiply at the birth rate attained by Israel's Arab population, within twenty years the Arabs will be in a majority.

One factor has not been taken into account: Jewish immigration, which could restore the balance, if large enough. In recent years immigration has dropped and become a fraction of the annual natural increase. Now the Israeli Government has called for more Jewish settlers from Western countries. A figure of 30,000 a year has been suggested as a possible target, but few Israeli planners think this is being realistic, and most do not expect more than a few thousand serious immigrants a year from the United States, Britain, South Africa, and Western Europe.

The *aliya* (immigration) from the Middle East countries is nearing its end, as Prime Minister Eshkol has noted. "Perhaps a few more tens of thousands will come," he told a B'nai B'rith conference. "Russian Jewry is still behind the Iron Curtain," he continued, "and that curtain is getting thicker and more impenetrable." The only remaining source is "the Jews of the free world, the Jews of the West."

22. *The New York Times*, October 30, 1967.

23. *Jewish Observer and Middle East Review*, quoted by London *Times*, August 23, 1967; *Evening Standard*, April 19, 1967.

Later Eshkol confirmed, during a Knesset debate, that the Soviet Union had halted the steady trickle of Russian Jews which had been one of Israel's open secrets for years. Moscow had approved this immigration from its borders but demanded it not be made public because of the probable Arab reaction. But after the June war the Soviet Union cut its diplomatic relations with Israel and banned any further immigration.[24]

Because of the strained relations with the Kremlin, and the unlikelihood that these will improve in the next few years, Israel cannot count on large-scale future immigration from Eastern Europe, although some countries—such as Rumania—will continue to take an independent line and permit their Jews to leave for Israel if they so wish. With Western Jews unlikely to respond for a number of social, economic, and psychological reasons, and such sources as North Africa and the Middle East itself drying up, the outlook for immigration is bleak. No serious Israeli official today takes this factor into account in outlining a program for the population acquired after the war.

There is one more possibility which is so dreadful that I can scarcely bring myself to contemplate it, let alone put it down on paper: that Israel will hold all the territories it now has and expel all or some of its more than a million Arabs into the deserts of the east and the south. Let us hope that the people in Israel who dare to think along these lines remain confined to the lunatic fringe and that desperation does not drive any recruits into their ranks.

This then is the choice Israel must make: between a tract of land four times as large as the 1948 state but containing a non-Jewish population which will make the Jews a minority long before the turn of the century, and an area similar to that of the State of Israel on June 4, with minor additions, but with a more manageable Arab minority of some 20 per cent.

It is a choice between land and people, between geography and demography. But it *is* a choice. Israel cannot have it both ways. It cannot choose the land without the people, unless it is prepared to act in the unmentionable manner I cannot contemplate.

24. AP dispatch from Jerusalem: *International Herald Tribune*, November 29, 1967.

Essentially, this is a question of identity. It is the question which has haunted the Zionist movement ever since the days of Herzl and has now risen again to torment Israel in the aftermath of its most glorious triumph. It is the problem of whether to be a European enclave in the Middle East or a Middle East country linked organically, spiritually, to other countries to the north, east, and south; whether to be just another state which belongs to the United Nations and has the usual trappings of statehood, embassies, ambassadors, and a flag, or a Jewish state, the culmination of an exile unprecedented in the history of man.

The debate within Israel today is between those who want a larger country, a more logical and viable strategic space, and are prepared to accept the human and social complications resulting from this desire, and those who would prefer a smaller country with a more homogeneous population, with only a small number of non-Jews, who would enjoy freedom within this Jewish state.

But what do we mean by a Jewish state? Is it a Jewish state merely because it has a Jewish majority? Or because its language is Hebrew? I do not believe this is the whole answer. If Israel is to fulfil its historical destiny as a state which will be as Jewish as England is English, *it must act in a Jewish manner*. It must be a *Jewish* state, not a Jewish *state*. By this I do not mean that it should impose the theology and practice of Judaism upon its individual citizens. Religion in our day and age is fundamentally a private matter and cannot be dictated by the state.

By "acting in a Jewish manner" I mean accepting the ethical and moral implications of our Jewish heritage. If we base our claim to the territory of Israel on our historical rights and the authority of the Bible, we must at the same time accept our obligations under this claim. We cannot select from the ethical imperative of Judaism those commandments which suit us, while rejecting those we find inconvenient. We cannot insist on "Unto thy seed have I given this land" (Genesis 15:18) while throwing off "One law shall be to the homeborn and the stranger" (Exodus 12:49). We cannot make a *political* claim based on certain passages of the Bible, while ignoring the *moral* demands which are inseparable from them.

The time has come to restore the spiritual element in Israel's national rebirth which runs from Achad Ha'am and A. D. Gordon through Chaim Weizmann and Moshe Sharett to Magnes and Buber, and which has been subdued and suppressed in the desperate struggles of the last thirty years, when territorial and political goals replaced all other valid ideals. Instead of *proclaiming* that it is a Jewish state, Israel should *demonstrate* that it is one.

I believe the young people of Israel—a new kind of Jew, idealistic yet secular—are yearning for just such a change in the spiritual climate of the only country they call home. There is an emptiness, a great moral hunger—a yearning for an ideal to replace the ideal of Zionism which has been realized. The sabras, the Jews born in Israel, are taking their rightful place as masters of the country's destiny, and the next Prime Minister after Eshkol will almost certainly be a sabra. If a government composed largely of or at least headed by sabras can channel the latent idealism of the youth, Israel can enter a tremendously exciting period. But the youth will have to be offered more than continuous wars and an armed struggle.

Do we have the courage to act as authentic Jews? To *be* Jews instead of theorizing about being Jews? Are we ready to fuse principles and action in an organic Jewish existence in our own land? And what would this mean in practice?

It would mean, first of all, following the precept "Justice, justice follow" (Deuteronomy 16:20). It means showing understanding and compassion toward others who have suffered exile. It means accepting Israel's destiny as a truly democratic country in which members of all religions and nationalities would have equal rights. It means placing the foundations of Israel's new life firmly upon justice and law, not merely upon the momentary supremacy of force and power.

Because I seek this authentic Jewish existence and believe Israel can be the instrument of its realization, I am distressed when men whose lives and persons embody Jewish values act in what seems to me an un-Jewish way. I am distressed when the Chief Rabbi of Israel lays down a Halachic ruling and proclaims it orthodox religious doctrine that "Jerusalem and the Land of Israel are holy to us. The land was promised to us by the Almighty and all the prophets foretold its return to us. Therefore it is forbidden for any

Jew even to consider returning any part whatsoever of the land of our forefathers."[25]

I am distressed when a leading Hebrew poet, Natan Alterman, declares: "Now, and only now, are we in the Land of Israel."[26]

I am distressed when a group of prominent Israelis, including Alterman, the writers Moshe Shamir and Haim Hazaz, university professors and army chiefs, form a Movement to Oppose the Return of Conquered Areas and state solemnly that "a withdrawal from the occupied territories is a betrayal of the Zionist ideal." I am distressed when the leaders of this movement, including some of the most distinguished men and women in Israel, claim that anyone who is ready to achieve a settlement with the Arabs by giving up parts of the historical homeland is surrendering his Zionist dream.[27]

And in my distress I want to ask the Chief Rabbi, Alterman, Shamir, Hazaz, and the other leaders of Israeli opinion:

If you wish to hold all the territories which once formed part of historic Israel, are you prepared to grant the non-Jews living in them full and equal rights, as the Bible itself commands you to do? Are you ready to give them voting rights and a share in the national destiny commensurate with their numbers? And when, in ten or twenty years, their numbers exceed the number of Jews in the historic boundaries, will you accept the rule of the Arab majority for the sake of these ancient frontiers?

For if anyone is contemplating holding these territories without granting the non-Jews living in them equal civil rights and without accepting their rightful presence, then I say he is acting in an un-Jewish way under the guise of a Jewish mask.

For if there is one thing above all that no Jew can do and remain a Jew it is to oppress another human being or a nation. No Jew can desire to secure his freedom over the body of another man, whether Jew or non-Jew. We did not come to the Land of Israel to oppress the people already living in that country. And if we seek to resolve the present dilemma by holding tight to the land and "persuading" its non-Jews to go, then I say this would

25. Harold Jackson in the *Guardian*, October 30, 1967.
26. Quoted by Israel Eldad, "Moshe Dayan Causing Confusion or Stirring Up the Devil?" *Haaretz*, September 15, 1967.
27. *Jerusalem Post*, September 25, 1967.

be a betrayal of Zionism, and a cynical, brutal betrayal, because the most oppressed people in the world would be turning into oppressors while still posing as victims.

I did not come to Israel to oppress anyone. I left South Africa to seek freedom and a genuine Jewish existence in my own land. I wished neither to oppress nor to be oppressed. I cherished the noble words of Martin Buber, who said in 1921:

"As it enters the sphere of world history once more, and becomes again the standard-bearer of its own fate, the Jewish people, which has constituted a persecuted minority in all the countries of the world for two thousand years, rejects with abhorrence the nationalistic methods of national domination, whose victim it itself has long been. We do not aspire to return to the land with which we have inseparable historical and spiritual ties in order to suppress another people or to dominate it."[28]

And because I do not believe it is possible to hold these territories while acting justly; because they can only be held with the aid of oppressive measures, martial law, expulsions, and persecution; because to insist on holding them while closing our eyes to the moral and political trap they represent would be unpardonable blindness—for all these reasons I say we must not link the retention of all these lands with the ultimate ideal of Zionism. The Bible can certainly be a moral and spiritual signpost, but an Israeli Government cannot conduct foreign affairs with the story of Genesis as a position paper.

If the Israeli Government yields to the extremists within the country and indeed within the Cabinet itself and decides to annex the West Bank and make the Jordan River Israel's eastern frontier, I believe we will be playing into the Arabs' hands. There are clear indications that Nasser's policy, formed with advice from Moscow, is to hold tight and hope that Israel's longer lines of communications, the need to keep so many civilians mobilized, and sporadic guerrilla activity in the occupied areas will eventually force Jerusalem to withdraw unilaterally without the need for painful Arab concessions.

Certainly it is tempting to think of borders in which, for the

28. Address to 12th Zionist Congress in Carlsbad, 1921: published in *Nation and World*, a collection of Martin Buber's essays on topical affairs (in Hebrew), World Zionist Executive, Jerusalem, 1961, p. 287.

first time in nineteen years, no place in Israel is within reach of Arab guns. But Israel must draw a clear distinction between temporary security maintained by force and a real, lasting security in which the Arabs too would have a stake. And when I hear Eshkol speak of "Greater Israel"; when the Israeli press and radio refer to "Yehuda and Shomron"—Judea and Samaria—rather than the West Bank; when I hear of Arab villages like Jiftliq being razed to the ground and thousands of Palestinian refugees being made homeless again—I began to fear that Isaac Deutscher was right when he quoted the German saying: *Man kann sich totsiegen:* "You can rush yourself victoriously into your grave."

And Deutscher issued a warning which no observer of current trends within Israel can brush aside:

"The Israelis have bitten off much more than they can swallow. . . . Will Israel expel the mass of Arabs in order to hold 'securely' the conquered lands? This would create a new refugee problem, more dangerous and larger than the old one. Will they give up the conquered territories? No, say most of their leaders. . . . None of the Israeli parties is prepared even to contemplate a binational Arab-Israeli state. Meanwhile great numbers of Arabs have been 'induced' to leave their homes on the Jordan. . . . Yes, this victory is worse for Israel than a defeat. Far from giving Israel a higher degree of security, it has rendered it much more insecure. If Arab revenge and extermination is what the Israelis feared, they have behaved as if they were bent on turning a bogey into an actual menace."[29]

And I cannot help but add, with a heavy heart:

If Israel insists on holding all the land it now holds and uses coercive and anti-Arab measures to maintain a Jewish majority, it will have no future except as a Middle East Rhodesia. Peace will be impossible. Israel will remain a ghetto, an armed ghetto practicing a refined type of apartheid. And if that will not be a betrayal of Zionism, then I do not know what Zionism is.

The question for me is not one of world public opinion—although the same circles which cheered Israel's victory in June will be only too ready to take the side of the Arab underdog if it

29. Interview with Isaac Deutscher, *New Left Review*, July–August 1967, p. 39.

appears that Israel is expelling Arabs or denying them civil rights. Michael Frayn summed this up brilliantly in an article in the London *Observer* soon after the war, in a letter addressed to "My Dear Israel":

"We could have overlooked your becoming involved in war; it happens to the best of us at times. What we cannot so easily forgive is your insistence on *winning* the war—particularly in such a brash and violent fashion.

"What makes your behavior all the more perplexing is that when the war commenced you enjoyed the approval and sympathy of polite society as a whole. . . . We shouldn't have let you down! If things had gone badly, we had ships standing by which could have evacuated *several thousand* Israeli survivors—who would have had the *unreserved sympathy* of the entire world!

"But you took it upon yourselves to win, and you have no doubt learnt, to your cost, what the world thinks of nations that win wars. . . . I hope I have said enough to make the family's feelings clear. Now, *how are you to make amends?*"[30]

What disturbs me is not the fear of adverse world reaction. Neither is it the threat of possible sanctions by the UN. It is in fact quite possible to imagine Israel holding its present area for years to come, if it is prepared to use strong-arm methods to do so. It will take at least two years, and probably longer, before Egypt will regain the military strength it possessed on June 4, and Israel is not standing still. The Soviet Union will not undertake military action against Israel or encourage the Arabs to do so. The only hold Moscow has over Israel is the Jews it keeps hostage in the Soviet Union, but it cannot release them without irrevocably angering the Arabs.

The only Power which could press Israel to withdraw from the occupied Arab lands is the United States. And it will not press Israel to do this without firm Arab guarantees and binding peace treaties. There are several reasons for this:

¶ *The United States has no interest in the Suez Canal being opened.* As long as the canal is closed, Russian supplies for North Vietnam have to be shipped from the Black Sea the long

30. Michael Frayn, "My Dear Israel," London *Observer*, June 25, 1967.

way round via the Cape of Good Hope, instead of through the Middle East. Vietnam is a far more major issue than Israeli-Arab relations, in the view of the White House. And anything which hampers Soviet assistance to Hanoi is desirable.

¶ *Since the canal was closed Soviet influence in the Yemen, Somalia, and other Red Sea countries has declined, because of the delay in communications.* With Britain pulling out of Aden and cutting down its commitments east of Suez, Washington wants to prevent Moscow expanding into this vacuum and controlling the Indian Ocean and the Persian Gulf.

¶ *The United States has sold considerable quantities of oil to Western Europe since the Israeli-Arab war.* With a large deficit expected for 1968–1969, this has been an unexpected but welcome windfall.

¶ *Last, but not least, is the fact that the United States has a tradition of sympathy with Israel, going back to President Truman's immediate recognition of the State in 1948.* During the 1968 Presidential elections every aspiring Democratic and Republican candidate expressed strong support for Israel. It is unlikely that a policy of unilateral pressure on Israel will ever prove popular with the American public.

No, I am not concerned so much with world opinion or possible international sanctions. What worries me far more is whether Israel, having won a magnificent victory, not only because of its iron and steel, but because of its heart, its faith and courage, can now have the wisdom to realize that "the Arabs may *obey* force, but they *respect* justice."[31] The question is whether Israel can now, in the moment of its greatest triumph, have the insight to see that it holds the seed of peace in its hand, if it has the humility to plant it.

The United States is not going to press Israel into unilateral action. The UN is not going to pass a motion calling for sanctions. The Soviet Union has no hold over Israel, and the Arabs are still confused and divided by the shock of the catastrophe. Everyone recognizes that these are facts. Abba Eban summed the

31. Robert Stephens, "How the Arabs See Their Choices," London *Observer*, July 16, 1967.

situation up succinctly, in one of his rare flashes of blunt talk:

"Nobody is going to send fleets or armies simply to get us out, and they cannot get us to move from the cease-fire line except under the terms of any agreed peace settlement, including a frontier demarcation."[32]

But it does not follow from this that Israel can scorn the world and do as it pleases. As I see it, it means that Israel should take the initiative if it genuinely, truly seeks peace. Because no one else is going to take the initiative—and if Israel does not, it runs the risk of sinking into an illusory kind of security, the acceptance of the present borders almost through inertia and complacency. And this would merely postpone a future confrontation until the Arabs felt ready for one or the region's accumulated tensions spill over into war again as they did in June.

If Israel truly wishes to take the initiative toward a firm security, resting on more lasting foundations than a temporary military advantage, it must do two things:

¶ *It must acknowledge the state's moral obligation toward the former inhabitants of Palestine and undertake a just and honorable solution of their human and social problems.* This must not be linked to a peace settlement and should be undertaken independently of any peace settlement, as a prior step toward it.

All historical upheavals involve human suffering. But Israel, which was founded so that refugees and exiles could lead creative, productive lives, is duty-bound to try to reduce this suffering to the minimum and to alleviate the anguish of those who themselves became refugees and exiles in 1948.

Later in this book I shall describe in detail how I believe this can be done. It is enough to say here that this is the crux of the Israeli-Arab dispute. Israel should now make this unilateral commitment not out of any desire to use it as a bargaining point, but—as John F. Kennedy said—"because it is right." Perhaps if we had pledged to eliminate the refugee problem earlier, the wars of 1956 and 1967 would not have been fought.

¶ *Israel must accept its destiny as an integral part of the Middle*

32. Television interview with Eban in Washington: *International Herald Tribune*, November 13, 1967.

East and act upon this recognition of its role. This means among others changing the concept of Israel as a Jewish state, in which non-Jews were tolerated on sufferance, and replacing this with the idea of a multiracial state, in which the Jews will be the majority, but all races, national groups, and sects will have equal rights and will share in the country's destiny.

This means recognizing that the Arabs find it difficult to accept us and hence taking steps to make it easier for them to do so. It means encouraging the moderate Arabs by displaying our readiness to meet them, and by making it easier for the moderate Arabs to resist their extremists.

I believe that if we can do these two things, and express them in appropriate action, we can change the course of events in the Middle East as dramatically as we changed them on June 5, 1967.

If we follow an authentically Jewish path in our dealings with the Arabs in our midst and the neighboring peoples, we shall regain the affinity we had with these peoples throughout so much of our history.

But as long as Israel clings vainly to its image as an appendage to Europe, it will be unable to play the role history has assigned to it, as an indisputably Middle East nation based on Western democratic patterns and multiracial cooperation. When the Zionist movement rejected such alternative proposals as Herzl's Uganda territory and staked its whole future on the return to Palestine, it decided the orientation of the future State of Israel. Fate has decreed that the Jews and Arabs of Israel and the Arabs of the Middle East are to share a single geopolitical region. The great goal of the second phase of Israel's rebirth should be to reopen the lines of communication with its immediate environment, so that Western concepts and techniques can flow through it to the East and so that Eastern wisdom and knowledge of the region can flow through it to the West. Israel must rediscover its age-old link with Semitic culture, while bringing to this reunion the experience gained during its 1,878 years of enforced sojourn among the nations of the world. Then it will be expressing the historic purpose for which it was created. The Zionist struggle and the culminating resolution of 1947 will be seen in perspective, first by discerning Arabs and then by the masses, as acts of historic justice which restored to the Middle East a vital and essential catalytic element.

But in order to obtain the justice it deserves Israel must give justice. It must not base its security and territorial integrity purely upon the right of conquest—for then, can Israel deny the Arabs a right it claims for itself? Surely the preeminence of violence is not the most profound message Israel can bring back to the region from its long and painful exile.

As for myself, I say with Albert Camus: "I should like to be able to love my country and justice too." I hope that the leaders of my country will act resolutely, firmly, while remembering that justice and compassion are values the Jews were the first to give the world.

Toward the close of his life the old, blind Dr. Chaim Weizmann told the United Nations Special Commission on Palestine: "God has chosen the small nations as a vessel through which he sends his best messages to the world, and it is perhaps not too much to think that once strife is at an end and peace and the work of construction begins, and the old wanderer comes back to his old inheritance—perhaps once more a message of peace will come out of this country to a world which stands sorely in need of such a message."[33]

This is a noble vision for the future—an ideal which does not negate Zionism, but enlarges it. This would be a truer conception of a Greater Israel: not one based on force, armor and acquisition, but a new and broader ideal in which Israel can join forces with its Arab neighbors and the Jews of the world to develop not only Israel itself, but the entire Middle East. This is the challenge to Israel.

As the leadership of Israel passes from the pioneer generation of Diaspora Zionists to the sabras—the Jews born in Israel—the question is whether this ideal can inspire this generation of Israelis. To answer this question we will have to look at the sabras and their views on the present crisis, as expressed in the words of their representative leaders.

33. UNSCOP proceedings, Official Record, Vol. III, p. 82.

8 | *Allon and Dayan: The Sabras Take Over*

THE LEADERSHIP of Israel is still in the hands of Russian and Polish Zionists who came as pioneers forty or fifty years ago. Prime Minister Levi Eshkol, who turned 72 in October 1967, came to Palestine from the Ukraine in 1914. Mrs. Golda Meir, former Secretary General of the Labor Party, was born in Kiev in 1898. Other Mapai Ministers are 66, 68, and 65, and came to Palestine in the 1920s.

But not only the Israeli Cabinet is dominated by Eastern European Jews. Among trade union officials, in the civil service and the Jewish Agency, talking to Israeli diplomats, one is constantly surprised by the overwhelming number of men and women who were born in Russia or Poland or are the children of *halutzim* (pioneers) from these countries.

Most of these pioneers came from middle-class homes and were part of the "back-to-the-land" movement which revolted against the traditional Jewish occupations of business and the professions. They came to Palestine to do manual labor and live in the new socialist settlements which were the cells of the future Jewish society. Eshkol's career in Israel is absolutely typical. He was a farm laborer and a member of *Hashomer*—the groups which guarded the earliest Jewish colonies. Later he became a member of Kibbutz Degania Beit, a trade union organizer, and head of the Jewish Agency's Settlement Department. When Israel was established he helped to build up the country's military industry and then was coopted into the Cabinet as Finance Minister.

But the old back-to-the-land ideology is no longer valid today, when Israel's economy is orientated towards greater industrial production and Western-style technology. The kibbutzim are still a great moral influence. But they make up only 4 per cent of the total population, and they proved inadequate to absorb the waves of urban-dwelling new immigrants who flocked in after 1948. Also, the intensive farming methods used today mean that fewer people can grow the country's food. If real peace with the Arabs ever comes, Israel might well decide to import more of its food and use its resources to produce more industrial goods for export. The emphasis today is on management, marketing, the application of scientific techniques. The older generation, with its neo-Tolstoyan call for a Jewish return to nature, has been left behind by Israel's self-propelled growth.

The generation of Ben-Gurion and Eshkol represents the *halutz* period of Israel's rebirth. It was an astonishing and glorious period. But many younger Israelis believe this generation has had its day. One reason for this feeling is demographic. Just over 40 per cent of the Jewish population are sabras, or Israeli-born. More than 30 per cent are Asian or African Jews. The European Jews are in a minority, and the generation of Mapai leadership is about 6 per cent of the Jewish population. The demand for a change at the top has a solid grass roots foundation.[1]

One intellectual whose family has lived in Palestine for five generations put it this way:

"I believe that the men who have been brought up in the Diaspora (dispersion) cannot help unconsciously taking over some of its attitudes. They have done their part. Now we must have a man who was born here, who thinks and feels as we do."[2]

Already native-born leaders are taking over key roles in the Cabinet and the army. The men who planned the astonishing 1967 victory were born in Palestine. Many of their soldiers were immigrants from North Africa and the Middle East who came to Israel in the 1950s or were born there. Unless a large Russian emigration takes place, which is more unlikely now than before the war, the leadership of Israel soon will pass to the sabras, with the Oriental Jews as their partners.

1. Michael Wolfers in London *Times*, July 15, 1967.
2. Quoted by David Spanier, "Demand for a New Kind of Leader," *London Times*, September 15, 1967.

Who are the sabras? What are their views on Israel's identity and future? What do they feel about the Arabs? Are they Jews as we think of Jews or Eastern Mediterranean Semites?

If we accept that the next generation will be a sabra one, then the answers to these questions become both fascinating and crucial. For myself, I find the study of the sabra soul endlessly intriguing. I know many of the leading Israeli-born Hebrew writers and intellectuals, most of whose ideas are a closed book to Western Jewry because of the language gap. They are, I am convinced, not merely a new generation of Jews but a new Jew altogether. In their personalities, values, and spiritual identity lies the clue to Israel's role in the last third of this century and beyond.

The simple and basic fact about the sabras is that they are not Zionists. They were born in the land. They did not need to join a Zionist organization and make the physical and psychological journey to the territory of their fathers. As one sabra writer, O. Hillel, has said: "My Zionism finished the moment I was born here."[3] Indeed the Hebrew word Zionut—Zionism—is used sarcastically for any sermonizing or high-minded talk unbacked by action.

It follows from this that the sabras see the problems of Israel from the inside out, and not from the outside moving toward the inside, like the old-style Zionists. They are concerned with Israel's security and progress and not overworried about adverse world reactions to anything which advances this aim. The sabras accuse the Old Guard of being too sensitive to international criticism and hint that this comes from the centuries of minority living among the non-Jews. The sabras have never lived on sufferance as a minority. They have no inhibitions about the Gentiles or the neighbors, no inferiority complexes. Some people think this very absence of Jewish timidity and caution is a complex—and a peculiarly sabra one.

The sabras are secular Jews, by and large. Of course there are sabra children of orthodox parents who are fanatically religious with an almost Puritanical zeal. But sabras are on the whole not synagogue-goers. They are not supplicants. They despise the

3. *Maariv*, March 19, 1965.

European Jews for having yielded so meekly to the Germans and for having gone quietly to the gas chambers with a prayer on their lips. They associate Jewish orthodoxy with passivity. And the sabras are above all not passive. They are dynamic, tough, hard, ruthless if necessary. It is as if the Jewish will to survive has fused with a flint-like feel of the hot difficult terrain to produce men who grow out of the Negev and the Galilee as if they had stayed behind when the Romans drove the Jews out in 70 C. E.

Because the sabras are secular in outlook and because they feel at home in this country as no Zionist Jew born in Warsaw or the Ukraine ever could feel at home, they often—but not always—have a sense of kinship with other indigenous peoples of the Middle East. Many sabras have told me they feel closer to an Arab from Nazareth than to a Jew from Hampstead or the Bronx. An Israeli poet who came to Palestine as a child says: "It was not Herzl or Weizmann who brought me to the Land of Israel, but the Arab docker who transported me from the ship to the shore of Jaffa."[4] And the painter Nachum Gutman—admittedly not a sabra, but a Russian Jew who grew up as a child under the Turks and has lived in Tel Aviv from its beginning sixty years ago—explains:

"My love of the Arabs is endless. The charm of their culture is overwhelming. There is much beauty in them that even they don't realize is there.

"The older Jewish painters saw things Jewish with the eyes of Diaspora Jews. We younger artists began to see things in terms of the Mediterranean atmosphere. In the 1920s we became conscious of sources and wanted to create something local. . . .

"Should I talk like an anti-Semite? Well, we have vandalously ruined the landscape, the character of the land itself. What is Israel's largest wall? The sea . . . a blue wall. Which colors have we put next to it? White, ochre, gray. That is vandalism! Look at Venice, Alexandria, the original Old Jaffa—reds, blues, yellows, greens!

"The Arabs built instinctively—and just look at their forms,

4. Avot Yeshurun: quoted in *The Modern Hebrew Poem Itself*, edited by Stanley Burnshaw, T. Carmi, and Ezra Spicehandler (New York: Holt, Rinehart and Winston, 1965).

their colors. Our architects are all Western-minded, and they have spoiled the Tel Aviv seashore and are spoiling Tiberias and Safed. Even Old Jaffa is being renovated in dull European colors. Instead of learning from the Arabs, we destroy what they built and put up Hiltons."[5]

Many sabras unconsciously prefer a Middle East pattern of living to an American or European one. They tend to gravitate to Oriental-style cafes and restaurants. Biblical and classical Hebrew was prayer-oriented and had no slang. So for their four-letter words the sabras borrow from Arabic. Modern Israeli dances and songs are often modeled on such Arab forms as the *debka*. The national passion for archaeology is also a way of reaching back in time for roots that exist in no other country. For a sabra the history of the Jews in Poland is simply the history of Poland. It does not touch him. His history is the history of Palestine, and he shares this with other Palestinians—Moslems, Christians, Druse, Maronites, Armenians, and Bedouin.

But the sabra is not an indulgent "Levantine" in the sense that many European Jews misuse the word: an idle, soft individual without much pride or ambition. He combines a liking for Eastern habits of living with a fiercely Western attitude to knowledge, work, morals, and existence. The best sabras combine Eastern and Western traits in a poised harmony which perhaps explains their lack of self-consciousness.

What we have, then, is not just a subculture of the orthodox Jewish culture, but a totally new phenomenon in Jewish life: Jews who feel at home in a Middle East environment, yet have sharply defined Western attitudes; who accept their identity as Jews, but have discarded the religious separatism of their grandparents or parents. This is not a sect, but the beginning of a new nation distinct from other Western or Eastern Jews. As Professor Georges Friedmann puts it:

"There is no Jewish nation. There is an Israel nation. The state that came into existence as the result of Herzl's prophecies is not a 'Jewish state.' The Israeli state is creating an imperious national

5. *Jerusalem Post*, September 26, 1965.

community that is conscious of itself, but does not include in that consciousness belonging to a 'Jewish people.' "⁶

I believe the best hope of a peace settlement with the Arabs is the prospect of an Israeli Cabinet consisting mainly of sabras, with a sabra Prime Minister. Perhaps only leaders who were themselves born in the Middle East will be able to see the Arabs as potential partners, not as military or economic rivals.

But is this assumption correct? Is it a subjective theory of mine, based on intimate contact with sabras in every walk of life? What really are the views of the leading sabra contenders for high political office? More specifically, how do they propose to resolve the present deadlock and make a stable peace with the Arabs?

Two men are mentioned in the same breath whenever anyone talks about the successor to Levi Eshkol. Moshe Dayan is 53 and Yigal Allon is 50. By Israeli standards this is young. In fact, the politicians of their generation are usually referred to as *ha'tsi'irim* —"the young men" or the Young Turks. It is not surprising that Senator Edward Kennedy once asked students in Jerusalem why such a young country should have such old leaders.⁷ But then Israeli elder statesmen never resign. They die in harness or cling stubbornly to office until they are forced out by the Hebraic version of a Greek tragedy which afflicted Ben-Gurion at the end of his long career.

What sort of men are Allon and Dayan? How would their attaining supreme office affect Israel's chances of peace?

Superficially, the two men have much in common. Both are outstanding military figures who first became nationally prominent in the 1948 war. Both grew up on farms in northern Israel— Allon at Kvar Tabor in Lower Galilee, Dayan on Kibbutz Degania Alef and then on Moshav Nahalal in the Valley of Jezreel. Both have considerable charm and exert a magnetic spell over their followers.

But then the differences start to emerge, with as much force as the gathering personal struggle between them seems to indicate.

6. Georges Friedmann, *The End of the Jewish People?* (London: Hutchinson, 1967), p. 230.
7. *Report from Israel, The Economist,* July 29, 1967.

Dayan is blunt, crude, unsophisticated. He is a genuine icon-oclast. He pays no attention to moral scruples and does pretty much what he wants—or as much as he can get away with. He is motivated by an inner power which ignores obstacles or sweeps them away in the rush to his target, which he cannot bear not to reach.

He has little time for the game of international politics or such weak-kneed bodies as the United Nations. I heard him tell an audience in Tel Aviv: "Anyone who thinks we have to obtain any Great Power's agreement and permission before acting is a political infant."[8] And in an article he summed up his basic political philosophy when he said: "What the Jews do is more important than what the Arabs say."[9] This parallels the saying of his mentor, David Ben-Gurion, that "what counts is not what the Arabs think, but what the Jews do."

Dayan is a cynical realist who is concerned only with the end results and not by the attractiveness of the means used to get them. Three days before the 1956 Sinai campaign began he told his staff:

"Israelis will have to behave like a cyclist pedaling uphill and finding an unexpected opportunity to hold onto the tail of a truck. This should continue until our roads part."[10]

The fact that Israel was hitching onto the Anglo-French truck and later denied it knew it was passing by does not seem to trouble Dayan, whose drastic vision of the world leaves no room for a bad conscience. In this and in other ways he is curiously un-Jewish, as if the rebirth in Israel had wiped out all those "ineffectual" Diaspora traits of doubt and spiritual yearnings. He is cold and unemotional. He is intolerant and not a warm family man. He is a loner, self-contained and with few loyalties apart from his passionate devotion to Israel. Above all, he is a soldier, a military man who revels in war and feels cramped by the humdrum of Israel's everyday political infighting.

One cannot help admiring his frankness, his uncompromising

8. *Yediot Aharonot*, March 14, 1965.
9. *Haaretz*, January 14, 1964.
10. Moshe Dayan, *Diary of the Sinai Campaign* (in Hebrew): quoted by Francis Ofner in London *Observer*, September 26, 1965.

way of telling the truth as he sees it, his natural flamboyance. But one wonders too whether Dayan, if he ever became Prime Minister, would have the patience for the Parliamentary committees and the slow grind of government which go with the job. It is difficult to see Dayan bargaining with trade union leaders about wages or social problems, or spending much time studying economic reports.

Dayan was born on May 20, 1915. His parents were *halutzim* from Russia, and he grew up on a farm. But he was soon drawn into the Haganah, the Jewish underground movement. In 1939 he was captured and sent to Acre jail.

Two years later he was released to help the British fight the Vichy French in Syria and was attached to an Australian unit as a scout. He lost his left eye there when he was hit by a bullet, and his slightly opaque black patch has become his trademark.

After World War II Dayan returned to the Haganah, and during the 1948 war with the Arabs he commanded the Jerusalem front. Ben-Gurion recognized his military genius and took him under his wing. In 1953 Dayan became Chief of Staff and prepared the ground for the 1956 Sinai campaign, which foreshadowed the 1967 victory.

After retiring from the army he became Minister of Agriculture under Ben-Gurion. But in 1963 Ben-Gurion left the government, and such followers of "the old man" as Dayan and Peres followed him into exile, after an uneasy period of office in Eshkol's Cabinet. Although Dayan admires Ben-Gurion, he does not obey him blindly, and now that he is within striking distance of the top leadership he sticks to his own counsel.

In many ways Dayan reminds me of the South African Boers I learned to know as a boy. He would fit easily into Ian Smith's UDI Rhodesia. He has the same elemental views, the same lack of interest in what the rest of the world thinks. Whenever I hear Dayan speak I recall the warning of the Swiss historian Jakob Christoph Burckhardt against "the terrible simplifiers." Take almost any statement of Dayan's and read it. You will see that at some point he presents two stark alternatives and demands a choice between them. He has an either-or mind. Everything is seen in black and white extremes. But politics is, as Disraeli said, the art of the possible. It is a gray art, a skill which requires a knowledge of compromise and flexibility. Dayan is not a stereotyped party politician. This is his strength—and his weakness.

Toward Arabs he displays the same blunt approach. He does not like them. But he has respect for the ones who oppose him, although he will fight them. He has often said that those Arabs who do not want to live in Israel should leave it. He is capable of surprise gestures toward Arab soldiers, like the off-the-cuff visit he paid to Egyptian officers in Atlit prisoner of war camp just before they were repatriated. He told the one hundred officers, who included four generals, he had come to wish them godspeed and to have a frank talk on Israeli-Arab relations.

"We can live in mutual respect and peace," he said. He asked them to remember Israel's wishes for peace and coexistence and to understand "that in the midst of the Arab world surrounding it, there exists a Jewish state." It is characteristic of the man that, having made this gesture, he spoke to the officers in English, although he speaks Arabic fluently.[11]

Allon is a very different personality: subtler, more sophisticated, more aware of the world outside Israel. His two years at St. Antony's College, Oxford, studying economics, philosophy, and political science probably contributed to this. But his active membership of a kibbutz also helps to root him in the constructive everyday life of Israel. Although he too is a military man, he is not a professional soldier and is concerned with problems wider than security strategy.

Allon grew up near Mount Tabor and was familiar with Arab life in Galilee villages. He speaks Arabic fluently and has more feeling than Dayan for the ordinary Arab fellah, or farmer. People on his kibbutz say he maintains friendly ties with the Arab villages in the vicinity and often invites Arabs to his home.

He helped to found this kibbutz, Ginossar, on the shores of the Sea of Galilee. His wife runs the guest house. Allon manages to take off at least two days a week from his ministerial duties so that he can be on the kibbutz.

11. *The New York Times*, January 17, 1968.

As a youth he studied agriculture at the Kadoorie College near his village of Kfar Tabor and then had a brief spell at the Hebrew University. In 1941 Allon helped to form the Palmach, the elite striking force of the Haganah. As commander of its first company, he cooperated in the Allied invasion of Syria and Lebanon which drove out the pro-Nazi French.

During the 1948 war he commanded the forces that liberated Upper Galilee. He became famous as the conqueror of Safed, Lod, Ramle, the Jerusalem Corridor, and the Negev. He expulsed the Egyptian army from the Beersheba area and northern Sinai and then took Eilat. In the Faluja pocket he met a young Egyptian officer named Gamal Abdel Nasser. The two men talked about the Middle East and the need for social change in the Arab world. Nasser has said that Allon is the one Israeli he would be prepared to meet for peace talks. And Allon calls Nasser "my old friend."

After the war Allon went to England. In 1961 he became Minister of Labor. He retained a special interest in security matters and is a key member of the Cabinet's inner Defense Committee, which approves all major decisions. For the last three years he has been an obvious contender for Eshkol's mantle when the latter would retire.

Allon is a deeper man than Dayan. He has a far more complex view of life and a greater understanding of the non-military pressures—social, economic, and spiritual—which can also lead to wars.

He is a humane man who takes no delight in war for war's sake. In May 1956 I happened to be on a visit to Johannesburg. Allon was on a lecture tour to South Africa. I met him there and took some letters home to his wife and family, as I was returning to Israel before him.

It was the time of the fedayeen raids, and the mood which led to the Sinai offensive was already in the air. I went along to hear Allon talk to a mass rally of South African Zionist youth. The speakers who preceded him called for Israeli reprisal actions to put an end to the fedayeen raids. Nothing would have been easier for this visiting Israeli military hero than to fit into this atmosphere and deliver a belligerent speech full of threats and bluster.

But Allon did not do this. He spoke to the young Zionists about the meaning of war; the Jews and Arabs who would die in a conflict; the diversion from productive and constructive aims which it represented. He told them he hated war because he had seen it and did not want Israel to go to war again unless it had to act in self-defense. When I left the hall that night I remember feeling that Allon could be a leader not only of Israelis, but also of Arabs.

The great difference between Allon and Dayan in terms of their Middle East policies is that one believes in the possibility of Jewish-Arab cooperation and the other doesn't. Allon has frequently spoken about the need to develop the entire region for the benefit of all its peoples. Dayan, on the other hand, has little interest in active cooperation with Israel's neighbors and is concerned first and foremost about developing the land lying within Israel's garrisoned borders.

To use my definitions, Allon is a "Middle Easterner" who sees Israel's future within a regional framework. Dayan is a "European" who wants to strengthen the fortress against the invaders outside.

Because of these inherently opposed points of view—which perhaps represent ambivalent aspects of the sabra mentality—the two men hold different opinions on how to end the present deadlock. But here a surprising shift occurs. When it comes to analyzing their statements since the June war, the pat definitions of "hawk" and "dove" break down. In the same way that Ben-Gurion is now thinking about a Palestinian state, like his former left-wing Mapam opponents, so the views expressed by Dayan and Allon cut across party lines and reflect each man's experience, suspicions, and deepest beliefs.

As an Israeli who is concerned above all with the quality of life inside Israel, Dayan does not want to dilute this "Jewishness" with a large Arab minority. He is attracted by the idea of keeping all the territory now under Israeli control. "Speaking purely theoretically," he told the army newspaper *Bamachaneh*, "I doubt whether we could find more ideal borders than the present lines." But, he added quickly, "the ideal frontiers may not be realistic."[12]

12. *Guardian*, October 2, 1967.

In other words, Dayan has weighed the advantages of a frontier from which Israel could move into key Arab capitals in the event of war against the disadvantages of large numbers of resident Arabs, and he would prefer a smaller territory containing fewer non-Jews.

But Israel of the future should embrace the areas with emotional and historical significance for the Jewish people:

"Foreigners must realize that with all the strategic importance to Israel of Sinai, the Golan Heights and the Tiran Strait, the mountain range west of the Jordan lies at the heart of Jewish history.

"If you have the book of the Bible and the people of the Book, then you also have the land of the Bible—of the judges and of the patriarchs—in Jerusalem, Hebron, Jericho, and thereabout."

What he was saying, Dayan added, "may not be a political program, but what is more important—the fulfillment of a people's ancestral dreams."[13]

This speech was made in August 1967, very soon after the victory, when Dayan still thought of a West Bank absorbed into Israel. Some of his statements then seemed to express the hope that the West Bank Arabs would leave to live among the Jordanians on the East Bank. Thus he told the press on July 25: "If I had to make a choice to live under my own people—whether I admire kings or not—or under foreign domination, I would have gone to my own people."[14] And he made it clear that there was no room for the Palestinian refugees in the occupied territories or in Israel:

"One million Jews have replaced the Arabs and whether it's moral or not, there simply isn't room."[15]

Dayan initiated the policy of allowing West Bank Arabs to cross freely to the East Bank—apparently in the hope that many of them would not want to return. He encouraged refugees from the Gaza Strip to leave for Hebron by laying on trucks and by closing a blind eye to anyone who wanted to go from Hebron to Amman.

13. *International Herald Tribune*, August 11, 1967.
14. *Haaretz*, July 26, 1967.
15. Interview with Henry Brandon, *Sunday Times*, September 10, 1967.

But the West Bank Arabs did not respond to these open invitations to abandon their homes and lands. By the end of the year it became obvious that the West Bank could be integrated by Israel only if the Arab residents were taken along with it. This has led Dayan to change his views on Israel's future boundaries. In January 1968 he listed what he thought Israel should demand:

¶ Secure borders. In the west, this means holding onto the Tiran Strait. "This is essential for us, and we can neither abandon it to Egypt nor rely on the UN to guard it."

¶ In the east, secure borders must be accompanied by peaceful relations with whoever is Israel's "partner"—whether King Hussein or the Palestinian Arabs.

¶ The Arab refugees must be resettled permanently, and there must be full freedom of worship and access to holy places and historic sites.

¶ As for the occupied territories, Dayan is convinced the policy of minimum interference and allowing maximum contact with Jordan is paying dividends: "We must tell the Arabs of Nablus: 'All we want from you is non-intervention in our security. . . . Whatever the final settlement, you can live without being cut off from the Arab world.' The Jordan River, which I see as Israel's security border, need not separate the West Bank from the Arab world or lock its inhabitants into a Jewish ghetto." Dayan believes this policy is helping to defeat Arab nationalist terrorism. West Bank residents, he says, are already urging Hussein to make peace: "They would be happy if the earth were to swallow us up. But they are terrified at the thought of Arab armies trying to 'liberate' them, because they fear there would be no survivors."

¶ The Israeli Defense Minister was not optimistic about the chances of an early peace. The Arab states and the Soviet Union, he felt, were determined to eject Israel from the territory conquered in June 1967 and would not accept the cease-fire lines. But the decision whether there would be a fourth Arab-Israeli war would be the Kremlin's. If Moscow and Cairo could not oust Israel by political methods, they might try force. Another war, if it came, would be tougher than the 1967 one, as the Arab attack would be coordinated, making full use of the combined strength of Iraq, Jordan, and Syria in the north and Egypt in the south. The Arabs themselves would not risk another war, "but if the Russians decide they must fight they will fight."

¶ A separate peace with Hussein is ruled out, in Dayan's opinion, because Nasser and the Soviet leaders would see such a settlement as an Israeli concession to the United States. This would only encourage Cairo and Moscow to press all the harder. The only front that really mattered was the Suez Canal, where Israel confronted Egypt: "If war starts there it can drag in other countries. But Jordan will not start a war."

§ The best chance of altering the situation lay in "imponderables" such as the difficulties and pressures that President Nasser was undergoing: "I hope he is having a very hard time, economically, domestically, and politically. This patronage—that the Russians direct things for him—it is doubtful if he likes it. And he has domestic troubles. Perhaps he will say, 'We will come to an arrangement with Israel and get out of the mess.' "[16]

The West Bank, then, should remain under Israeli *occupation*, with an autonomous *administration*. As Dayan explained to Joseph Alsop, all that Israel needs is to insure that no enemy troops cross the Jordan. For this purpose, Israel requires only the use of the main roads and a few strongpoints on the heights above the river. But the West Bank Arabs should run their own non-military affairs:

"We must not interfere, become involved, issue permits, make regulations, name administrators, become rulers. For if we do, it will be bad for us."[17]

Notice that Dayan does not talk about economic or political cooperation with a possible Palestine Arab state. He is not interested in a confederation or in any wider grouping which could open the way to mutual trading and development programs. His reasons for preferring Palestinian autonomy for the West Bank are completely negative. He often sounds wistful about the

16. *Haaretz*, January 19, 1968; London *Times*, January 20; *Jewish Observer and Middle East Review*, January 26.

17. Joseph Alsop, "Moshe Dayan's Motto," *International Herald Tribune*, September 12, 1967.

territory up to the Jordan, as if hopeful that a large Arab exodus—spontaneous or assisted—would take place so that it could become part of Israel.

Allon, on the other hand, has always believed that Jews and Arabs would one day cooperate within the region they were destined to share. In 1959, recalling his meeting with Colonel Gamal Abdel Nasser eleven years earlier, he wrote:

"This region is normally regarded as an underdeveloped area. But, at the same time, it offers to its peoples tremendous hopes, if properly developed and harnessed for the welfare of its peoples. We have in this area enough natural wealth, oil and water, minerals and manpower, know-how and technological ability, to make the Middle East the envy of other less blessed regions. We stand at the crossroads of the world's great communications routes.

"From every point of view—economic and political, cultural and strategic—I believe that the ultimate solution for the entire region lies in the creation of a regional organization, a Middle East commonwealth of sovereign nations interdependent on each other for economic, political, cultural, scientific, and defensive cooperation. This confederation would not only secure adequate national autonomy for all member states, but also ensure the presence of an efficient organization to prevent conflict within the region and to establish it as a powerful instrument able to eradicate poverty, disease, and illiteracy and to make a considerable contribution to the peace of the world."[18]

This is a concept close to Eban's Open Region and one which Allon stayed close to after he entered the Cabinet. Many Israeli writers and public figures have charted a similar vision. But few have been able to do so much to implement it.

After the June 1967 war Allon spoke of the need to reach a peace which would be dignified and would not perpetuate the Arabs' humiliation. His "old friend" President Nasser, he remarked, had told the Khartoum summit conference that there were two choices before the Arab countries—surrender or re-

18. Quoted by John Biggs-Davison, M.P., in British House of Commons: *Hansard*, July 6, 1967, columns 2,070–2,071.

sistance—and that he preferred to resist, because this represented the spirit of Arab nationalism.

"I think he is utterly wrong," Allon said. "These are not the only alternatives. Peace is not surrender. Direct negotiation between us and any Arab government, including Egypt, may lead to a solution of peace with honor."

But, he warned, if the Arab leaders refused to draw the lessons from the war, Israel would be compelled to take a stubborn position in its own defense. "Time is not on their side, and I cannot see their point here. Israel's own system of defense may entail unpleasant facts for them, which may be difficult to alter in the future." The sooner the Arab leaders negotiated, without preconditions, the better it would be.[19]

Allon also hinted that Israel was ready to negotiate piecemeal on individual issues, the solution of which would benefit both sides. While reiterating that an overall settlement could only be achieved on the basis of peace treaties and safeguards for Israel's securities, he listed several "piecemeal issues": the question of free navigation, a refugee settlement, and the unhindered flow of tourist traffic.[20]

But as the weeks went by and the chances of talks with any of the Arabs on any issue grew dimmer, Allon showed increasing private and public impatience. His speeches began reflecting his feeling that Israel should stay on the cease-fire lines until permanent, recognized, safe borders were drawn up.

"We are determined to stick to the new borders," he told a gathering in Haifa. "Not because we are aggressors—but because we know withdrawal would eliminate the chance of peace."

The United Nations and the Great Powers had had nineteen years in which to help settle the Arab-Israeli dispute. "But far from doing so, they failed even to prevent wars." A partial withdrawal would not make it easier to start talks with the Arabs. And, Allon declared, the settlement movement should establish new villages in areas occupied since the war, as they were "crying out for an Israeli presence."[21]

19. David Spanier in London *Times*, September 5, 1967.
20. *Financial Times*, September 26, 1967.
21. *Lamerhav*, November 19, 1967; *Guardian*, November 20, 1967.

The Jordan River, Allon now thinks, should be Israel's eastern border. This would run through the middle of the Dead Sea and give Israel "geographical depth and a comfortable strategic situation."

He admits that the area contains "400,000 refugees and hundreds of thousands of Arabs" and that "in the course of years this fact will create political problems."[22]

The solution, he has argued in the Cabinet, is to set up paramilitary settlements, similar to those established by *Nahal*, the corps of soldier farmers that carry out the dual job of cultivating the land and protecting the borders. He wants these settlements to "strike roots" in the Golan Heights of Syria, the Jordan Valley, the Hebron Hills, and the southern Gaza Strip.

The Minister of Labor maintained that these military farm outposts were necessary from a security point of view. But he told a conference of Kibbutz Hameuchad kibbutzim belonging to his party, Achdut Ha'avoda, that settlements in the Syrian Heights would be historically justified. Because of numerous references in the Old Testament, "the Golan Hills are no less Israeli than Hebron and Nablus."[23]

The first of these settlements have now been set up in Banias, a hilltop site in Syria near one of the Jordan's sources, and at Kfar Etzion, the site of a kibbutz wiped out by Jordan in 1948. Other settlements are being planned for the Gaza Strip and the West Bank.

Some of Allon's admirers, including myself, have been disappointed by his latest postwar pronouncements. He seems to be falling into the same defeatist posture as Dayan and to be relinquishing any Israeli initiative which could prevent a slide back into the paralyzed status quo that existed before June 1967.

His proposal for Israeli semi-military settlements in the occupied areas also seems unfortunate. It must inevitably raise doubts about Israel's intentions and sincerity. If Israel really means to hand back the West Bank to Jordan or an Arab state of Palestine if peace is signed, why should it entrench itself so deeply? And what will happen to the new kibbutzim when Israel pulls out? Putting

22. *Daily Telegraph*, August 16, 1967.
23. Terence Smith in *The New York Times*, August 17, 1967.

armed farmers in an area is not the best possible preparation for abandoning it when peace comes.

Those who are following Allon's career closely now, knowing that he is the leading contender for Eshkol's post, concede that Dayan's hard line is forcing him to take a tough stand in order to avoid being accused of soft-centered naïveté toward the Arabs. But they feel too that a potential leader's task is to lead and to point to the constructive way ahead, rather than to retreat into the tired old fortress mentality.

Dayan wants a Jewish state leading its own life and not adulterated by too many Arabs, and so he rejects the extra land and its people. Allon believes in the possibility of cooperation, if the Arabs would only see reason, and so he wants to hold the land and the burdensome Arab people in it until peace talks can begin.

Both positions contain weaknesses. Neither is a totally "European" or "Middle East" stance. Both are half-solutions based on disappointment and a growing despair. But what is needed now is a dynamic attack on a situation which is starting to stagnate again. The question is whether either Dayan or Allon can summon up the faith and drive needed to power a forceful Israeli peace campaign, the thrust of which would involve imaginative gestures toward the Arab moderates.

I listened to a talk on the BBC recently by an Egyptian writer who spent six weeks in Israel between July and September 1967. This man, Waguih Ghali, a Copt, wrote a novel several years ago in which he tried to remind the Egyptians of the Jewish suffering in Nazi Germany and Eastern Europe and made a plea for peace with Israel. The book also criticized the corruptness of the Egyptian army officer class. As a result Ghali fell foul of the Nasser regime, left Egypt, and now lives in Europe.

The novel was translated into Hebrew. It was well received and read by many people. When, after the war, Ghali applied for a visa to visit Israel, he was given one—the first Egyptian to visit Israel, apart from another journalist who came for a few days several years ago.

Ghali met Israelis of many different backgrounds, including Arabs. He talked with members of the Cabinet, members of the Knesset, and officials of the Israeli Foreign Ministry. He notes that he was always "very politely and kindly treated." Because he is an Egyptian, he did not ask "platitudinous questions" or accept "cliche answers."

One of the things that struck him was that "the nearer I came to the government, the higher the official, the less likely he was to be Palestinian or Middle Eastern either in origin or in outlook."

"The men responsible for Israel's policies," he points out, "are all of European extraction. Men like Dayan and Allon may have been born in Israel, but that does not make them Middle Eastern in outlook, for they have been brought up by East European parents. There's a very great difference in outlook and behavior between a Jew whose culture and background are genuinely Middle Eastern and a Jew with a Western or European orientation."

At the end of the war, Ghali says, Israel was in a position "to make some sort of 'grand gesture' toward the Arabs, to tell the Arabs that Israelis are Palestinian and not European." But "no such gesture is forthcoming. There is not one genuinely Palestinian Jew in the government. It is a government which despises any affinity with the Arabs and even, to a lesser extent, the Oriental Jews."

If Israel wants to have peace with the Arabs, it should support the progressive movements in the Middle East. "It should tell the Arabs: 'We are not the tools for imperialist designs on the Arab world.'" Israel should acknowledge that the 1956 Suez war was its greatest mistake—because it shook many Arabs like Ghali himself, who were not anti-Israel.

Real peace, in this Egyptian's opinion, can come only if Israel wills it. And he sees this will for peace coming about "only when and if the government of Israel is composed of Israelis who feel an affinity with the Arabs, and not with the West."[24]

This view by an Egyptian who is not hostile to Israel is important because it raises the question I asked earlier: Would a government composed largely of sabras, with a sabra Prime Minister, undertake the shift in emphasis which would make a new approach possible?

24. *The Listener*, January 11, 1968.

As things stand, this is more than a theoretical question. With an election in the offing, and Prime Minister Eshkol, at 72, anxious to retire when he can hand over the office to a handpicked successor, it is likely that either Dayan or Allon will become Israel's first sabra Prime Minister.

The formation of the Israeli Labor Party in January 1968 means also that for the first time there is a party in the Knesset controlling almost a majority of the 120 seats. This party brings together three smaller parties. Eshkol's Mapai, with Allon's Achdut Ha'avoda, ran a joint list in the general elections held on November 2, 1965, although they kept separate party machines and newspapers. This list—The Alignment—won 45 seats. The third member of the new party is Rafi—the breakaway group headed by Ben-Gurion and Dayan, which left Mapai after failing to unseat Eshkol. In the 1965 election Rafi won 10 seats. But Ben-Gurion has flatly refused to follow Dayan, Peres, and his other protégés back into Mapai, or to accept Eshkol as Prime Minister. He will remain in the Knesset as an independent—a solitary role for a man who was Israel's first Prime Minister.

This means that the Israeli Labor Party—*Mifleget Ha'avoda Ha'Yisraelit*—will have 45 Mapai-Achdut seats and nine Rafi members—a total of 54. With the Arab members affiliated to Mapai, it commands 58 seats. There is pressure on the left-wing party Mapam (the United Workers Party) to join the new unified party, which would then resemble something like the British Labor Party: a national workers' party in which left, right, and center trends coexist. Mapam has eight seats, and if it decides it cannot play an effective independent role and joins the ILP, the new party would have 66 votes, or an absolute majority—the first time any Knesset faction has enjoyed this position. Even if Mapam does not join the Mapai-Achdut-Rafi bloc, it would vote with it against the right-wing National Unity coalition on most vital issues.

So the man who succeeds Eshkol will take over a large integrated labor party and stand an excellent chance of being Prime Minister. This is the real significance of the struggle between Allon and Dayan. Dayan's motive in joining Eshkol and Allon, despite Ben-Gurion's vehement opposition, is to try to take over the party from within. Eshkol's motive in taking him in is to absorb his attack and neutralize him. Both men are confident of victory. But as the leadership fight intensifies, Allon and Dayan are bound to adopt more hawk-like public postures, with disturbing effects on the mood in the region.

Eshkol can of course stay on in office, if he feels Allon—his own chosen candidate—is not yet sufficiently strong to hold his own. We cannot also overlook the chance that another less likely aspirant might draw level with the two front-runners. Finance Minister Pinchas Sapir is fifeen years younger than Eshkol and has some support among Mapai leaders who fear both Allon and Dayan. But Sapir is identified with Israel's recent and current economic *mitun*, or slowdown, and is not popular among the general public.

Foreign Minister Abba Eban enjoys considerable prestige and admiration in Israel today. But his image is that of a brilliant international spokesman for Israel's cause, not of a man of action capable of military decisions. He does not have the advantage of an outstanding security career, like Allon and Dayan. And this is almost mandatory in the present climate of Israel—a fact I personally regret, because Eban is the most able exponent of the Middle Eastern school in the Cabinet.

Another name sometimes mentioned is that of Professor Yigael Yadin. Although he has scrupulously stayed out of Israel's political infighting, he has built up a worldwide reputation as an archaeologist and hints from time to time that he would return to political life if the nation asked him. Yadin is an autocratic man with rigid views perhaps even more hawkish than Dayan's. But he has no base of power within the party's grassroots and no springboard from which to launch a comeback—although he might be called in to join a tough-minded future Cabinet, particularly if Dayan wins the race.

For the first time, then, Israel will witness a contest between two able and formidable sabra aspirants. This struggle for control of the nation comes at a critical time. It is more than a battle between princes for the king's crown. It heralds the passing of the torch from the Diaspora-born Zionists to the native Israelis. One of these Israelis, Allon, is a man whose vision of a Middle East confederation has been eroded and perhaps blurred by years of Arab enmity. Another, Dayan, is a cynical advocate of realpolitik who could astonish everyone by one of his mercurial changes of course toward sworn adversaries like Nasser and Hussein. The contest will be grim, and it will take place against a background which will prevent any punches being pulled. No matter who wins, the outcome can decide Israel's orientation through the 1970s, and it will have the most fateful implications for the future of the West Bank, the Gaza Strip, and all the territory now held in bondage.

9 Jordan, Hussein, and the West Bank

ON THE MORNING of June 5, 1967, shortly after the first wave of the Israeli air strike had gone in against Egypt, Israeli Prime Minister Eshkol sent the following message to King Hussein of Jordan, via General Odd Bull, Chief of Staff of the UN Truce Supervisory Organization:

"We shall not initiate any action whatsoever against Jordan. However, should Jordan open hostilities, we shall react with all our might and he (King Hussein) will have to bear the full responsibility for all the consequences."

General Bull confirmed later that he had conveyed this message to the King.[1]

Yet, despite this warning, shortly after 8:30 A.M. bursts of firing were heard coming from the Old City of Jerusalem, and soon afterward shells began falling on the Israeli part of the city. Perhaps Hussein did not then believe the Israeli claim that the Egyptian Air Force had already been crippled and the war had virtually been won in that crucial first hour. Another possibility is that he was no longer in control of his armed forces, who were now taking their orders from the Egyptian General Riadh, who had arrived in Amman a few days earlier to set up an advance command post.

Whether Hussein acted impulsively or whether his army threatened to revolt unless he attacked Israel, one thing is certain: in deciding to shell Israeli Jerusalem he made the worst mistake of his career. It cost him half his kingdom—and it could still cost

1. Randolph S. Churchill and Winston S. Churchill, *The Six Day War*, (London: Heinemann, 1967), pp. 127–128.

him his throne. It inflicted enormous suffering on thousands of Palestinian Arabs who were made homeless for the second time in nineteen years. And it placed the future of Jordan as an independent country in serious doubt.

In order to understand the dimensions of the disaster that followed Hussein's miscalculation, the first thing to be realized is that even in peacetime Jordan's economy was shaky. Over 90 per cent of prewar Jordan was desert. The productive area along the Jordan River's West Bank—now controlled by Israel—made up about one quarter of the cultivated land. But its importance to the economy was far greater than this percentage. It supplied fresh supplies for consumption on the arid East Bank of the Jordan and for export to such countries as Iraq and Kuwait, which are short of vegetables and fruit.

In 1966 Jordan's foreign currency earnings were $158 million (at the old, $2.80 rate of sterling exchange). Official estimates in July 1967 put the loss of these earnings as a result of the war at $67.2 million—the entire $33.6 million brought in by tourism, $28 million lost from remittances to the West Bank by breadwinners in other Arab countries, and $5.6 million from reduced agricultural exports.

Foreign currency reserves after the war stood at about $252 million, and the balance of payments deficit in 1966 was only $2.8 million. But this was in fact an artificial figure kept down by grants from the United States and Britain totaling $41 million and grants of $27 million from other Arab countries. In addition UNRWA (United Nations Relief and Works Agency) contributed $15.7 million. These figures show up the stark fact that—as one correspondent reported from Amman a month after the war— "the Jordan budget is the greatest balancing act since Blondin crossed the Niagara Falls, and now the pole has suddenly been wrenched away."[2]

Before the 1967 catastrophe Jordan's economy had been making promising progress. Between 1959 and 1964 the country's income rose by 65 per cent, and its growth rate was 5 per cent a year.[3] Development plans on the boards included a seven-year scheme

2. Harold Jackson in the *Guardian*, July 11, 1967.
3. *Atlantic Monthly* survey of the Middle East, September 1966.

for extracting potash from the Dead Sea by building dikes across the southern end of the lake and an irrigation project for the Jordan Valley. But today Jordan can no longer afford these projects, which would cost more than half its current gross national product.

Because of this structural weakness in Jordan's economy and the intolerable burden created by the refugees flooding in from the West Bank, Israel's leaders hoped that Hussein would be ready to come to terms with them, even if this meant signing a separate peace treaty. Informed sources in Jerusalem thought the King would be under pressure to negotiate with Israel and could not refuse to do so unless he wanted to lose his annual $27 million subsidy from the United States.

Hussein himself always has been a surprisingly popular figure in Israel. The Israelis admire his courage, his survival skill, his dash and style. They knew he was a target for Arab extremists, and, on the sound Middle East principle that "the enemy of my enemy is my friend," they watched his efforts to stay in power with admiration, although they were careful not to give him the kiss of death by saying this in public.

As late as May 1967—only a few weeks before Hussein's dramatic embrace with Nasser at Cairo Airport—Cairo Radio was attacking the young King as a traitor who should share the fate of his grandfather King Abdullah, who was assassinated in 1951 in front of his grandson. "Hussein's throne is the target," Achmed Sa'id declared on November 29, 1966. "It should fall so that Israel may fall."[4] And Achmed Shukairy, chairman of the Palestine Liberation Organization, called the King, in a fiery speech broadcast to Jordan from a Cairo radio transmitter, "the tyrant of Amman ... who has betrayed God, the Prophet, and Palestine."[5]

Although Israel reluctantly carried out a massive reprisal operation against a Jordanian village in November 1966, its leaders hoped that Hussein would arrive at some type of *modus vivendi* with Israel in the course of time and would meanwhile keep the borders quiet and avoid internal agitation. It did not escape ob-

---

4. Quoted by W. A. C. Adie in "China and the Middle East," *The World Today*, August 1967, p. 323.
5. *The New York Times*, December 28, 1966.

servers in Jerusalem that President Bourguiba's celebrated press conference at which he first proposed negotiations with Israel was held in the Old City of Jerusalem, clearly with Hussein's consent. Although the King kept a discreet silence throughout the Tunisian President's visit, it was widely felt in Israel that he shared his unorthodox views on peaceful coexistence with Israel.

Indeed, Hussein sometimes sounded like Bourguiba, particularly after he broke with Shukairy and refused to allow his country to be used as a base for guerrilla warfare against Israel. Replying to Shukairy, the King called for an end to the refugee camps and said they should be closed so that the refugees could earn their own living. They should not be allowed to remain behind barbed wire, living in squalor and depending on world charity.

Hussein—who was the first Arab leader to suggest emptying the camps—added:

"We reject the philosophy which says that through keeping the refugees at starvation level their feelings of hatred will be nurtured and thus their desire for revenge strengthened."[6]

He has stated that the Hashemite Kingdom of Jordan is the legitimate heir of the projected Arab state proclaimed by the United Nations General Assembly on November 29, 1947, as part and parcel of the partition of Palestine into Jewish and Arab states. This Arab state never came into being, and in 1949 King Abdullah annexed the West Bank area, inhabited almost entirely by Palestinians. Hussein invariably addresses his subjects—in both the West Bank and Transjordan—as "members of the great Jordan family."[7] He has announced that any former Palestinian Arab can settle in Jordan and become a Jordanian citizen.

In December 1966 Hussein went even further when he remarked that the Arabs and Israel should concentrate on fighting not one another but "the real enemies—the barren mountains and deserts which we all have to try to control for the good of our people."[8]

In view of this apparent moderation, Israel waited to see

6. London *Jewish Chronicle*, June 24, 1966.
7. *Jerusalem Post*, July 1, 1965.
8. Interview with Dr. Michael Evenari, *The New York Times*, December 18, 1966.

whether Hussein could persuade his Arab colleagues to adopt a moderate attitude toward Israel or at least not to hinder him if he wanted to go it alone to the conference table. Hints and rumors began to circulate from Amman. Dana Adams Schmidt reported that Jordan was ready for "an elaborate armistice agreement," with a UN force occupying sensitive positions on both sides of the border and unlimited Israeli access to the Wailing Wall and other Jewish holy places in Jordanian territory.[9] Jordanian diplomats abroad also suggested that an arrangement enabling the two sides to coexist could be reached through mediation, if Israel would withdraw from the West Bank and in particular from the Old City of Jerusalem.

Israeli Prime Minister Eshkol revealed later that King Hussein had approached Israel through unnamed go-betweens before the Arab summit conference in Khartoum in August.

Hussein had asked Israel: "Is there anything to talk about?" Israel replied—according to Eshkol—that conditions could only be discussed in direct negotiations at a conference table. This was rejected by Hussein.[10]

The Khartoum summit conference took what the world considered a "moderate" approach to Israel. But it flatly refused to consider the possibility of any Arab state recognizing Israel. This put Hussein in a difficult situation. His ability to survive and pull his country out of the wreckage depended upon defying combined Arab opinion and running the risk of being accused of stabbing the Arab cause in the back. But if he did nothing Israel would simply remain in the West Bank and the Old City, and these territories and their revenue would be lost to him forever. The Hashemite Kingdom would be reduced to a sliver of desert kept alive by handouts from abroad and permanently on the brink of disappearing from the map.

It was in this mood that Hussein flew to the United States at the end of October 1967 for talks with President Johnson. En route he stopped in Paris, where he told a press conference: "We are not against the right of any nation to exist." Pressed to say whether Israel could be considered a nation, he answered: "I sup-

9. *The New York Times,* July 12, 1967.
10. *Daily Telegraph,* October 5, 1967.

pose it is a nation, whether we like it or not, isn't it?" But he qualified this by rejecting any separate peace between Israel and Jordan and denouncing Israel's "aggression" and "ruthlessness." Jordan, he said, "was victimized by people who were themselves victimized by others and not by us"—a clear reference to the Nazi extermination of Jews.[11]

This two-edged approach of Hussein's—hinting at a possible accommodation with Israel, but immediately protecting himself against charges of treason and covering his flanks by reverting to the usual propaganda line—was even more obvious in the United States. Speaking on the CBS television program *Face the Nation*, he indicated that the Arabs were now prepared to recognize "the right of all the people of the area to live in peace." Asked if that meant all the states of the area, he replied:

"All who live in it. That would mean all states, yes."

He also said he thought the right of free passage for Israeli ships in the Suez Canal could be granted, "if the right conditions were reached." But these "right conditions," he insisted, meant that Israel must withdraw totally from all occupied territory before talks could begin—a condition wholly unacceptable to Israel and completely unrealistic in the present position of Israeli dominance and Arab weakness.[12]

Two nights later he spoke at Georgetown University in Washington, D.C. Here he again referred to the need to accept the facts of Israel's existence. The Arabs might, however, not choose to recognize Israel formally, just as they and the United States chose not to recognize China. He expressed the hope that Israel would modify its insistence on direct negotiations, "just as we have modified our position toward accepting a political settlement."

Hussein disclosed that the views he was expressing were also essentially those of President Nasser. But he appeared only concerned with finding a formula under which Israel could be persuaded to withdraw from Arab territory. He did not seem to accept the continued existence of the State of Israel. This is the only possible interpretation of such statements as: "When the structure of our future society has been completed, we are con-

11. *International Herald Tribune*, October 27, 1967.
12. *The New York Times*, November 6, 1967.

fident that the Jews themselves will decide to renounce their present separatism and their unrealistic political position." Finally the King said: "Perhaps the development in the Arab world would one day lead to the de-Zionization of Israel."

These remarks seemed to belie his statement to the National Press Club earlier the same day that his aim was "not simply a settlement of the present difficulties" but a "lasting peace." One reporter who heard both Hussein's speeches that day wrote: "The King raised very grave doubts that even he, even now, is thinking in terms of a permanent settlement between Israel and the Arab states."[13]

Another journalist who listened to both speeches in Washington commented: "Little that the King has said, apart from his view that the search center on the United Nations, is calculated to persuade the Israelis to negotiate with him, or any other Arab leader, through a representative."[14]

Hussein's talks with President Johnson and American officials were unproductive. He fell into the common Arab error of assuming that Israel obeys Washington's dictates and hence that firm U.S. pressure could make Israel withdraw from the West Bank. Apart from the evidence that U.S. and Israeli interests now accord far more than they did at the time of the 1956 war, for instance, the truth is that Israel follows a toughly independent line on many domestic issues and does not submit meekly to the White House. It is a fact, for example, that after the war President Johnson had a personal message conveyed to Prime Minister Eshkol asking that whatever the Israelis did about the Jordanian half of Jerusalem, they should on no account make any statement about it. The Israeli Government paid no attention to this cautionary message, and the announcement that they were going to annex the Old City was made very soon afterwards.[15]

Far from pressing Israel to withdraw without recognition or peace talks—a pointless exercise—the Johnson Administration attempted to persuade Hussein to settle with Israel on a piecemeal basis, without following the other Arab states into a blind alley.

13. Richard Scott in the Guardian, November 8, 1967.
14. J. D. S. Graham in the Financial Times, November 8, 1967.
15. Ibid., November 21, 1967.

Hussein did not feel ready to do this. The United States made it plain it would not sink more money into Jordan's shattered economy unless the King took a more realistic position. In January 1968 the United States informed Jordan that it could not expect any budgetary assistance during 1968. While the ostensible reason was that three oil-rich Arab states had given Jordan $162 million, many observers believed Hussein was being punished for declaring war on Israel and for refusing to accept the realities of defeat.[16]

Since Hussein's fruitless journey to the United States the Middle East situation has hardened again. Facing unrest among his officers and economic bankruptcy, President Nasser has fallen back on sullen slogans and the hope that Israel will weary of the strain involved in holding onto its new land. The Syrians still are living in their unreal world of wishful thinking, in which defeat is revenge and peace means defeat. The UN's special envoy to the Middle East, Dr. Gunnar Jarring, was making the rounds of the Arab capitals and Jerusalem. But almost no one was hopeful about his chances of even warming the ice. Soviet arms were still flowing to the Arab world, now accompanied by thousands of Russian "advisers" to see they were properly handled. Harmony in the Middle East looked as far away as ever.

In this atmsophere of enmity jelling over again, what should Israel do? Can it do anything? And would this further its real interests or harm them?

Before outlining the course of action I think Israel should take, let me note the assumptions on which this course of action is based:

¶ *Israel should encourage the signs of moderation in the Arab world and make it easier for moderate leaders to press their point of view in inter-Arab forums.* The cause of peace will not be helped if middle-of-the-road leaders are led by despair and opposition by Algeria and Syria to fall back into extremist postures.

¶ *Israel's supreme national objective is not more territory, but a lasting and workable peace.* More land is an illusion if it is accompanied by greater problems and less security. The goal

16. *International Herald Tribune,* January 9, 1968; *Daily Telegraph,* January 9, 1968.

must remain peace within Israel's present borders, with adjustments where handing back strategic locations would vitally endanger Israel's *real* security, as distinct from the tempting mirage of more ground and people.

¶ *It follows from this that the advocates of the Greater Israel idea are misguided.* Accepting their program would lead Israel into a trap which would eliminate any chance of peace for decades to come and would pose grave moral and social problems for Israel.

Two hundred fifty distinguished Israelis—including such respected men as Professors Ernest Simon and Zvi Werblowsky and former Justice Minister Pinhas Rosen—have signed a statement opposing the demand that Israel should hold on to all the occupied lands. Their views were given added weight recently by the Chief of Staff during the June war, Major General Yitzhak Rabin, who also dissociated himself from the Greater Israel movement. He told *Davar:* "Our main aim is peace. We must be prepared to make concessions over the cease-fire lines which we now hold."[17] I endorse wholeheartedly what Professor J. L. Talmon said in a letter to Professor Arnold Toynbee after the war:

"I recoil from the idea of Jews lording it over others. It is at variance with the image of Judaism I cherish, and the example of other nations makes me fear the dangers to the moral fiber, the psychological balance, and spiritual values lying in wait for a master race."[18]

¶ *Nasser is at present both unwilling and unable to respond to any Israeli move.* He might do so at a later stage if other countries prepare the ground.

Tunisia's known moderation cannot solve the immediate problem, since it is in the second ring of Arab states, far removed from the arena. Lebanon would favor a settlement between Israel and Jordan, but its Christian majority will not act alone and will not sign a separate peace with Israel.

Algeria and Syria will remain opposed to any settlement with Israel for years to come, even if other Arab states sign peace

17. *Jewish Observer and Middle East Review,* January 19, 1968.
18. *Encounter,* October 1967, p. 77.

treaties. As the country which has lost most from the war, Jordan is the most desperately in need of peace so that it can heal its wounds. But Amman cannot now agree unilaterally to meet with Israel unless Israel makes it possible for Hussein to do so by avoiding any abysmal loss of prestige on his part, if he agrees to be the first Arab leader to negotiate.

¶ *Israel must abandon the hope of a general peace settlement with all its Arab neighbors and think in terms of a piecemeal approach toward each Arab country in turn.* Every Arab state has a different interlocking complex of relations with Israel. Their economies, social structure, and ethnic composition vary tremendously. Each Arab government has its own scale of national priorities. Each would emphasize different problems during any peace talks. No single ceiling approach to all these diverse countries can be applied.

Israel's policy should be flexible and aimed at reaching agreements with those states who are most vitally concerned to recover territory, prestige, or natural assets. In this way a chain reaction can be begun which will isolate the more moderate states from the intransigents, whose territory Israel would continue to hold until such day that they were ready to come to the conference table.

¶ *As Jordan is the weakest link in the present chain of renewed Arab hostility, Israel should first of all concentrate its efforts on attaining negotiations with Jordan.* Only if these fail conclusively should other alternatives for the West Bank be considered, it being clearly understood that these would be less preferable to a full settlement with Hussein.

With these guiding principles in mind, I propose that the Israeli Government take the following steps:

¶ Proclaim that there is no conflict between the self-determination of the Palestinian Arab people and the self-determination of the Jewish population of Israel.

¶ Declare that it wishes to see a territory designated as the national territory of the Palestinian Arabs, in the same way that the State of Israel is the national homeland of the Jewish people.

¶ Affirm that all Palestinian Arabs, from any country in the

Middle East, should be entitled to immigrate to this territory and settle there in perpetuity, with the due protection of international law and the United Nations.

¶ Announce its determination to resolve the refugee problem so that the UN resolutions of 1947–1948 would be met and separate Jewish and Arab states would exist in what was formerly Palestine, with the refugee issue no longer forming a barrier to cooperation and possibly federation between the Jewish and Arab states, as envisaged by the United Nations General Assembly in its resolution of November 29, 1947.

¶ Note that the Hashemite Kingdom of Jordan has declared that all former Palestinians are free to immigrate to that country and become citizens. Hence the Israeli Government expresses the view that the Kingdom of Jordan is the natural embodiment of the Arab state projected by the United Nations and that Jordan physically contains much of the territory intended to form part of the original Arab state.

¶ Incorporate the Gaza Strip, which was destined to form part of the Arab state under the 1947 plan, with the Kingdom of Jordan, the whole territory to form a homeland for the Palestinian Arab people, in which this people could attain full self-determination and national liberation, as the Jewish people did in Israel.

¶ Declare its readiness to meet with the Government of Jordan to settle all outstanding differences between the two countries and to initiate a program of active cooperation in the development of natural resources, the improvement of communications, the joint exploitation of tourist resources, and other projects designed to increase living standards and inaugurate an era of progress and constructive endeavor.

Simultaneously, to dramatize this declaration and make the maximum impact on opinion in Jordan and the Arab world, Israel should demonstrate its goodwill by offering immediate cooperation with Jordan on a project of major importance. I can suggest no more effective way of doing this than by turning the former Hebrew University and Hadassah Medical School premises on Mount Scopus into a health center for the entire Middle East.

Israel should invite the Arab citizens of Jordan and other

Middle East lands to use the center's facilities, under the auspices of an international health authority—perhaps the World Health Organization. Here Arab and Israeli doctors could work side by side, compiling data from their respective countries and developing ways of combating malaria, trachoma, and the other diseases. which are so rife in the Middle East. Mount Scopus could become a focal point of regional medical research and a positive element in scientific cooperation.

The old campus of the Hebrew University has not been in use since 1948. A new and far larger campus has been built in the Israeli sector of Jerusalem, and it has far outstripped the older campus. Even now that the Mount Scopus site is available again, it is doubtful whether it will be practical to turn it into an annex of the new university. How much more fitting it would be if Israel offered this site, with all its symbolic associations and its superb location in the Holy City, as an international center of peaceful efforts to eradicate disease and to improve the health of all the peoples of the Middle East!

Setting up what could become a world-famous center of medical research also would demonstrate that Israel does not intend to hold the city of Jerusalem for its own exclusive use but wishes it to become once more a cosmopolitan city where Arab and Jew, Greek and Armenian, Christian and Samaritan mingle and where ideas cross-fertilize one another, as they have done throughout the Holy City's long and unique history.

I do not ignore for a moment the political difficulties which would lie in the way of the solution I have proposed. But I believe it would overcome Hussein's hesitation and prompt him to negotiate. An all-out attack on the refugee problem, initiated and powered by Israel, is the missing factor which would turn the balance and enable him to agree to a separate peace agreement without the risk of being overthrown by popular feeling.

Many Arabs recognize today that Jordan contains the largest concentration of former Palestinians. Jordan and the Gaza Strip together would hold over 80 per cent of the Palestinian Arab people. If the new state is formed and the idea takes hold, other Palestinians now living in Lebanon and Syria—even in Israel itself —might want to settle there instead of putting down new roots in their present host countries. Jordan would be linked with the Gaza Strip by a corridor through Israeli territory. There would be a natural flow of refugees from the camps in the Gaza Strip to the less crowded and more fertile West Bank. Israel already is encouraging this flow. The density of the Gaza Strip population is four times as great as that of Holland, one of the most densely populated countries in the world.[19] During the Egyptian military occupation there was 40 per cent unemployment among the non-refugee population. The refugees themselves worked only clandestinely, as they forfeited their right to UNRWA rations if they earned more than fifteen Egyptian pounds a month.[20]

The refugees were never permitted to become Egyptian citizens or even to move away from the Gaza Strip. They were in effect penned into this belt of sand dunes and prickly pear bush, an area twenty-five miles by five miles, and encouraged to turn their frustration and bitterness against Israel. Small wonder that when Israel lifted restrictions on travel to the West Bank thousands of families traveled to Hebron and from there to other West Bank towns or to Amman on the East Bank.

The biggest obstacle in the way is likely to be the status of Jerusalem. The Israeli Government has said that this is not negotiable. And in saying this it is unquestionably reflecting the unanimous feeling of Israel's Jewish citizens. Nobody who saw the scenes at the Jaffa Gate on June 29, 1967, when the barriers which had divided the city for nineteen years were blown up and thousands of Israelis and Jordanians poured into one another's streets, can believe that any Israeli government could hand the Old City back and survive for more than a day.

This is something Hussein will have to accept as a condition Israel cannot surrender, in the same way that he cannot surrender his demand that the refugees be given justice. Israel can and should make concessions on the refugees and on other major issues. But Jerusalem will remain a united city, under a municipal government of Arabs and Jews. It should not be beyond the skill of the negotiators to devise a way of maintaining Amman's

19. Interview with Arthur L. Geaney, UNRWA director in the Gaza Strip: *Jerusalem Post*, September 1, 1967.
20. Moshe Brilliant in London *Times*, August 31, 1967.

presence without violating Israel's future sovereignty. A Lebanese columnist has suggested that the West Bank be returned to Jordan without Jerusalem, but that the Jordanian flag should fly over Islamic and Christian shrines.[21] An interfaith committee could be appointed to supervise the holy places and facilitate pilgrimages. Israel would allow considerable latitude in religious matters and grant complete freedom of worship to all sects, provided the city remained an integrated one, without sections of it being torn off to placate external pressures.

Israel should proclaim this plan for an amended version of the 1947 partition with all the vigor and authority at its command. It should do its utmost to persuade all sources of influence in Amman, ranging from President Bourguiba to Washington, that it is in earnest and that it means business. The package deal should include a mutual nonaggression pact and minor border readjustments at strategic points, by joint consent.

Only if King Hussein finally rejects this package deal should Israel reluctantly turn to the leaders of the West Bank and offer to set up an autonomous Palestinian state which would be demilitarized and inevitably under its protection.

Support for this idea has grown in recent months, after it appeared that Hussein was not prepared to accept Israel's terms for a separate peace. A group of leading Jordanian Arabs, headed by Dr. Hamdi Tati Faruky, has called for the formation of a state made up of the West Bank and the Gaza Strip and led by a "Palestinian Government." They proposed that the state should be under direct United Nations trusteeship for five years. After this time the Arab League would join the UN to exercise a less strict control.

Faruky, a Ramallah notable who was at one time exiled by Hussein to Syria for his Ba'ath sympathies, said relations between the new state and Israel would be based on the "good neighbor" principle. He added hopefully that in the event of a conflict between Israel and any Arab nation "strict neutrality would be observed."

The group said it planned to send delegations to various Arab capitals to seek approval for the scheme and to explain it to Arab

21. Dispatch from Beirut: London *Times*, January 1, 1968.

leaders. If the Arabs outside Jordan refused to give their assent—and the spokesmen in Jerusalem admitted this was possible—a plebiscite would be held in the West Bank and the Gaza Strip.[22]

Dr. Faruky explained later that Palestinians felt ill used by the Great Powers and by the Arab countries and needed some piece of land to call their own. The solution, in his opinion, would be to reawaken the UN partition plan and to create a Palestinian territory.

"If Israel wants peace, she has to pay for it—with the partition plan amended," he said. His new state would be under United Nations supervision but with leanings toward Jordan. But he listed two conditions which seemed tough enough to kill the plan before it got off the ground. He demanded that the new state include a section of northern Israel and that the initiative for the plan should come from Egypt and without any approaches to Israel.[23]

Another West Bank notable, Dr. Aziz Sheharde, Acting President of the West Bank High Court of Appeal and the President of the Ramallah Chamber of Commerce, claimed at a press conference in September 1967 that almost two-thirds of the West Bank population opposed a return to Jordan and wanted an independent Palestinian state.

Sheharde pointed out that the Palestinians have been the main victims of two out of the three Israeli-Arab wars in the last two decades. They now wanted a durable peace with Israel and were willing to accept a demilitarized status for the West Bank and an alliance with Israel. But they wanted a modified status for Jerusalem which would allow them free access to the Holy Places and the Arab city.[24]

He claimed the support of over two hundred well-known local Arabs, including Aref el Aref, the writer and historian, the former Jordanian Governor of the Old City, Anwar Khatib, and the principal local leaders of Nablus, Jenin, and Tulkarm.

But, Sheharde complained, Israel had not encouraged his initiative. "Israel calls for peace with the Arab states but says nothing

22. Agence France Presse dispatch from Jerusalem: London *Times*, October 28, 1967.
23. "Divided Aims in Palestine," London *Times*, November 20, 1967.
24. *Maariv*, September 7, 1967.

about the Palestinians." He expressed his readiness to negotiate with the Israeli authorities on the constitutional basis of the proposed "autonomous Palestinian entity."[25]

It is possible that if Hussein feels unable to accept even a far-seeing Israeli offer such as I have outlined, the Eshkol Administration might seriously consider some of these proposals, which up to now have been treated politely but with reserve.

However, I personally am apprehensive about the idea of a Palestine Bantustan which could become a convenient source of cheap labor and without great care could easily decline to near-colonial status. I share fully the misgivings of Professor J. L. Talmon, who wrote to Arnold Toynbee:

"I dislike the idea of a separate little autonomous Arab State on the West Bank of Jordan which would be a camouflaged Israeli protectorate. Not only because I doubt its economic viability, am apprehensive of the crushing financial and administrative burden it is sure to impose on Israel, fear its irredentism, and the grave security problems arising out of it."

But while he prayed that "we shall not be compelled to assume that role," which would mean the Jews of Israel lording it over others, he feared it might happen "if an arrangement with Jordan proves impossible and the other Arab states refuse to establish peace with Israel."[26]

Although forming a separate Palestinian state would, in my opinion, be less desirable than a full Israeli-Jordanian link, there is no doubt that the Palestine Arabs have undergone an agonizing soul-searching since the war. During the twentieth century these people have been under Turkish, British, Jordanian, and now Israeli occupation. These regimes have deprived them of their land, their homes and their livelihood. They are tired and dispirited. They no longer believe the extremists who rant about Israel's future destruction, and they are seeking a better deal than anyone has given them up to now.

One of the most hopeful signs of this reappraisal has been the rebellion against Achmed Shukairy and the way he was forced to resign as chairman of the Palestine Liberation Organization. For

25. *Financial Times*, September 8, 1967.
26. *Encounter, loc. cit.*

years Shukairy has displayed the vicious demagogy, the boastful-ness, and deceit which led directly to the Arab defeat in 1967. His tirades made perfect Israeli propaganda, and his cocky, Franco-like poses aroused nothing but ridicule, even in the Arab world itself.

At the beginning of December 1967 seven members of the Cairo-based PLO executive demanded Shukairy's resignation. Mohammed Sobaih, president of the General Union of Pales-tinian Students, accused Shukairy of giving away guerrilla secrets and making hotheaded, inaccurate statements. He said Shukairy's statement before the war that it would be a "war of annihilation" had provided the Israelis with valuable propaganda and helped them to justify their air strike on June 5.

Sobaih added that a large section of the Palestine liberation movement was unwilling to overthrow the Israeli Government if this would mean "the mass killing of Israeli citizens, including children and the old."[27]

The movement to depose Shukairy gathered force when groups representing Palestinian students, workers, writers, and women pooled their support. Shukairy dismissed the seven rebels—half his committee—on December 12. But they refused to go. On Decem-ber 24 Shukairy himself resigned and was replaced by Yahia Ham-mudah, a well-known left-wing leader who agitated against both the British and Zionists in Palestine before 1948 and went to jail. A lawyer by training, he has spent considerable time east of the Iron Curtain.

In his first public statement after taking office, Hammudah made the most moderate proposals to come from any recognized Palestinian leader for many years. It was "obviously ridiculous," he admitted, to ask all Jews who have emigrated to Israel since 1948 to return to their countries of origin, as the PLO had de-manded under Shukairy. "We need the Jew and he needs us," he told the Beirut paper Al Nahar.

Hammudah called for the creation of a "Jewish-Arab state of Palestine" and said the Jews should abandon Zionism and all the sectarian, "racist," and religious tenets associated with the State of Israel.

27. Dispatch from Cairo: Guardian, December 21, 1967.

But, as if recognizing that this would never be seriously considered by Israel, the new chief of the PLO suggested that the Jews could hold to Zionism and still cooperate with the Arabs in a Palestinian state if they would return to the Arabs the property taken from them and devote their efforts to building up areas not developed before 1948.

"We must face facts," he added, "and not demand the impossible. Everything is done now, and it would be stupid to demand that the Jews should return to their original homes." Demagogy and impetuosity were gone for ever. The armed struggle must be conducted by a political leadership uniting the various organizations involved, he said. This was seen as a bid to control the activities of the Fatah group, which took its orders from Damascus.[28]

It goes without saying that Hammudah's proposals are unacceptable to Israel. But this does not mean we cannot appreciate how far he has come from Shukairy. Instead of regarding his program as something Israel has to accept or reject once and for all, we should see it as the opening bid in the debate over a possible *modus vivendi*. We should try to make the leap of imagination necessary to understand the bewilderment and confusion of the Palestine Arabs and should take the first step toward them. Let us admit that they also have a case. They also have suffered. Let us give them an opportunity to show that they will not be misled any more by leaders who offer them nothing but blood and deceit. Let us show them a different path, and let us lead them along it for our mutual benefit.

For let us be quite clear in our own minds about the alternatives if the Arabs do not make peace with us and we continue to hold all the territory we now hold, with its hostile people. In this case we have nothing to look forward to but years of grim internal struggle, sabotage, and political unrest. It is happening already. The Israeli military authorities in the Gaza Strip imposed a total day-and-night curfew on some 200,000 Arabs on January 17, 1968. This followed mounting terrorism in which hand grenades were thrown and mines were planted. Suspected members of the PLO

28. Joe Alex Morris in *Los Angeles Times*, January 5, 1968; Moshe Brilliant in London *Times*, January 5, 1968.

were arrested and schools, shops, and offices in Gaza were closed.[29]

Similar incidents were taking place all over the West Bank and even in Galilee, which forms part of Israel proper. The situation was starting to resemble the years of bitter underground warfare in the 1930s and 1940s, with one ironic difference: the Israelis now were playing the role played then by the British Mandatory Power authorities, with the Arabs as the freedom fighters. It is a dismal thought that we now are sentencing Arabs to life imprisonment under the same laws used by the British to hang and imprison Jewish patriots twenty years ago.

If Israel tries to hold on to the West Bank and the Gaza Strip without giving the local population civil rights and democratic representation, it will knowingly be running the risk of becoming a Middle East Portugal or Rhodesia, suppressing national freedom movements through savage laws and an iron oppression. It would be a tragic outcome for the Jewish national liberation movement which set out so boldly to return to the Land of Israel seventy years ago.

In a penetrating study published by the Institute of Strategic Studies, Michael Howard, Professor of War Studies at London University, and Robert Hunter, Lecturer in International Relations at the London School of Economics, warned that Israel's ability to come to terms with its Arab minority would determine the country's future security. "There was not much scope for guerrillas in the Sinai Desert; but among a large, discontented Arab population in Israel itself, who knows?"

Howard and Hunter did not suggest that events in Israel would take the course of those in Algeria, Vietnam, or southern Africa: "The advantages of terrain enjoyed by guerrillas in North Africa and Southeast Asia are not to be found in the Sinai Desert or the restricted area of the West Bank, although Jordan, Syria, and the Lebanon could still provide sanctuary for the forces of a new 'liberation front.'

"But a renewal of the kind of intercommunal friction—the sniper at the upper window, the grenade lobbed into the coffeehouse—that was so common under the (British) Mandate is by

29. London *Times*, January 19, 1968.

no means to be ruled out. If a fourth Arab-Israeli war occurs, this is the shape it is likely to take, and the military brilliance recently displayed by the Israeli nation and its leaders will not be very relevant to its conduct."

"If Israeli statesmanship does not match up to her military achievements," they summed up their on-the-spot findings, "her victories may, like so many other victories in the past, bear very bitter fruit."[30]

It is in order to avoid these future dangers—of a strategically secure frontier drawn around a strategically insecure population— that we must make it possible for Hussein to come to the conference table, with or without the leaders of the Palestine Arabs. The worst thing of all is the absence of any decision at all about the occupied territories. The Arabs remember the fate of the Mayor of Gaza at the time of the Israeli occupation in 1956–1957. He cooperated with the Israeli authorities. But when the Egyptians returned to Gaza he was executed. As long as there is uncertainty the Arabs will refuse to take the risk of being branded as collaborators. And this uncertainty will create nervousness and lead to terrorist actions springing from either conviction or despair.

Israel must act, soon and boldly. The internal debate will continue, probably for years. But a decision cannot be delayed. Let us remember that Israel is at its greatest when we act positively and with faith. And let us realize that the Arabs are fated to share this land with us. Then we will know how to distinguish between acts of realistic vision and illusory "security" measures and how to rest our security and that of the region upon solid foundations.

30. *Sunday Times*, October 8, 1967.

10 *A Program for the Refugees*

ANY DISCUSSION on how to attain a Middle East settlement soon becomes a debate on how to solve the Palestinian refugee problem. Some groups consider it a stumbling block in the road to peace; others consider it the key. But it is certainly the crux, the clue to any lasting rapprochement between Arabs and Israelis. No peace initiative which ignores or sidesteps it stands any chance of unfreezing the glacier. The 1967 war did not change this basic fact of life in the region. If anything, the war emphasized the human nature of this problem and demonstrated that it cannot be solved by ordinary military means.

The official body charged with catering for these former residents of Palestine is the United Nations Relief and Works Agency for Palestine Refugees (UNRWA). In the middle of 1967, before the fighting broke out, 1,325,000 people were registered with UNRWA. Sixty camps in the four Arab host countries—Jordan, Gaza, Lebanon, and Syria—accommodated about 38 per cent of the refugees. The rest found whatever accommodation they could.

UNRWA is a little-publicized but hard-working organization. It supplies rations of 1,500 calories per person per day in summer and 1,600 calories in winter. It runs over 100 health centers and 8 mobile clinics. It operates 400 agency schools which educate 190,000 children. UNRWA is rightly placing increasing emphasis on vocational training. In 1967 nearly 3,000 students graduated from some 30 trade and professional centers. Wherever these people will ultimately live, they will face a future of self-support and self-respect for themselves and their families.

Almost every UN General Assembly since 1948 has been occupied with this festering problem. To date UNRWA has spent nearly $600 million. Its 1965 expenditure was $37.8 million, and the 1966 budget was $38.6 million. Over 90 per cent of this total has been contributed by four Western countries: the United States—about 70 per cent; Britain—17 per cent; Canada—3 per cent; and France—2 per cent.

Yet the problem is no nearer a solution than it was in 1948 when the refugees fled from Palestine. On December 15, 1965, the UN General Assembly voted to extend UNRWA's mandate to June 1969. The United States delegate served notice that his country would not pay more than 70 per cent of the total annual costs and would cut its 1966 contribution by $1 million in line with this decision. As a result UNRWA faced a deficit of $4.2 million at the end of 1966.

Even before the 1967 hostilities, then, the refugee problem was becoming more complex from year to year as the number of classified refugees grew and the nations of the world showed an increasing reluctance to shoulder the burden of merely keeping the refugees alive on iron rations, without taking serious steps to eliminate the problem once and for all.

This increasing complexity was in direct contradiction to the view widely held by official Israeli circles, namely, that if Israel could only stand firm and resist the onslaught of the Arab countries and the Great Powers, the refugees would gradually give up all hope of returning and settle down in the Arab lands through a process of normal adjustment.

Expert opinion did not support this belief. In an authoritative study,[1] F. Th. Witkamp drew a parallel between the social pattern in the Arab refugee camps and other refugee environments, including the Nazi concentration camps. He noted the emergence of a professional refugee mentality among the Arabs:

"Low vitality, a loss of independence ('I can't do it myself any more'), a growing lack of initiative ('I'll be looked after anyway'), a reluctance to accept responsibility for one's own life even where this has been possible ('What's the use of it anyway?')."

---

1. F. Th. Witkamp, *The Refugee Problem in the Middle East*, Bulletin of the Research Group for European Migration Problems, The Hague, January–March 1957.

Other typical reactions reported by Witkamp were:

"Life in camp is just a bad dream. Soon all will be what it used to be."

"Why repair a tent or clean up rubbish when you don't get paid for it?"

Some of the refugees are unable to adjust themselves to the facts of the situation and are obsessed with the thought of a return to the land of their fathers. Others have resigned themselves to their predicament:

"Their bewilderment at the sudden changes, and the fighting, the interventions, the UN resolutions, all these incomprehensible things, have been dissolved in a kind of abysmal apathy. In the daytime they listlessly sit around somewhere in the sun in the stench of the latrines, and quarrel a little about food, resigned to the noise and the bickering of camp life. They only seem to wake up when they discuss their one remaining hope: to go back to Palestine, back to their piece of land and the hut that was their home. But the clay hut is no more, the soil has been tilled by tractors, and the longer they turn this last hope round in their fingers like a rosary, the more worn it will become."

Witkamp concluded his survey with a dire prediction:

"The longer the refugees live in camps, the more difficult adaptation (to a normal life) will be."

A United States delegate to the UN General Assembly, Carl Rowan, also has warned:

"As the years go by, each of the two sides stands fixed in the same rigid attitudes, somehow hoping in the face of all logic that some miraculous development will occur that will destroy the arguments of the adversaries and permit the problem to be worked out according to its point of view.

"But . . . such a development is unlikely. All have heard spokesmen from both sides boast that 'time is on our side.' It is time we all freed ourselves of this self-deception. So long as this dispute exists, with all the passions that we have once again heard expressed, time is on the side of danger and despair."[2]

And the Commissioner-General of UNRWA, Laurence Michel-

2. Address to the Special Political Committee of the UN General Assembly on December 11, 1962: U.S. Information Service dispatch, December 12, 1962.

more, told the General Assembly in his 1965 report that the refugee problem "has not grown any less complex or less dangerous to the peace and stability of the region." The attitude and feeling of the refugees continues unchanged, he said:

"From their standpoint, a nation has been obliterated and a population arbitrarily deprived of its birthright. That injustice still festers in their minds and they hold the United Nations responsible for their lot and for extending assistance to them until a solution can be found to their problems."[3]

The problem has grown more serious from year to year because it is a human problem; because humanitarian concern and political expediency appeared—erroneously—to be opposed to one another; and because the refugees' plight was exploited by unscrupulous Arab agitators who tried to turn them into guerrillas in the constant war of nerves along Israel's frontiers.

All attempts to end the stalemate have begun from Clause 11 of the resolution adopted by the UN General Assembly in December 1948, at the end of the hostilities in Palestine. The General Assembly resolved "that the refugees wishing to return to their homes and live at peace with their neighbors should be permitted to do so at the earliest practicable date, and that compensation should be paid for the property of those choosing not to return and for loss of or damage to property which, under principles of international law or equity, should be made good by the Governments or authorities responsible."[4]

These twin principles—of repatriation and compensation—have been reaffirmed by every General Assembly that has dealt with the problem since then, usually by an almost unanimous vote—with Israel sometimes the only dissident voice. Every mediator who has tried to solve this problem—one of the thorniest and most persistent in international affairs—has employed this directive as a starting point.

The most daring and far-reaching attempt to unravel the refugee

3. *Report of the Commissioner-General of the United Nations Relief and Works Agency for Palestine Refugees in the Near East, 1 July 1964–30 June 1965,* General Assembly, Official Records of 20th Session, Supplement No. 13 (A/6013).

4. Resolution 194 (III): Palestine—Progress Report of the UN Mediator, adopted by the General Assembly on December 11, 1948.

dilemma was made in August 1961, when the UN Conciliation Commission for Palestine appointed Dr. Joseph E. Johnson, President of the Carnegie Endowment for International Peace, as its special representative to the Middle East, charged with finding "practical means of seeking progress in the Palestine Arab refugee problem," in the language of his original instructions.

For the next eighteen months Dr. Johnson left his academic pursuits and tackled the roots of the problem *in situ*. It was—he told the 24th American Assembly in October 1963—"a fascinating, frustrating and, at times, infuriating experience."[5] He traveled to the Middle East for personal inspections of refugee camps and exhaustive talks with Israeli and Arab leaders. When he returned to UN headquarters he submitted detailed proposals for repatriating some refugees to Israel and resettling the rest in the Arab countries.

Neither Dr. Johnson's proposals nor the Arab and Israeli reactions to them ever have been published officially. But he himself referred his audience at the American Assembly to "several essentially accurate accounts"[6] which appeared in the *Christian Science Monitor*, the *Chicago Daily News*, and other papers.

In confidential documents dated August 31, 1962, and September 6, 1962, the UN special representative outlined concrete proposals for consideration by Middle East governments. These included:

¶ The appointment of a new UN administrator and staff charged with carrying out the December 1948 General Assembly resolution on repatriation or compensation.

¶ Individual refugees and heads of families would be given confidential questionnaires. They would make a "preliminary" choice, keeping the right to change their minds later.

Possible choices would include:

a) Return to former property in Israel;

b) Return to alternative location in Israel;

5. Address to the 24th American Assembly, Arden House, Harriman, N.Y,. on October 24, 1963: published by the American Assembly, Columbia University, New York, p. 10.

6. *Ibid.*

c) Resettlement in Arab countries;

d) Resettlement elsewhere in the world.

¶ UN agents would consult Israel on repatriation possibilities and would discuss resettlement with the Arab countries and other countries specified by the refugees themselves in the preliminary questionnaires.

¶ Israel would be asked not to set a maximum number of refugees it would admit. However, Israel would reserve the right to reject individual Arabs as security risks, subject to overall UN surveillance and review.

¶ A special UN fund would be set up to help the refugees become integrated. It would be financed by voluntary contributions from governments and the world public. Israel would be expected to make a substantial contribution to the fund.

¶ Israel would be required to pay indemnities to Arabs who lost property in Israel. The UN and such friendly countries as the United States would assist Israel in bearing this financial burden.

¶ The expenses of the UN administrator and agents would go into the regular UN budget, assessed against all member states (including Communist and Arab countries, which had not paid cash for the UN relief program hitherto).

¶ The UN agents would be "coordinators" and "catalysts," with the responsibility to inform the individual refugees about their rights and to see that they understood and obtained them. Illiterates, for example, would be given special assistance.

¶ All refugees would be entitled to a UN fund indemnity covering the hardships they had undergone (along the lines of a veteran's bonus).

¶ The four Arab host governments and Israel would be invited to name representatives to a council of advisers to the UN administrator.

¶ Although refugees would indicate preferences on their questionnaires, they would be told from the start that they would not necessarily get their first choice.[7]

In effect, Dr. Johnson proposed finding out for the first time

7. Milt Freudenheim in *Chicago Daily News,* October 1, 1962.

exactly how many of the refugees really wanted to go back to their former homes, now that these homes were in Israel. The UN administrator and his staff would interview the refugees individually and privately, explaining the alternatives. Those choosing repatriation would be allowed to go, subject to an Israeli veto on individual security risks. Others would receive compensation.

The underlying assumption was that—despite vigorous public protestations to the contrary—the great majority of the refugees would in fact choose to be resettled in Arab countries, where the social environment would be more congenial than in Israel. However, they would have been offered the right to return—and they could regard this as a sort of vindication and as implementing the 1948 resolution.

One of the virtues of the Johnson plan was that it would require an absolute minimum of formal approval by the parties. The Arabs would not have to accept it in the usual diplomatic sense. They would only have to stand aside, *de* facto, and let the UN carry it out. Israel would have to make it clear that it would cooperate in good faith, rejecting only persons genuinely believed to be spies or saboteurs. But it would be entitled to say "no" in specific cases where it felt its security was threatened.[8]

The Kennedy Administration—and President Kennedy himself —threw the whole weight of their prestige behind this attempt to persuade the Arab states and Israel to permit an important breakthrough toward peace in the Middle East. The United States was the most important member of the Conciliation Commission, and progress on the refugees depended largely on the views of Washington, which paid over two-thirds of UNRWA's annual bill. Secretary of State Dean Rusk underlined this deep U.S. interest in making a start toward solving the refugee problem when he talked with the Israeli Foreign Minister, Mrs. Golda Meir, and with key Arab leaders attending the 1962–1963 session of the UN General Assembly.[9]

Dr. Johnson's proposals sought "to establish a middle ground between the Arabs' insistence that all refugees be 'allowed to return to their homes,' and Israel's contention that this solution

8. William R. Frye in the *Christian Science Monitor*, October 4, 1962.
9. *Ibid.*

was no longer practicable because the refugees' homes had either been destroyed in the war or were now occupied by Jewish refugees —many from Arab lands."[10] The Conciliation Commission envoy displayed an unusual awareness of the psychological nuances of the situation. Perhaps no other neutral observer has probed more deeply into the psycho-political roots of the deadlock, with a merciless, almost clinical objectivity no Middle Easterner could hope to match, and at the same time with a wise and human understanding of the national obsessions and defense mechanisms blocking a reasonable solution. He noted the Israelis' "dedication, a sense of purpose, that is truly inspiring—and sometimes frightening." "Many Arab leaders," he remarked, "are troubled by a sense of failure, a feeling that they have been consistently on the losing side . . . have failed to redeem their pledge to their people and particularly to the Palestinian Arabs."[11]

Other statesmen have tried to launch a frontal attack on the refugee problem. Johnson's approach was infinitely subtler, more flexible, less direct. He showed a perceptive understanding of sensitive Middle East psychologies on both sides of the barrier. Under his plan, neither side would lose face. Neither party would be called upon to "subscribe publicly to a formal agreement acceptable to the other." Instead, he proposed "a kind of tacit acquiescence"—"a willingness to permit the practical measures to be taken and to cooperate in them, without insisting that everything be spelled out in a public document."[12]

His escalated plan contained the kernel of the only possible solution which would meet the stand taken by the UN General Assembly and could give the refugees "substantial justice" ("as substantial as they could ever hope to receive"). Its implementation would have meant that "neither the Arabs nor Israel would get what they want. Both would have to give up something." The Arabs would have "to abandon a propaganda weapon they have cherished for a decade and a half," while Israel "would have to

10. George E. Gruen, *The Arab Refugee Problem and the United Nations*, published by the American Jewish Committee's Institute of Human Relations, April 1966. This is one of the best short summaries of the problem.
11. Address to the 24th American Assembly, pp. 5–6.
12. *Ibid.*, p. 13.

take in some refugees it does not want" (which Johnson estimated at "fewer than one-tenth of the total of true refugees and their descendants"). But the refugees' hopelessness "would be transformed into hope and expectation of a future, of a decent life as members of normal societies." And, Johnson hoped and continues to believe, "erosion of the Palestine question would begin, to the benefit of the refugees, of Israel, of the Arab states, of the United Nations and the world at large, and of the United States."[13]

Addressing the General Assembly, U.S. delegate Carl Rowan praised Dr. Johnson's "dedication, persistence, and realism."[14] But the parties concerned were cool toward the proposals, for very different reasons. Israel feared too many refugees would return; the Arabs feared too few would want to go back, thus exploding their claim that all the Palestinian Arabs sought repatriation. Both rejected the plan and refused to enter into practical discussions on its implementation. As Johnson himself noted later, Israel found his proposals "unacceptable," and "the Arabs did not in the circumstances find in them a suitable basis for progress."[15]

But neither side wanted to be the first to come out into the open by denouncing the plan outright. Each side hoped that the other would lose patience and criticize the Johnson proposals openly, so that it could be blamed for the failure of a plan which both sides resisted equally bitterly. Neither Israel nor the Arabs were ready to take the initial step toward a solution, to abandon the propaganda positions built up so diligently over the years. Inertia and ennui triumphed over imagination, as happens so often in the Middle East. Israel and the Arabs ultimately agreed on only one thing: that Johnson's proposals should not be made public and should be pigeonholed. The Conciliation Commission's special representative was forced to concede defeat. On February 1, 1963, Dr. Johnson resigned and went back to the Carnegie

13. *Ibid.*, p. 14.
14. Address to the Special Political Committee of the UN General Assembly, *op. cit.*
15. Address to the 24th American Assembly, p. 10.

Endowment. The sigh of relief could be heard all the way from Cairo and Jerusalem to United Nations headquarters. The only losers, as usual, were the refugees themselves.

So ended the last all-out attempt to break the log jam that is holding up a Middle East reconciliation. The Johnson plan was never given a chance to get off the ground before it was shot down. But it is not dead. I believe Dr. Johnson's recommendations were rejected not because they were wildly impractical, not because they would not have cleared the camps, but *because they could have worked*. This tragic and frustrating episode is one of the best illustrations of my basic thesis: that Israel and the Arabs would rather maintain the present no-peace, no-war climate than accept any international program under which the other side might be granted concessions that would enable it to score points in the propaganda battle.

If adopted, Johnson's suggestions could have changed the whole nature of the Arab-Israeli relationship. Tension in the region would have been reduced; tentative contacts would have begun, without any formal recognition or loss of face; the UN's role in the region would have been strengthened and made more positive. The 1964–1965 clash over the Jordan waters probably would have been averted. And there would have been no third round in 1967. By the end of the 1960s the refugee program would have been moving into the practical phase of setting up new villages, paying compensation, and cutting down UNRWA's budget.

But the governments of the region could not make this revolutionary adjustment, which would have given the Kennedy Administration its first major breakthrough in Israeli-Arab relations. The fact that the plan was turned down does not mean that it was faulty, only that it was ahead of the political and psychological conditions in 1962. But the thrust of the Johnson plan is still valid and timely. Any future attempt to resolve the refugee deadlock will have to start from the 1962 recommendations and build upon them. Whatever name is eventually given to the plan that solves the Arab refugee problem, it will be the Johnson plan brought up-to-date. It remains a signpost to the only solution which is sober, realistic, and just.

After Johnson's resignation and President Kennedy's assassina-

tion later that year the refugee question was allowed to lie
dormant. Policy planners in Washington felt neither Israel nor
the Arabs were ready to take the bold moves which would have
been necessary for progress. More time was needed for developments in the region to catch up with Johnson's perceptive and
imaginative thinking. The United States decided to continue
supporting UNRWA, while waiting for an opportunity to introduce another peacemaking attempt bent on tackling the refugee problem as the first step in a possible détente.

Throughout this entire period various groups in Israel called for
a Government initiative to resolve the refugee problem, without
waiting for peace talks. This was one of the main themes at the
New Outlook symposium on "New Paths to Israeli-Arab Peace,"
held in Tel Aviv in 1963.

One of the most consistent advocates of an Israeli initiative
was Archbishop George Hakim, head of the Greek Catholic
community in Israel and undoubtedly the leading Arab figure in
the country until his appointment as Greek Catholic Patriarch of
the Middle East in the fall of 1967, when he moved to Damascus.

Apart from being the most influential Christian leader in Israel,
Maximos V Hakim, as he is now, became in a sense the recognized
spokesman of all the 300,000 Arabs living in Israel, in the absence
of any comparable Moslem leader. He protested vigorously and
fearlessly against any injustices to the Arab community. At the
same time, he believed in the possibility of Jewish-Arab cooperation within Israel and urged the members of his flock to join the
Histadrut, Israel's General Labor Federation. During the June
1967 war he called upon his followers to remain loyal to the
state. At the Vatican Ecumenical Council he supported the
Jewish schema and fought for its approval, despite strong opposition from other bishops living in Arab capitals.

But Hakim always had a mind of his own, and in his talks with
the Israeli Government he stressed the importance of eliminating
the grievances and suffering of the refugees who had lived in the
territory now occupied by Israel.

I remember a long conversation with him on this topic, before
the 1967 war. Characteristically, our interview had to be post-
poned because the Archbishop had to travel to Lebanon that

weekend. He was the only Israeli Arab leader who was able to move up and down between Israel and the neighboring lands as if the frontiers did not exist. Because of this he was in close touch with the mood of the refugees in the four Arab host countries.

As he had done so many times before, Hakim reiterated to me his belief that Israel should take the initiative on the refugees. "The solution of this problem is the key to Israeli-Arab peace," he said. "I have said many times—and I will go on saying it—that Israel could start solving this question today by paying compensation to the many refugees who are ready to conduct negotiations on accepting compensation, and to waive their claim to repatriation as a result."

I asked him whether he thought many refugees were ready to enter into practical talks with Israel.

"Yes," he replied emphatically. "I know for a fact that a very significant number of refugees are prepared to come to terms with Israel and to settle their claims once and for all, in return for fair compensation. But the Israeli Government doesn't seem willing to do anything in this direction. I have suggested this to the right quarters in Jerusalem, time and time again. But there haven't been any concrete offers which were solid enough to start the ball rolling."

What did Hakim propose on the refugees?

"With the help of the United States and its many friends, Israel should earmark several million dollars a year for compensation to former Palestinians who are entitled to it. This compensation should be paid fairly and justly, not as a propaganda move. This is a question of the refugees' human and civil rights, not of charity. Then, instead of waiting another nineteen or twenty years, 1 per cent—2 per cent—3 per cent of the problem will be solved for a start. And this process would continue and expand. These people would be gained for peace, instead of hating Israel, continuing to feel bitter and making propaganda against the Jews who are living in their former homes."

The Archbishop explained that the "crucial 20 per cent" of the refugees are the intelligentsia, the articulate displaced people who are influential in Arab politics and are circulating the vehement anti-Israel line. These people owned most of the land and property left behind in 1948.

"They are the ones you should try to reach," Hakim said emphatically. "The other 80 per cent are mainly small landowners who owned less than five *dunams* of land–1.25 acres–before the 1948 war. The couple of hundred dollars they will get for their land will not solve their problem, and it will not be enough to resettle them. This is a different problem: an international one. And most of the money will have to come from international funds, such as the UN or the World Bank. Here compensation by Israel would not be adequate. But Israel could do a great deal to eliminate the problem of the crucial 20 per cent."

"Are the refugees really prepared today to accept compensation from Israel?"

"Certainly. Thousands of refugees are only waiting for the first sign from Israel to submit their property deeds to some neutral body, to have them verified and checked, and to receive their compensation—in return for which they would sign a document waiving any further claims against Israel."

"Would Lebanon and Jordan allow their refugees to accept money from Israel?" I asked.

"Yes," Archbiship Hakim replied. "Or at least they will turn a blind eye. For example, in 1953 the Israeli Government unfroze £3 million in refugee bank deposits. This money was returned to Arab owners across the armistice lines *on an individual basis*, with the aid of the UN and without the official consent of the Arab governments in the countries concerned, but with their full knowledge. This shows that what I am suggesting is perfectly feasible."

"What about the Gaza Strip?"

"The refugees there might not accept the offer at first. But this will come in time, when the former Palestinians in other countries accept and are paid fairly and honestly for their property. This will have an impact.

"Perhaps at first only a small number of refugees will take up Israel's offer. But slowly this number will grow. I am absolutely certain about this. They will see other people—their families and friends—accepting Israel's offer and making a fresh start, rehabilitating themselves and their children, leaving the camps. This will encourage others to do the same. Instead of waiting hopelessly, more and more refugees will find the way to approach Israel and to settle their claims once and for all."

The Archbishop thought that many refugees are ready to emigrate to countries outside the Middle East: the United States, Canada, Latin America. If they could obtain fair compensation, this would enable them to make the move.

What about those refugees who want to return to Israel?

"I think it is too late for any large-scale return. The solution has been delayed until there is not enough land available. In any case, few of the refugees really want to come back today."

What percentage would choose repatriation to Israel before any other alternative?

Hakim shook his head. "Not more than 10 per cent. Probably even less. On the contrary, if the gates were opened, some Arabs now living in Israel would leave for the neighboring countries.

"The important thing is that Israel should make a constructive offer, backed by money, to refugees *on an individual basis*. Goodwill alone is not enough. And money alone is not enough. You need both. Goodwill and money: that is the formula.

"The Arab governments will never give their consent officially. But unofficially they will close their eyes. The main thing is to start."

Hakim sighed. He is an imposing, gray-bearded man, who speaks his mind forthrightly and *dugri*, as the Arabs say—straight from the shoulder. And his eyes flashed as he said: "I have spoken to people in the Israeli Government—important people—and told them: you have so much money for development, for settlement. Why don't you set aside a token sum of $5 to 10 million every year—from the United Jewish Appeal, the Israel Bond Drive, or any other source of foreign currency—to start paying compensation to the refugees?

"They listen to me. But nothing seems to happen. Nothing concrete is being done. And this is a great pity. Apart from the human aspect of the problem, you are missing an opportunity to do something, to bring peace closer. These are the people you are going to have to live with. And you surely do not want them to be your perpetual enemies. Act with goodwill and sincerely, and you will see what an effect this will have on the whole region.

"What an opportunity you missed after Bourguiba's initiative! If, when he had spoken, Israel had done something, made a definite move, offered something like the proposals I have been outlining, this would have had an impact. But you didn't do it. Israel only welcomed Bourguiba's initiative after he abandoned it. Yes, it was a missed opportunity."

The Archbishop was silent for a moment as he looked through the window of his study at the Bay of Haifa and the hills of Galilee beyond. Then he added quietly:

"Remember always that the refugees can be an obstacle. But they can also be a bridge, if you go about things the right way."

Since this conversation history has, I believe, given Israel another opportunity to grasp the nettle of the refugees and take decisive action for a solution. As usual in human affairs, this opportunity has arisen unexpectedly, in a way nobody could possibly have foreseen: as the aftermath of the third round in June 1967, which placed so many of the Palestinian Arabs under Israeli rule.

When the Israeli army occupied the West Bank the local population began moving eastward. The refugee camps around Jericho and the towns along the Jordan were virtually emptied as people crossed the river into what was left of the Hashemite Kingdom. The years of propaganda had convinced the Arabs that the Israelis would massacre them, and they fled in panic.

No one knows exactly how many Arabs crossed into the East Bank and became refugees—many of them for the second time. UN circles put the figure at 150,000. Other estimates go as high as 200,000.

After several weeks, when the people on the East Bank saw that the Israelis were treating the civilian population fairly and life on the West Bank was returning to normal, they began infiltrating back. But by then Israel was facing the problem of the occupied areas, and government policy was to prevent the return of former West Bank inhabitants.

Under pressure from the United States, the Israeli Government announced on July 2 that Arabs who had been living on the West

Bank and had crossed over to the East Bank would be allowed to return to their former places of residence, provided they did so not later than August 10.

This threw the ball into the Jordanian court. The question was whether Amman would allow the refugees to return to what was now Israeli-occupied territory.

The next stage was a protracted wrangle over the wording of the International Red Cross documents to be used in the return. Jordan objected to the use of the words "State of Israel" in the heading, but eventually agreed to the form "Israel," which would not imply recognition of the state. Each side accused the other of trying to exploit the dispute over the wording for political purposes.

All this bickering ate up valuable time and made the August 10 deadline unrealistic, as the actual crossing was delayed. Israel extended the closing date to August 31, and the first crossings were made on August 18. The Swiss Red Cross officials who were supervising the return pointed out that 170,000 refugees wished to return. But the Allenby Bridge near Jericho and another farther north could handle only 2,000 to 3,000 a day. In the twelve days left before the deadline only a fraction of the total number could be brought over.

At this stage Jordan made a colossal error. The Jordanian Finance Minister, Mr. Majali, appealed to former residents of the West Bank to go back to occupied territory quickly "to become a thorn in the flesh of the aggressor." Jordan, which was facing an impossible situation because of the homeless people pouring in across the river, was so anxious for them to leave that it offered three months' food supplies and £1 10s ($4.20) to everyone who agreed to go back. Amman was anxious to conceal its desire to rid itself of the new refugees and tried to disguise this by creating the impression that returning to Israeli-held territory was in some way patriotic. But this naturally angered the Israeli authorities and made them suspicious—particularly when King Hussein repeated the "thorn in Israel's flesh" appeal a few days later.

Israel began creating even more difficulties than it had previously placed in the way of the returnees. For example, they were not allowed to bring back cars, livestock, or heavy goods. Sometimes some members of a family were given permission to return and others were held back. Eventually only about 14,000 refugees actually returned by the end of August. Under further United States pressure, Israel agreed to admit a further few thousand refugees with proper papers. But the great majority of the 150,000 –200,000 people who fled in June were never given a chance of returning.

The plight of those who are now living in camps east of the Jordan River was described by the British journalist John Mossman:

"At the Jordan government Wadi Dhi El camp on the Mafraq road north of Amman, which accommodates 11,500 refugees in tents, I saw hundreds of children playing in rotting refuse heaps. They are all underfed. The water supply is hardly enough for 1,000. There are no latrines.

"One doctor told me: 'It is surprising there is not a serious epidemic yet. But when the wet, cold winter sets in I am horrified to think of the disease and suffering there will be.'"[16]

Another British reporter, Neville Brown, wrote in the *New Statesman*, a journal generally sympathetic to Israel:

"The daily food ration in the best of the camps basically consists of two eggs, some melon, a loaf of bread, and one good meal of rice and stew. This provides a diet which is bulky enough but markedly deficient in proteins and vitamins. . . . But the present calorie scale would be quite insufficient for the winter, and it is uncertain if either the UN or the Jordan government will be able to improve it."

Most of the accommodation in the camps, Brown noted, consisted of small and flimsy American "beach tents" which had to take eight people:

"No floorboards are provided and each person has only one blanket. Even as early as September it can be bitterly cold at night in the Jordan hills and so it is absurd of Mr. Eban to say, as he has done, that there is no humanitarian reason why those who are refugees for the second time should be on the West Bank of

16. John Mossman in *Daily Telegraph*, August 10, 1967.

Jordan as opposed to the East. About 60,000 places now stand empty in hutted UNRWA camps on the West Bank."[17]

In January 1968 Jordan did in fact have its worst weather in fifty years. Some villages were a foot deep in snow, and at least thirteen people died of exposure. Many refugees suffered bitterly in their inadequate tents out on the highlands around Amman.

Although the situation in Jordan was most serious because of climatic and objective reasons, the outlook was grim for all the refugees, because UNRWA was suddenly faced with greater needs and less money to spend.

Laurence Michelmore, the UNRWA Commissioner-General, estimated in December 1967 that the agency would need about $47.5 million in 1968–1969, mostly to continue carrying out its former mandate but also to deal with the new influx of homeless people caused by the war.

The extra cost of these emergency operations arising from the war would be $5.7 million, he estimated. But all the signs were that the contributions to UNRWA were actually below the 1967 level. At a pledging conference in New York at the beginning of December, thirty-three governments undertook to contribute a total of $26,270,340—or appreciably less than the previous year's pledges, despite the increased needs.[18]

The Israeli Government's policy appears to be to aggravate the refugee problem and create almost intolerable pressures on Hussein's overstrained economy, in order to force him to come to terms. I believe this is a fundamental error of judgment and policy. It can only lead to increased support for the Arab guerillas operating in occupied Jordan, and this in turn will make it even more difficult for Hussein to take the bold step of making a separate peace and breaking away from the official Arab line. Perpetuating the misery of the refugees and turning the screw will only breed more bitterness and store up more hatred for Israel. It will play into the hands of the Arab resistance movements by making their recruiting easier and reviving a Jordanian national mood of vengeance. If Israel genuinely wants to persuade the Arabs to live

17. Neville Brown, "Jordan's Despairing Refugees," *New Statesman,* September 29, 1967.
18. London *Times,* December 13, 1967.

in peace with it, the worst possible tactics are to pile suffering on
suffering in the refugee camps, to the point of desperation.

For eighteen years I have been a member of a group in Israel,
headed by the late Martin Buber, who believed the Israeli Government should take the initiative in resolving the refugee problem
once and for all as the first step toward a peace settlement. We
did not manage to convince the authorities in Jerusalem that this
would change the climate between Israel and the Arabs, partly
because the refugees were virtually hostages of the Arab governments concerned and would have come under heavy pressure to
demand repatriation as the only alternative.

But now the situation has changed radically as the result of
the war. Over half the Palestinian refugees now live under
temporary Israeli rule. Israel controls territory which is vitally
important for refugee resettlement plans, even if these areas are
eventually evacuated and turned over to the appropriate Arab
governments. Above all, the wishes of these refugees now can be
ascertained directly, through Israeli government agencies, instead
of indirectly through other governments or UNRWA.

The time has come to solve the refugee problem through a
dynamic Israeli initiative, *without linking this directly with a
peace treaty*. I believe this is the most important result of the war
and the occupation of territory: that Israel now has this solution
within its grasp for the first time. This opportunity must not be
lost, and we should not allow it to be frittered away by a lack of
imagination or daring on our part.

I believe we should take this decisive action for various reasons:

¶ Because it will strengthen the position of the moderates in
  Jordan, Lebanon, and Egypt and make it more likely that King
  Hussein will feel politically able to negotiate a settlement, even
  if this is initially confined to the refugee issue.

¶ Because it will clarify the dilemma of the occupied territories
  and show how many Palestinians want an independent state
  linked with Israel and Jordan and how many wish to remain
  an integral part of the Hashemite Kingdom.

¶ Because it will answer international arguments that Israel is
  indifferent to the miserable condition of the refugees and indeed

wishes to deepen their desperation in order to bring them to the conference table.

¶ Because Israel should be more interested than any other Middle East state in eliminating this problem and emptying the camps. Because this should be one of the most urgent aims of national policy. Because the presence of discontented refugees whose numbers grow from year to year threatens stability and is a festering wound infecting the entire region.

¶ Finally—but not least important—because we are Jews. Because we have been the arch-refugees of history. Because we refugees did not come to the Land of Israel to create other refugees. Because we do not seek to purchase our freedom by degrading other victims of history. Because if we want justice we must give justice. Because if in returning to Israel the Jews have lost all their compassion then that return will be a disaster. Professor Norman Bentwich spoke for me and for others who think this should be a cardinal aim of Israel's policy when he declared:

"The important thing now is to make a start, and not to allow the attitude of hatred, bitterness, and uncharitableness to persist unchallenged. That, I feel, is a Jewish and Israeli, as well as an international, challenge and responsibility."[19]

Any bold and significant Israeli initiative on the refugee problem would have to contain two decisive elements:

1. It would have to precede and be separate from an overall settlement of all our outstanding problems with the Arabs. This does not in any way imply that we renounce our claims against the Arabs. The Jews who were forced to leave Arab countries have a legitimate right to compensation for the property they left behind. These demands will be pressed at the negotiating table. But the Palestinian refugee situation is too dangerous a time bomb to ignore until that day comes. The best chance a Jewish Israeli who comes from Egypt or Iraq has of obtaining compensation for his abandoned property is if Israel begins paying compensation to Jordanian or Lebanese Arabs who originally come from Palestine.

Israel should abandon its long-standing policy of a refugee

19. Letter to *Jewish Observer and Middle East Review*, July 9, 1965.

settlement within the framework of peace talks, and declare its determination to solve this problem *before* a peace settlement and without linking the two issues. It should announce a unilateral initiative, accompanied by a detailed program, without making this conditional upon the political recognition of the State of Israel by the Arab countries. In short, it should take the crucial and essential step of isolating the refugee problem from the overall complex of Arab-Israeli differences and treating it as a question on its own.

2. The approach must be constructive, forward-looking, generous. No useful purpose is served any longer by the endless rehashing of arguments about who was to blame for the Palestinian Arab exodus in 1948. There is weighty evidence indicating that many of the present refugees were urged to leave by their leaders. But it is also known that many Arabs fled from areas taken over by the Israeli army and that the policy was to make them leave. What *is* clear is that the Palestinian Arabs who left their homes, whether they followed their leaders' orders or were forced out, were helpless victims of the kind every war leaves behind us human flotsam and jetsam. They should not have to suffer from this generation to the next because their leaders made mistakes or because their homes became part of the battlefield. The issue of whether they left of their own accord or were pushed out does not affect the question of compensation. This is a basic human and legal right which is the refugee's sole means of defense in a relentless world.

With these guideposts in mind, I propose the following step-by-step, five-point plan for an Israeli initiative aimed at breaking the refugee deadlock:

1) Refugee Compensation Fund

Israel should announce the establishment of a central fund for the payment of individual compensation to refugees and their families. The fund should have an initial capital of at least $200 million. There should be no difficulty in raising this sum as a loan from the World Bank or some other international authority. This compensation will be paid to all refugees who declare that it fully satisfies their claims against Israel and hence waive their right to repatriation—in other words, those who, in the language of Paragraph 11 of the 1948 resolution, "choose not to return."

From an Israeli standpoint, this payment will be made sooner or later. There has been much vague talk of paying compensation, but we have never made it possible for the refugees to submit specific claims which could be met from an existing fund. We have never put our money on the table.

The proposed fund will do this for the first time. It will enable those refugees who wish to remain among their Arab kinfolk—and they are the great majority—to obtain the capital with which to start a new life. They will be removed from the UNRWA relief rolls and will become citizens of their present countries of residence or any other country to which they choose to emigrate.

2) Limited Repatriation Project

Simultaneously Israel should declare its readiness to accept back a small but fixed annual number of refugees, in line with the country's absorptive capacity: 5,000–10,000 a year would be a reasonable figure. Lists would be opened in all the refugee camps and people repatriated on a first-come, first-served basis.

Every returnee would have to sign a declaration of readiness to become an Israeli citizen and to abide by the country's laws. Israel would be entitled to reject applications on legitimate security grounds. The first refugees to apply and to be absorbed probably will be relatives of Arabs already living in Israel, and this scheme can in fact be considered an extension of the family reunion program.

No more than the fixed number would be taken back each year, no matter how large or small the number of people on the lists. This will eliminate the Israeli nightmare of being swamped by a flood of returning Arabs. On the other hand, if the number of candidates for repatriation fell short of the annual fixed figure,

Israel could fairly claim that it had offered to implement Paragraph 11, but that a return to Israel was clearly less popular than resettlement in the Arab lands.

3) Repatriation and Resettlement Authority

The United Nations should set up a Repatriation and Resettlement Authority (UNRRA), along the lines of the Mixed Armistice Commissions, *i.e.*, with Arab members, Israelis concerned with refugee activities, and a UN chairman. This body would administer the Refugee Compensation Fund and supervise the register of applicants for repatriation. It would also undertake joint development projects, *i.e.*, the creation of new villages for refugees who would accept compensation, the construction of vocational schools for refugee youth and similar schemes aimed at helping the refugees to become economically self-sufficient.

This authority was proposed by the Institute of Mediterranean Affairs, in its 1958 proposals for solving the refugee problem.[20] It has also been advocated by Dr. Shimon Shereshevsky, editor of the *Ichud* journal *Ner*, and the *New Outlook* group, which has conducted several studies of the refugee problem.

Under present conditions it is difficult to see any official Arabs agreeing to serve on the RRA. However, if Israel announced an imaginative onslaught on the refugee question, some nonpolitical Arab personages probably could be persuaded to cooperate with the UN and Israel, on condition that only non-official Israelis became members of the authority. The experts selected could include town planners, economists, sociologists, humanitarians, religious figures, and other men of goodwill who do not serve their governments in any official capacity. At the Mediterranean Colloquia held in Florence our experience was that Israelis and Arabs could find common ground based on their professional interests, as long as government officials and diplomats were excluded. The RRA should be based on similar principles in the beginning, although in the course of time it could be expanded to include offi-

20. *The Palestine Refugee Problem*, published by the Institute for Mediterranean Affairs, New York, 1958.

cial representatives and such Arab countries (*e.g.*, Syria) who will boycott it at the beginning.

4) Pioneer Corps

The Israeli Government should set up a volunteer organization of Jewish and Arab citizens of Israel and Arabs from the refugee host countries, along the lines of the U.S. Peace Corps and Israel's own technical cooperation teams in the African states.

At first these Jews and Arabs would work in refugee camps and towns with a high concentration of refugees, such as Jericho. Their function would be to improve living conditions and health standards, combat illiteracy, and help to modernize farming techniques. At a later stage, when the compensation-cum-repatriation program enters the practical stage, they would work in the new villages to be set up in the Arab countries and in Israel. Here the remarkable work done by Mussa Alami in Jordan could serve as a pointer to the possibilities of training refugee youth for reclamation work among their own people. Cecil Hourani, President Bourguiba's former adviser on Palestinian affairs, has described Alami's project in Jericho as "perhaps the most interesting agricultural, social, and educational experiment being conducted in the Middle East today."[21]

Israel is justifiably proud of its technical aid projects in the new African, Asian, and Latin American states. In the past nine years this country with a population of under three million people has sent out 2,000 separate missions in 62 countries, from Nepal to Venezuela, from Thailand to Dahomey. Recent projects have included organizing the postal services in Ethiopia and the police force in Malawi, harnessing solar energy in Mali and educating the blind in Sierra Leone.[22]

Since 1960 Israel has sent out over 1,700 experts—1,211 to Africa,

21. Cecil Hourani, *The Arab Development Society's Project in Jericho, Jordan,* in *Social Change and Economic Development,* UNESCO, 1963 (reprinted from the International Social Science Bulletin, Vol. V, No. 4).

22. Hugh Hanning, "Israel's Exports of Knowledge," *Guardian,* December 11, 1967.

178 to Asia, 144 to Latin America, and 178 to the Mediterranean area. The fields covered included agricultural planning and training, medicine, teaching, commerce, finance, aviation, and transportation. About 9,000 students—half of them from African countries—have come to Israel to study farming, cooperation and trade unionism, community development, youth leadership, industrial techniques, and health practices.

I propose that we should use this impressive reservoir of skill and expertise in our own region, to solve the most pressing of our immediate problems: the conversion of the refugees from unskilled displaced persons to productive skilled workers and artisans. There is no reason why we should prove less successful in the hills of Galilee, the mountain passes of the Triangle or the sands of Sinai than we have been in the highlands of Kenya and the savannahs of Senegal.

What this Pioneer Corps could do is to bring together Oriental, Arabic-speaking Israeli Jews, Arab citizens of Israel, and Palestinians from Jordan and Lebanon in a new venture which would spearhead modern ideas and know-how in the Middle East. Here is a role for the neglected Arabs of Israel, who could act as a bridge between the Jews of the state and the Arabs of the neighboring lands.

That these Arabs would respond to an opportunity to show their potential I know from my own experience. During the late 1950s and early 1960s I assisted the American Friends Service Committee (Quakers) in running their very successful summer work camps in Israel, at which Arabs, Druse, and Jews from Israel and students from the United States, West Germany, Denmark, and other countries laid roads to Arab villages and erected buildings in Jewish settlements. I am certain many Arabs and Druses in Israel would be ready to take part in a dynamic program of rehabilitation in the West Bank, the Gaza Strip, and Northern Sinai, if the Israeli Government threw its whole weight behind the corps and presented it in the proper light to the potential recruits, as a challenge and an opportunity to advance the cause of progress

23. Ritchie Calder, "Israel's Health Conference," *New Statesman*, September 1, 1967.

in the region and help the refugees to adjust to the changes in their lives and economic prospects.

5) Review of Progress

After these parallel programs have been operating for two or three years the UNRRA should report to the General Assembly on its progress and on the number of refugees removed from the rolls after having either received compensation or been repatriated. In the light of the experience gained during this period, the General Assembly would make its recommendations for further steps toward a final solution, the pattern of which should be starting to emerge by this time. It would also be clear by then which of the Arab host countries was ready to cooperate fully in the projects and which still refused to join a constructive initiative by Israel.

This five-point program should be announced by the Israeli government as a package deal, on some suitable occasion such as the opening of the UN General Assembly. It should be carefully prepared. Detailed outlines of the projects should be published in Hebrew, Arabic, French, and English. Information about the program should be beamed at the refugee centers by radio and through the new Israeli television service in Arabic. Registration forms should be circulated through the agency of the UN, and refugees should be encouraged to apply on an individual basis directly to their local UNRWA office. Recruits to the Pioneer Corps should be sought in kibbutzim, among Oriental Jews serving in the army, and from the ranks of Israeli Arab graduates from high school, who usually have great difficulty finding jobs in the Israeli labor market and might be ready to serve a two-year stint in the corps. Palestinian refugee camps should also be visited, with emphasis on secondary school graduates who wish to contribute toward raising the living standards of their own people and furthering their own training and higher education.

I believe that if the Israeli Government announced this program and set it moving with the full weight of its authority, it could launch an irreversible chain reaction. For the first time since 1948 the refugees would be offered a genuine choice, not between two abstract phrases, but between two concrete, realizable possibilities. Tension over refugee bitterness would start funneling off. Even though some Arab countries would attack Israel's initiative and refuse to take part, there would be enough initial response from the refugees themselves to get the plan off the drawing boards. Contacts between Israel and some of the Arab governments would develop in the course of cooperation on practical, constructive measures to relieve human suffering, without a stand on a final peace settlement having to be taken immediately. By pegging the operation at a relatively modest level during the first two or three years, the RRA would be able to study the human and psycho-political factors involved. By the end of three years it should be possible to put up at least one new community of former refugees —partly agricultural, partly urban, and partly industrial—which could serve as a pilot project for further communities.[24]

Most important of all, the refugees will be "reintegrated into the economic life of the Near East." They will no longer be "a liability, but, more justly, an asset for the future . . . and a reservoir of manpower which in the desirable general economic development will assist in the creation of higher standards for the whole population."[25] I do not think this is against Israel's interests.

Many Israelis feel vaguely uneasy about the existence of the Arab refugees. It troubles them, although this lack of ease is not widely verbalized and remains suppressed. But as long as the refugee problem continues to plague us it will provide a fertile source of virulent anti-Israeli propaganda. It is a fact that many countries extremely friendly to Israel are unhappy about the intransigent position we have hitherto taken on the refugees. Taking the lead in settling this problem once and for all will eliminate this focal point of anti-Israel agitation and increase goodwill for

24. Speaking in the British House of Lords on June 28, 1967, Lord Byers proposed the construction of new communities of about 50,000 refugees in various parts of the Arab world. These could be financed by long-term loans at low rates of interest repayable over thirty or forty years when the communities become prosperous. (See London *Times*, June 29, 1967.)

25. *Proposals for the Continuation of United Nations Assistance to Palestine Refugees*, document submitted by UN Secretary-General Dag Hammarskjöld to the General Assembly on June 15, 1959 (A/4121). This far-reaching and imaginative report focused on the Arab refugees' economic potential and their role in the future development of the Middle East.

the state in the world. An Israeli initiative launching a massive attack on the refugee stalemate would be welcomed by public opinion abroad, Jews in many lands, and sizeable sections of the Israeli population.

Since the June 1967 war there have been signs that Israel was considering a new approach to the refugees. Israeli sources in New York told the London *Times* in December 1967 that a "far-reaching plan for the resettlement of most of the 1,600,000 Arab refugees displaced by wars in the Middle East" was about to be submitted by Israel to the United Nations. These Israeli sources hinted at a five-year approach to the problem, to include "a broad-based economic and agrarian reconstruction of the mainly barren territories where the Arab refugees now eke out an existence." It was suggested that this project could be based on the Tennessee Valley Authority and similar schemes in Iran and Vietnam planned by David Lilienthal.[26]

This was encouraging news, as it indicated that the Israeli authorities were thinking along constructive and progressive lines. Observers noted with satisfaction that the Cabinet decided in July to appoint a seven-man committee to study the problem and submit recommendations. The members of the committee—Professors A. Dvoretzki, S. N. Eisenstadt, R. Bachi and D. Patinkin, Major General Zvi Tsur of the Defense Ministry, Dr. Ya'akov Arnon, Director General of the Finance Ministry, and Dr. Ra'anan Weitz, head of the Jewish Agency's Settlement Department—were asked "to draw up plans for the urban, suburban, and agricultural resettlement of the refugees."

At the same time, another committee has been dealing with the political aspects of the problem. Its members are Cabinet Ministers, assisted by a team of officials headed by Dr. Ya'akov Herzog, Director General of the Prime Minister's office. This committee's work is secret. But it is known that the divergence of views is wide and no unified approach has so far emerged.

The first, technical committee, on the other hand, has set down its findings in a number of printed reports submitted to the Government. But here too there was considerable disagreement on

26. London *Times*, December 14, 1967.

how the refugees could be absorbed into various parts of the territory held by Israel with the resources available at present or those which can be developed in the near future. Some of the experts favor a more urbanized society because it would mix more easily with Israel's higher standard of living. Others place the emphasis on agriculture because it matches the Arabs' traditional way of life. Some advocate separate Arab areas and Arab towns; others want the population to be mixed and think Jews and Arabs should live and work side by side.[27]

But none of these plans were submitted to the UN General Assembly at the end of 1967, as had originally been contemplated. This was partly because of failure to reach agreement on resettlement methods and partly because of uncertainty about the size of the territory Israel eventually would contain. Official Israeli statements now insist that the problem can only be solved on a regional basis and that not all the refugees living in the occupied areas can be absorbed in them. In other words, Israel still demands that peace treaties should be signed before the refugee problem can be tackled.

This is a slip back into defeatism, into impotence and inaction. As the chance of any peace treaty being signed is remote, the refugee problem will continue to snowball and fester unless it is tackled now. Even if work begins now, it is going to take fifteen to twenty years and about $3 billion to solve this neglected issue. The important thing is to begin. This should be Israel's top national priority. Instead of taking minor steps which do not add up to a cohesive and well-thought-out policy, Israel should strike boldly for peace, as it struck in war, by carrying out this major political, humanitarian, and demographic enterprise. There are times when an investment in human relations is also sound politics. This is one of those times.

27. Amos Ben-Vered in *Jewish Observer and Middle East Review*, January 19, 1968.

11 The Open Region

THE WORLD is moving toward the creation of regional blocs. The European Economic Community, the Organization of African Unity, and the Organization of American States are setting the pattern of the future, in which economic planning and overall political frameworks make for inner cohesion and integrated progress.

But the Middle East still is torn by sectional rivalries and blood feuds of medieval ferocity. Leaders in this part of the world tend to think in purely national terms. They are concerned almost exclusively with the security and advancement of their own countries. Where they go beyond this, it is to think in terms of groupings based on religious affiliation (*e.g.*, an Islamic alliance) or national affinity (*e.g.*, the Arab League). Yet one of the great lessons of the twentieth century is that full economic development can be attained only if geographical regions are seen as single organic entities, with every sovereign state located in this region being incorporated into the master plan and no country which wishes to join the bloc excluded for reasons of politics or prejudice.

Hardly any Middle East leaders proclaim the destiny of the region as one of the world's potentially great blocs, situated at the meeting place of Europe, Asia, and Africa. There is almost no sense of loyalty to the region as a whole, of dedication to its interests. Each country is seen as a separate entity, not essentially interrelated with its neighbors, or as one of the bricks in the general structure.

What the Middle East needs most today are men who have a burning love for their own lands and at the same time a greater dedication to the Middle East as a whole: men who are regional, as well as local, patriots. We must chart a new vision—of one functional, interconnected, interdependent territory seeking the inner cohesion it lacks today.

One of these rare regional patriots is the Lebanese statesman Dr. Charles Malik, who believes that "the great moments of the Near East are the judges of the world."[1] He is realistic enough to know that "the Near East has been given the choice between embracing the falsehoods of Europe and falling back upon its own inadequate past."[2] But he sees hope in the fact that there is an attempt to face the situation honestly:

"There is abroad in the Near East today a new critical spirit. It is dissatisfied with the given and is not afraid to voice its dissatisfaction. There is health and hope and freedom only in the daring knowledge and confession of the truth, whatever risks that may involve."[3]

"The Near East," Malik declares, "mirrors, by deposit or by reaction, the problems of the world."[4] Those who live and die in the region are granted the opportunity—which very few of them seize—"of beholding something eternal, of seeing right before their eyes the deepest problems of humanity almost in shimmering physical embodiment."[5] It is almost, he remarks in wonder, "as though there must be one place in the world to remind us all of the essential problematic character of human existence."[6]

Another Middle East statesman who thinks in regional terms is the Israeli Foreign Minister, Abba Eban. When he was Deputy Prime Minister he wrote a penetrating series of articles outlining his concept of the Open Region.

In Eban's opinion, the Middle East cannot be comprehended only in Arab terms. "The destination of this region lies not in an exclusive Arab unity, but in a creative diversity and pluralism."[7]

1. Dr. Charles Malik, "The Near East: The Search for Truth," *Foreign Affairs*, January 1952: in Sylvia G. Haim, *Arab Nationalism* (Berkeley and Los Angeles: University of California Press, 1962), p. 223.
2. *Ibid.*, p. 222.
3. *Ibid.*, p. 190.
4. *Ibid.*, p. 221.
5. *Ibid.*, p. 223.
6. *Ibid.*
7. Abba Eban, "Reality and Vision in the Middle East," *Foreign Affairs*, July 1965, p. 632.

The Middle East is not a purely Arab domain. Its destiny lies in "a pluralistic interaction of Asia, Europe, Africa; of Judaism, Christianity, and Islam."[8] And the pattern of the future is "a mood of tolerant variety"[9] which would respect the diverse national and ethnic strands in the regional tapestry and allow each country autonomy within the general framework.

"The most fruitful and natural regional concept"—in Eban's view—"is that of Mediterranean cooperation." The Mediterranean is "a central compact world, congenial to the free interaction of commerce and ideas and alien to exclusiveness." Yet here, "amidst all the conditions for a new emergence of human vitality, . . . we find statesmanship held down in implacable conflict."[10]

At the heart of this blocked road to progress lie the Arabs' siege of Israel and their refusal to recognize its existence. Israel lies at the crossroads of the Middle East. It is "small but wonderfully central." Opening the communication routes leading from it to the north, east, and south "would stimulate the life, thought, and commerce of the region beyond any level otherwise conceivable." Hence a regional bloc which would exclude Israel would not be in the best interests of the Middle East as a whole.[11]

"The issue"—according to Eban—"is whether the Arab and Jewish nations, which have been primary agents in the Mediterranean adventure, can transcend their conflict in dedication to a new Mediterranean future, in concert with a renascent Europe and an emerging Africa."[12]

He noted that "Israel and the Arabs are each accustomed to a self-regarding ethnocentric view of history." But today there is no way out of the impasse "except by thinking in larger categories than that of the single nation."[13]

Since writing these challenging words Mr. Eban has become the Foreign Minister of Israel and has brought to this high office the

---

8. Abba Eban, "Israel and the Arab Summit," *Jewish Observer and Middle East Review*, September 11, 1964.

9. Abba Eban, "Reality and Vision in the Middle East," *op. cit.*, p. 634.

10. *Ibid.*, pp. 635–636.

11. *Ibid.* p. 637.

12. *Ibid.*, p. 636.

13. Abba Eban, "Israel and the Arab Summit," *loc. cit.*

incisive vision and breadth of outlook which have marked his brilliant career. But he has also encountered the full weight of the practical difficulties involved in "thinking in larger categories" and in attaining any form of cooperation—even if this is utterly non-political—between Israel and the Arab states.

Within the Israeli Cabinet Eban continues to uphold what I have called the "Middle East" line, as opposed to the "European" approach. He has attempted to continue the search for Israel's regional identity and role—a search which ended when Moshe Sharett resigned as Foreign Minister in June 1956. During the stormy summer of 1967 and the immediate aftermath of Israel's lightning victory he argued consistently that Israeli policy should emphasize the possibility of cooperation, even if this seemed remote, and should not be bogged down in the vicious cycle of endless hostility with the Arab world.

In September 1967 Eban delivered a striking address to the Council of Europe's Consultative Assembly in Strasbourg. He called for the creation of a southern Mediterranean community in which Jews and Arabs would join to become a major international force. The first step, he declared, should be to form a free trade area embracing Jordan, Lebanon, and Israel; this could later be extended to other Arab nations. The Foreign Minister made it clear that Israel would place all its economic and industrial resources at the disposal of the community. But, he said, Israel could contemplate the creation of the community only if the Arabs agreed to a permanent peace that would do away with the present tensions and replace it by an era of cooperation.[14]

Eban added that economic integration between Israel, Lebanon, and Jordan was required by geography. He admitted that his views might sound utopian in the present climate. And of course the Arab League was quick to claim that Eban's speech was nothing but propaganda. Lebanese Prime Minister Rashid Karame also lost no time in rejecting the Israeli proposal and claiming that Israel's only aims were "to mislead and make propaganda to realize its aggressive plans."[15]

But in making this proposal Eban was in fact basing himself on

14. *Financial Times*, September 28, 1967.
15. Reuters dispatch from Beirut: *Guardian*, September 29, 1967.

recent historical fact. He was reportedly inspired by the 1952 call of the then French Premier, Robert Schuman, to pool French and German resources in order to avoid a future recurrence of the bloody conflicts between the two nations. This has led to the Franco-German reconciliation, the pooling of coal and steel resources within the framework of the European Economic Community, and the 1963 treaty of alliance.[16]

Anyone who forecast the current close ties between Paris and Bonn in 1945, at the end of World War II, would certainly have been dismissed as a utopian visionary, if not worse. Yet less than twenty years later this came about. Charting visions is in fact one of the ways history moves forward. The tractors and engineers follow behind ideas, and the committees have to be preceded by the dreamers.

I am not complaining about Mr. Eban's vision and projection into the future. On the contrary: my only quarrel with the Foreign Minister is that he has not gone far enough. If the Israeli Government sincerely feels regional cooperation is the pattern of the future and the prime target of national policy, then these ideas should be put forward as vigorously and forcefully as possible, with the full backing of effective government action at all levels.

The Israeli Government could establish Eban's Open Region concept as its grand design for the future by drafting a comprehensive blueprint for progress based on the assumption that a Middle East Economic Community sooner or later will come into being. Our best brains—our scientists, agricultural planners, sociologists, engineers, economists, and experts on all facets of the Arab world—should be formed into a team whose conclusions would be circulated among all the countries of the region, all members of the United Nations, and such interested bodies as the World Bank, the Food and Agriculture Organization, and other international development agencies.

This blueprint for an Organization of Middle East States should chart all possible forms of cooperation in communications, industrial development, and cultural advancement. It should make provision for:

16. *International Herald Tribune*, September 28, 1967.

§ Road and rail links between Cairo and Beirut via Tel Aviv and Haifa;

§ Highways from Amman to Haifa and Ashdod;

§ The joint exploitation of the Dead Sea minerals and the phosphates of the Negev and Transjordan by Jordan and Israel;

§ Joint development of Eilat and Aqaba ports;

§ Access from the Nile Valley to Jordan, Syria, and Iraq, through Israeli territory;

§ Inter-regional postal, telephone and wireless communications;

§ Plans for fostering tourism by eliminating the political cul-de-sacs which today hamper free movement between the countries of the region;

§ Studies of power potentials in the various states and the most suitable location of future plants;

§ Exchange of technical know-how in oil drilling, water control, irrigation, afforestation and the many other problems Israel and the Arab lands share in common;

§ Oceanographic research and the development of fishing in the Red Sea, the Indian Ocean, and the Mediterranean;[17]

§ The establishment of a Joint Economic Commission which would study plans for economic cooperation and present detailed cost programs and time schedules;

§ The removal of customs duties and tariff barriers as a means of promoting trade between the countries of the region;

§ The study of arid zones;

§ Reopening the oil pipeline to Haifa and constructing other pipelines;

§ Cultural exchange and research fellowships for Arab scholars at Israeli institutions of higher learning and for Israelis at Arab universities;

§ Joint archaeological research and expeditions;

§ Efforts to stop the flow of hashish from the centers of production in Iran to the markets in Egypt and North Africa via Jordan and the Negev;

17. "Within 50 years, man will move onto and into the sea, occupying it and exploiting it as an integral part of his use of this planet for recreation, minerals, food, waste disposal, military and transportation operations, and, as populations grow, for actual living space"—Dr. F.N. Spiess, head of the Marine Physical Laboratory of the University of California's Scripps Institute of Oceanography, quoted by *The New York Times*, July 17, 1966.

§ Joint control of locusts, Mediterranean fruit flies, and similar pests.

When this blueprint for a Middle East based on cooperation and not hostility is ready, Israel should launch it by initiating a specific project which would eventually form part of the overall scheme. I have already suggested that Israel should turn the former Hebrew University and Hadassah Medical School premises on Mount Scopus into a regional health center and open it to doctors and patients from all the Middle East. This is the kind of constructive idealism which is such a feature of life in Israel and which could become a source of benefit to the peoples of the entire region, if Israel takes the steps I have advocated.

Prime Minister Levi Eshkol has shown at times that he appreciates the need for an Israeli peace initiative which would build on the common ground between all inhabitants of the area. He has said that "Arabs and Israelis belong to the Near East from time immemorial. In hostility they and we suffer; in cooperation and peace they and we will prosper."[18]

On May 17, 1965, Mr. Eshkol presented a plan for Middle East peace to the Knesset, Israel's Parliament. He held out the possibility of "minor border adjustments, mutual and agreed, at certain points where there is hindrance to the daily pursuits of the populations." He outlined the advantages of economic cooperation and the benefits this could bring: "A climate of negotiation for peace will of course enable us to act together in restraint of the arms race and to cut down armaments in the region. The states . . . will be able to divert tremendous financial and human resources, now used for purposes of war, to the development of their economic and scientific potential." He proposed that Israel and the Arabs "sit down at the conference table without prior conditions and in full mutual respect, to start spinning the thread from the point where the armistice agreements left off—and the benefits will follow."[19]

But the Prime Minister's address was not accompanied by any

18. Address to Anglo-Israel Parliamentary group in London, March 30, 1965.
19. *Israel's Peace Plan*, statement by Prime Minister Eshkol in the Knesset on May 17, 1965, published by the Israeli Ministry for Foreign Affairs, Jerusalem.

concrete action or announcement which would dramatize Israel's determination to set the region on the path to peace and partnership. It remained just a speech. And this is not enough in the Middle East. There is no use for Israel to hold out a hand containing a piece of paper and expect somebody to grasp it. Our goodwill must be accompanied by something more tangible if it is to have the impact we need to overcome Arab suspicions.

We must mobilize for peace as we have shown we can mobilize for war. The energy, drive, and invention which won us the astonishing victory in Sinai, the West Bank, and the Syrian Heights must now be deployed to win the battle for peace in these same areas. We must demonstrate that we are ready to take the lead in a regional development program for the Eastern Mediterranean and to work together with our Arab neighbors. We must get this message across to the Arab masses in every way we can—using the new Arabic-language television service to illustrate modern farming methods, scientific research, and work on health problems, to show them what cooperation with Israel could mean for their own living standards and the future of their children. We must talk to the Arabs in their own terms. We should emphasize the huge sums of money being wasted on arms and point out that the value of the Egyptian army equipment destroyed by the Israeli army would have provided every refugee family with enough money to start its resettlement. We must show them how much money is spent on buying a jet fighter plane and training a crew and what could be done with this money if it was diverted to hospitals and schools.

But there is one pitfall we must avoid at all costs. Israel's considerable technical know-how must not be offered in a spirit of arrogance or a tone of superiority. Nor should it be employed as a weapon in the propaganda struggle with the Arabs. It should be offered in a spirit of responsibility, out of a genuine desire to help other Middle East nations improve the lot of their peoples and raise their living standards. Israel should also recognize with humility that it has much to learn from its neighbors, and that scientific and cultural exchange is a two-way street, not a Jewish monopoly.

And we must do something else if this experiment in cooperation is to succeed. We must accept Israeli's destiny as a pluralistic, multiracial state in a region which, as Abba Eban has so wisely acknowledged, is not the exclusive province of any one religion or race. We must set the tone for an ecumenical era in the Middle East, a time of greater tolerance and less prejudice and friction. And, as foreign policy begins at home and is essentially domestic policy projected onto the immediate environment, we should begin to turn Israel into a modern multiracial state in which all races, sects, and creeds would cooperate with the Jewish majority for the progress of the entire country and the benefit of all.

This will require bold and perhaps revolutionary changes in traditional thinking and social forms. It would mean that every school child—Jewish or Arab—should have at least an elementary knowledge of both official languages, Hebrew and Arabic. It would lead to more mixed Jewish-Arab schools. A start should be made with nurseries and kindergartens attended by Jewish and Arab children and run by educators from both peoples.[20] More Arab teachers and officials should be brought into the Ministry of Education and Culture—where the present chief of educational services for Arab schools, Yosef Gadish, an experienced and competent official, has one drawback: he cannot read and write Arabic.

The concept of Israel as a Western-style pluralistic democracy, led by its Jewish majority, also could lead to legislation separating state from synagogue and church and permitting civil marriage and divorce, which are banned at present. The Law of the Return might be amended, so that Jewish immigrants will not be entitled to enter automatically and non-Jews will not have an inferior status under the law. The Knesset should pass a bill prohibiting racial agitation or any discrimination in housing, employment, and public facilities on the grounds of race or religion. Israel would take the lead in educating Jews, Moslems, and Christians to live amicably side by side in the land sacred to all these three faiths. This is a lesson the world needs today, and it could perhaps be

20. In a letter to *New Outlook* Mrs. Bess Horowitz, director of the journal's New York office, made this proposal and added: "We cannot wait to *undo* fixed prejudices which are the result of isolation, alienation, and walls of non-communication. We might rather try to prevent their being built into the child."

Israel's greatest service to a century so troubled by racial violence, political fanaticism, and intolerance.

The Open Region might seem a wild vision now, after the bitter June war and at a time when the Arabs seem to be recovering slowly and preparing for a period of renewed tension. To speak at this dangerous time of Arab-Israeli cooperation in medical research and irrigation is to lay oneself wide open to attack by the cynics who abound on both sides in the Middle East.

But since the beginning of human civilization the Holy Land has been a cradle of men's dreams—of prophecies whose grandeur sustained mankind, even if the dreams themselves were never realized. In modern times too men have dreamed visions in this part of the world, and some of these have become everyday political facts. Only slightly more than twenty years ago Palestine was still under a British mandate, with the Jewish state a messianic image. Egypt was a monarchy, and the Suez Canal was controlled by an international, non-Egyptian company. Lebanon had only just gained its independence from France. Such countries as the Yemen were ruled by despots whose barbarism reduced their subjects virtually to the level of slaves.

Many things have changed since then, in these two brief decades. Time works its own revolutions. The Middle East is starting—cautiously, hesitantly, but surely—to heal itself from the idea that war against Israel is going to solve anything. The seeds of the ideas sown by President Bourguiba, Charles Malik, Cecil Hourani, and other far-seeing Arabs are bringing about a change which is painful but inevitable. Israel should do nothing to delay this process—and everything possible to encourage it.

Shortly before Bourguiba's first public statement on the need for an Israeli-Arab détente, the editor of the Tunisian weekly *Jeune Afrique*, Bashir Ben Yahmed, published a remarkable article proposing the formation of an Israeli-Arab Federation—"a United States of the Middle East." This idea, he remarked, "will look heretical to some, chimerical to others, and may cause suspicion among others."

Explaining his reasoning, Ben Yahmed said the State of Israel was "a reality which cannot be eradicated short of a war whose only certainties are the suffering and destruction that will follow.

The Arabs will never accept the status quo, and even less the permanent threat on their frontiers." Besides, Israel in its present form did not solve the Jewish problem.

"The real solution, therefore," he went on, "does not lie either in the consolidation of Israel—a Sisyphean labor—or in its destruction. It could lie in the disappearance of all the states in this region, their fusion into a Federation of Middle East States, in which Israel, having taken back part of the Arab refugees and compensated the others, would no longer be a sovereign and hostile state, but, like Texas or California, a federal state linked with the others within a framework which could be that of the United States of the Middle East.

"No more territorial problems or questions of living space; no more hostile armies absorbing half the budgets; no more competing external influences and an open door to all imperialisms; but a Federal State of the Middle East, encompassing some fifty million people, a market on the scale of modern industrial requirements, with natural resources which could be envied by other big federal states, such as Brazil, the U.S.A., and the U.S.S.R.

"And, above all, peace. And one of the biggest defeats inflicted on anti-Semitism for many, many years."[21]

Many people on both sides of the border would disagree with this heady vision of Bashir Ben Yahmed's. Some would prefer a confederation of autonomous states, rather than a federation. Others will be totally opposed to an arrangement embracing every country in the region.

But this is not important. We are not talking about an immediate decision, but about something for which the ground has to be prepared. What *is* important is to continue this as yet scarcely audible dialogue. To respond to every whisper. And to speak first and most loudly ourselves—in words and through deeds.

21. *Jeune Afrique*, December 27, 1964.

12 Lebanon, Syria, and Sinai

I HAVE SUGGESTED that Israel should adopt a piecemeal approach towards its relations with its immediate neighbors, treating each set of relations as a separate problem. We have already discussed possible ways of exploring an improvement in relations with Jordan—the country which suffered most from the last war and stands to gain most from cooperation with Israel. Now let us see what Israel can expect from its relationships with the other countries directly involved—Lebanon, Syria, and Egypt—and whether it can do anything to stabilize these relationships.

Lebanon did not take part in the fighting, although it paid its usual lip service to the Arab cause. But although Lebanese troops fired no shots and no shells fell on Lebanese territory, this does not mean the country was not affected by the war. One informed Western correspondent felt Lebanon was probably more confused than any other country about the war, "which threw into high relief the latent conflict between Levantine pragmatism and Arab emotion that runs under the surface of this urbane and civilized country."[1]

The war had an immediate impact on Lebanon's economy. In June the number of tourists fell by 59 per cent. The loss of Jerusalem hit tourism particularly badly: in 1966 about 65 per cent of European and American visitors planned to go to Jerusalem after Beirut. Middle East Airlines had a bad year; the construction industry slowed down almost to a halt; and less money flowed in from the rich oil-producing countries, so that economic activity was also sluggish.

1. Richard Johns in the *Financial Times*, August 17, 1967.

Lebanon is of course a member of the Arab League, committed in theory to the all-out struggle against Israel. But as the only Middle East state with a Christian majority, it silently accepts the convenience of another non-Moslem state to the south as a bulwark against possible Moslem hostility. This feeling of added security because Israel exists is rooted in such remembered traumas as the Druse massacre of the Maronites in 1860 and the 1958 threat to Lebanese security, when President Eisenhower sent in U.S. Marines to quell a Moslem revolt. And there is another cause of acute present concern: the presence of a predominantly Moslem refugee population from Palestine and an uneasy feeling that Moslems might outnumber Christians when the next census is taken. As the present Constitution is rooted in an assumed Maronite Christian majority, the discovery of a Moslem majority could cause an upheaval.

In this situation Lebanon would scarcely welcome the conquest of Israel by Nasserist forces. And it did not share the masochistic determination of some Arab countries to punish themselves for Israel's victories by losing revenue. Beirut's prosperity is based on trade with the West and the East. And it dislikes having this trade reduced for the sake of a fruitless holy war against Israel. "The Lebanese are patently the last people in the world willing, in Nasser's words, 'to live on dates' for the cause of Palestine."[2]

This twin desire to be part of the Arab front against Israel, and at least as patriotic as the Moslems, while continuing business as usual, led Beirut to take a path of realistic moderation after the war. This policy was outlined by Foreign Minister Georges Hakim in a major address to the United Nations General Assembly on October 6.

"The conditions are favorable for a peaceful settlement of the present crisis," Hakim asserted. "If peace is not achieved now, war will break out sooner or later. Time is not on the side of peace in the Middle East. The United Nations must act now, either in the Security Council or in the General Assembly."

Hakim noted that the State of Israel was created by the United Nations by the partition of Palestine in 1947 and that Israel became a state the following year. "Conditions of peace," he hinted,

2. *Ibid.*

"do not always result from diplomatic recognition, or negotiations, or peace treaties between states." World War II, for example, ended in 1945 and brought a peace to Europe which has lasted for twenty-two years, without peace negotiations or a peace treaty.

In his opinion, the withdrawal of Israeli forces from positions occupied during the June war "can be followed by the establishment of peaceful conditions guaranteeing the renunciation of the use of force and the security of all states in the region."

"But," the Lebanese Foreign Minister declared, "in view of the history of the Palestine question, there can be no recognition of Israel, negotiation with it, or conclusion of a peace treaty with Israel."[3]

In other words, Beirut sought some kind of under-the-counter arrangement in which relations with Israel would be normalized without any formal public actions ending the state of war. This was clearly unacceptable to Israel in its postwar mood. And, almost by definition, the Lebanese, who depended so much upon external trade and near-neutrality for their prosperity, were not going to take the bull by the horns in trying to mediate any such settlement between Nasser and Eshkol. Lebanon would continue to sit on the sidelines, wary and avoiding any extremes of anti-Israel hysteria or pro-Israel subterfuge, until it became clearer how the ground lay.

Beirut has not forgotten that one of the Aramco pipelines carrying crude oil from Saudi Arabia to Sidon, on the Lebanese coast, flows through the Syrian Heights, which are now in Israeli hands. In other words, Israel controls forty-five miles of this pipeline and can allow the oil to flow or block it at will. Israel receives no transit fees or other payments for the oil flowing through the occupied part of Syria. But it is obviously in Israel's interests to show that oil can flow routinely from one Arab country to another through Israeli-held land. Israel is willing to allow the oil through, and Lebanon is willing to receive it.[4]

This is a good example of the kind of silent but effective pragmatism Lebanon practices and would like to extend to Israel, which is a master of pragmatic politics. But despite this non-hostility—despite Israeli Foreign Minister Eban's proposal for

3. *International Herald Tribune*, October 7–8, 1967.
4. London *Times*, July 26, 1967; *Daily Telegraph*, July 27, 1967.

economic cooperation with Lebanon and Jordan—Israel cannot count on any separate Lebanese action in opposition to the hard Syrian and Algerian line. Beirut will watch with deep interest any Israeli moves toward a lasting settlement with King Hussein. But it will not react positively to these moves until they have had time to begin showing results. As always, Lebanon will play safe and walk its uncomfortable tightrope between its Jewish and Moslem neighbors.

We need not waste much space on the chances of Syria changing its virulent attitude to Israel. The Ba'ath leaders in Damascus believe in the inevitability of guerrilla warfare, not only because this is their gut ideology but because they think it the only military way. The Syrian Ba'ath Party newspaper *Al Ba'ath* has explained that "popular revolutionary war is the only way to counter Zionist challenges. Traditional wars exhaust the material resources of the Arabs. Popular war exhausts the enemy."[5]

The Syrian Government organ *Al Thawra* has strongly denounced "reactionary Arab regimes"—read King Hussein and perhaps President Nasser—who were "kneeling before the United States to help it achieve a compromise settlement to the Middle East crisis." The paper said the Arab masses would not permit any compromises with Israel.[6]

A Ba'ath manifesto issued in Damascus in September 1967 insisted that "Arab masses know full well that accepting compromises or solutions containing any form of compromise . . . means surrendering to the strategy of American imperialism, which seeks to impose peace through war."

"The Arab masses," the manifesto demanded, "must make more sacrifices and exert further efforts in order to preserve freedom and dignity."[7]

And *Al Ba'ath* expressed the mood being whipped up in Damascus when it exhorted its readers:

"Let us all prepare to die on the battleground, because this is better for us than to be wiped out in a war of eradication."[8]

Syria has rejected the British resolution adopted by the Security

5. Gavin Young in the London *Observer*, July 30, 1967.
6. Dispatch from Beirut: *The New York Times*, November 10, 1967.
7. *Ibid.*
8. *Financial Times*, July 6, 1967.

Council on November 22, 1967, which called for the withdrawal of Israeli forces from occupied Arab territories and the ending of Arab belligerence. Syrian Chief of State Nureddin Atassi has maintained that guerrilla warfare is a way of spreading terror in Israel and liberating Palestine from within. The Ba'ath wants an Arab national front to organize revolution inside Israel. And Syria has refused to attend Arab summit conferences together with King Hussein, President Bourguiba, and other "reactionary compromisers."

Soviet influence in Damascus is still strong, and Russian technicians will direct the building of a high dam on the Euphrates, under an agreement reached in December 1967. The Kremlin has undertaken to finance the first stage of the dam and to provide more than three hundred technicians.[9] There is no evidence that the Soviet Union is encouraging Syria's call for guerrilla warfare within Israel's occupied territories, and there are some signs that Moscow is in fact trying to restrain the militant Ba'ath hotheads. But while the Russians can exert a certain degree of pressure in Damascus, they cannot influence Fatah units in the field, which sometimes act independently. And Russia is always mindful of Peking's small but intense presence in the Syrian capital. There is almost no chance that the Ba'ath will suddenly turn more moderate, particularly as they are being encouraged by Algerian President Houari Boumédienne, as part of his campaign against Nasser for the leadership of the socialist element in the Arab world.

As long as the Syrians maintain their emotional extremism and talk of guerrilla war within Israel, they cannot expect Israel to do anything else but hold on to the Syrian Heights and take steps to prevent saboteurs getting through the security net. Holding the Syrian Heights indefinitely is in fact easier than holding almost any of the other occupied areas. The population consists of less than seven thousand Druse, who are not particularly pro-Syrian and are not creating any major security problems. The kibbutzim in the area can breathe freely for the first time in years. And Damascus lies an easy thirty miles away across the plain. Israeli public opinion will not easily tolerate a return of the Syrian tanks and guns. A United Nations force in the heights is unlikely to be

9. *Daily Telegraph*, December 29, 1967.

durable enough or to inspire sufficient confidence in its longevity. Unless Syria changes its tack, it will be the last Arab country to recover territory lost during the June war.

The situation with regard to the United Arab Republic is more complex. It comprises three separate territorial problems, apart from the overall problem of Israel's attitude to Cairo. These areas are the Gaza Strip, the Sinai Peninsula, and the Suez Canal.

It is almost certain that Israel will not return the Gaza Strip to Egypt. This territory was never Egyptian in the sense that the West Bank became Jordanian. The inhabitants of the Gaza Strip were not given Egyptian citizenship and could not travel freely to Cairo or settle outside the Strip. People living in Gaza, Khan Yunis, Rafah, and Deir el Balah have historical and emotional ties with Palestine and the West Bank, not with the Nile Valley or the Delta. This territory should, as I have proposed, be joined with the West Bank and the Hashemite Kingdom of Jordan to form the heir to the projected 1947 Arab state, with the Gaza Strip declared a demilitarized zone and removed from the arena of Israeli-Egyptian conflict.

The future of the Sinai Peninsula is inseparably linked with Israel's claims to free navigation through the Strait of Tiran and the Suez Canal. Israel's main interest is to prevent the peninsula being used again by the Egyptians as a springboard for attacking the south and the Negev. It will not agree to Egyptian bases being set up again in the desert. Although there are valuable mineral deposits in the area, and these now are being examined by Israeli geologists, the other main strategic reason for staying in the Sinai is the oilfield which has turned Israel into an oil-exporting country instead of an oil-importing one.

But keeping troops down in the desert with such long lines of communication is expensive and a drain on manpower. Because of this economic burden, it might be possible through skilful diplomacy to reach an agreement on a neutral, demilitarized zone in the peninsula, with both Israel and Egypt withdrawing to one side of a buffer area supervised by the United Nations. But this presupposes Egypt's agreement to Israel's free passage through the peninsula's waterways, in Suez and Tiran, and Nasser is not ready for this yet. Without guaranteed uninterrupted navigation Israel will not withdraw from the entire peninsula.

The idea of a neutral zone was in fact floated as a trial balloon by "informed sources in Cairo" in December 1967, who said President Nasser was willing to keep Egyptian forces out of part of the Sinai Peninsula if it was evacuated by Israeli forces and if Israel agreed to demilitarize an equal area on its side of the Egyptian-Israeli border. But the only other area of dispute where Cairo showed any readiness to come to terms was passage through the Strait of Tiran. Egyptian officials hinted that they would accept this pending a decision on their status by some international juridical body—presumably the International Court of Justice at The Hague.[10]

Israel would not accept any such attempt to transfer the issue to this court, where it could drag on for years without Israel being able to develop Eilat's port facilities because of the uncertainty. At present Israeli troops occupy Sharm el Sheikh, and even if the peninsula is evacuated one day Israeli public opinion is going to demand that this vital outpost remain manned by Israeli soldiers so that the strait will stay open. It will not be easy to persuade Israel to allow UN forces back to Sharm el Sheikh, after what happened in May 1967.

But Jerusalem was apparently ready to talk about the idea of a demilitarized zone in a part of the Sinai. Gunnar Jarring, the United Nations representative in the Middle East, took this up with both sides at the end of 1967. But the Swedish Ambassador to Moscow made progress on only two minor issues: an exchange of prisoners of war between Israel and Egypt and removing the fifteen foreign ships trapped in the Suez Canal since the war. On all other issues he found both sides dug in firmly in their entrenched positions, ready for a war of diplomatic attrition.

The editor of the Cairo paper *Al Ahram*, Mohammed Hassanein Heikal, who usually reflects Nasser's thinking, wrote in his regular Friday article on January 26, 1968, that Jarring's peace mission had failed. Heikal said Israel had proposed a four-point agenda for direct peace talks: the problem of frontiers, the refugee problem, freedom of navigation, and the lifting of the Arab economic boycott of Israel. All the Arab nations had rejected the Israeli pro-

10. Eric Pace in London *Times*, December 13, 1967.

posal, Heikal added, and so Jarring had failed to make any headway after two months.[11]

In other words, Egypt is not ready to allow Israeli ships through the Suez Canal and is not able to pay the political price this would involve at home. And without an open Suez Canal Israeli troops will not leave the East Bank of this waterway, which will stay closed, at a cost to Nasser of $300 million a year. The large oil companies are already saying that in ten years' time, with hundreds of 200,000-ton tankers rounding the Cape, the Suez will be just the world's largest ditch. And Israeli itself is building a 42-inch pipeline from Eilat to the Mediterranean and wants to ensure a share of the Middle East oil flow for this 160-mile, $90 million project.

But this does not mean that nothing should change in the Sinai while Israel holds it. There are things that can be done to develop the scanty resources of this area, which contains some of the most forbidding landscape outside the moon. But although farming is impossible in most of the peninsula, the coastal strip around El Arish has fertile soil and even today is famous for its date palms and green oases. To really develop, it needs only one thing: water.

It is here that Israel has an opportunity to start something moving that will show what can be done with a piece of near-desert and at the same time contribute toward settling some of the Arab refugees. The northern Sinai and the Gaza Strip would be a natural location for a desalting plant using the waters of the Mediterranean to fertilize land which cannot obtain water from any other source. As the first Middle East country to plan a desalting plant for its own coastal region, Israel could use its technical know-how to turn this arid piece of land into cultivated soil capable of supporting thousands of settlers.

The idea of an Israeli desalting plant was first presented by President Johnson in an address to the annual dinner of the American Committee for the Weizmann Institute of Science in February 1964.

"Water," he said then, "means life and opportunity and prosperity for those who never knew the meaning of these words.

11. Reuters dispatch from Cairo: London *Times*, January 26, 1968.

"Water can banish hunger, reclaim the desert, and change the course of history. . . .

"Water should never divide men—it should unite them.

"Water should never be a cause of war—it should always be a force for peace."[12]

Following this announcement, Israeli and American experts worked out plans for a mammoth nuclear-powered plant which will produce 100 million gallons of fresh water a day from the Mediterranean and also will generate 200 megawatts of electricity. The plant, whose total cost is estimated at $200 million, was originally scheduled to start operating commercially in the early 1970s. The site chosen was Nitzanim, on the Israeli coast, north of Ashqelon. But the project has been held up because of political disagreements between Israel and the United States over the type of nuclear fuel to be used. Israel wanted to use natural uranium; Washington favored enriched uranium. Problems arose also over the long-term U.S. government loan that was to finance the plant. While this project, which would have been the largest single joint U.S.-Israel venture, has not been officially abandoned, it can be considered frozen, with no practical work being done on planning or erecting the plant.

Nearly all the countries of the Middle East face acute water shortages. Yet many of them border on seas. If sea water can be desalted at commercial rates, this would have tremendous implications for arid lands everywhere in the Middle East and all over the world.

Several other Middle East lands already are thinking about desalting as an answer to their chronic water problems. The Ambassadors of four Middle East states—Saudi Arabia, Kuwait, Libya, and Iraq—were among a party of twenty Ambassadors who visited the brackish-water-conversion plant at Roswell, New Mexico, in 1965, at the invitation of President Johnson.

Commenting on the Roswell plant, Saudi Arabian Ambassador Ibrahim al Sowayel said:

"We have a serious water problem in the middle section of our country, which is mostly desert. I think this process will be of

12. United States Information Service release, February 7, 1964.

great use to my country, especially when it is developed and improved."

Kuwaiti Ambassador Talat al Ghoussein noted that his country had three desalting plants operated by American and British companies. He added that Kuwait did not have sufficient know-how to operate independently in this field.[13]

Desalting promises to become one of the most exciting technological breakthroughs of the 1970s. The United States Government will spend $185 million on saline water conversion for the period 1965–1970. President Johnson has said that success in the quest for large-scale economical desalting "could well change the condition of man throughout the world" and would "free mankind from nature's tyranny" by making it possible to "produce water when and where we need it and at a price we could afford." The desalting program would make "a most vital contribution to peace," the President stated when he signed the Saline Water Conversion Bill.[14]

Israel could be in at the ground floor in this promising new field. Although the Nitzanim project is frozen at present, there is no reason why similar plans should not be carried out if international financing can be arranged and adequate guarantees given against any military use of the plant. And Israel could offer to share its experience and desalting know-how with other interested Middle East governments and arid-zone lands.

Only a few weeks after the June 1967 war Edmund de Rothschild wrote a remarkable letter to the London *Times*. "Apart from peace itself," he stated, "the prime need in the Middle East is for water which can do so much to bring prosperity to the area." Mr. de Rothschild noted President Johnson's deep interest in the need to people desert areas, shown by the conference on the theme of "Water for Peace" held in Washington in May 1967. British industry and technology had made major contributions to desalting methods, and the Russians had cooperated with the United Kingdom and the United States in studies on possible areas where plants could be erected.

Mr. de Rothschild proposed the construction of three plants

13. *Ibid.*, August 30, 1965.
14. *Ibid.*, August 12, 1965.

"to provide 100 million gallons each for Israel and Jordan and possibly 50 million gallons for the Gaza Strip." The cost of a dual-purpose atomic desalting plant capable of producing 100 million gallons of water per day—in other words, about the size of the U.S.-Israeli plant—would be $170-210 million. If this water was to be cheap enough for agricultural use at the present time, a low-interest capital grant would be essential. De Rothschild proposed that this capital be raised and that the time was ripe to try to implement these major schemes.

"There is now a wonderful opportunity," he wrote, "of turning the present situation of turmoil in the Middle East to one in which all efforts are devoted to promoting the economic and social welfare of all the peoples of the area."[15]

This proposal was supported by Michael Ionides, an expert on Middle East water problems and author of *Water Resources of Trans-Jordan and Their Development.* He noted that the cost of desalted seawater in the present stage of technical advance might be slightly beyond normal commercial or economic feasibility. But, he went on, "we have to remember that ordinary standards of acceptable costs for water lose their meaning in a situation where the world community gives food and other supplies, at huge expense, to maintain refugees. If the money given to provide the food were used to supply the people with water so that they could grow the food themselves, there would be far more for the same cost. Everyone would be better off materially and the refugees would gain the dignity of men with a job in life, earning their own living. In any case the costs suggested by Mr. de Rothschild are insignificant compared with the cost of waging war every ten years and a running economic sore in between times."[16]

Israel could act on this proposal and enlist international support for the erection of a desalting plant serving the Gaza Strip and the northern Sinai around El Arish. This could be either an extension of the projected Israeli plant at Nitzanim or a new plant located at El Arish. Edmund de Rothschild has noted that Admiral Lewis

15. Letter to London *Times*, June 28, 1967.
16. Michael Ionides, "Producing More Water for the Middle East," London *Times*, June 29, 1967.
17. Letter to London *Times*, October 6, 1967.

Strauss, former chairman of the U.S. Atomic Energy Commission, interested General Eisenhower in the proposal and he agreed to sponsor the plan.[17]

Studies indicate that about 60,000 people—or 10,000 Arab refugee families—could be settled in the northern Sinai, if water is available. In addition to farming, fishing villages could be set up on the lines of the Israeli army settlement near the Sabhat Bardwil Lagoon, halfway between Port Said and El Arish. Here coconuts and other experimental crops are being planted.

The northern Sinai could become a world center of research into the problems of arid zones. The striking work done at the Beersheba Institute of Desert Research could be applied here to resettling refugees from the Gaza Strip or Bedouin from the Sinai itself, with the help of Israeli farmers and scientists. This work could start now, and its implementation does not depend upon a political settlement of the Suez and Tiran issues, which is not going to be a quick or easy task.

A group of British Members of Parliament has suggested that the United Nations should acquire the Sinai Peninsula either by purchase or long lease. Sixty-five MPs from all parties signed a motion initiated by the Parliamentary Group for World Government and presented to the British Government. They suggested that the peninsula could be used as "an assembly point and first base for a permanent UN world constabulary, a laboratory for the large-scale irrigation of arid zones by the desalination of sea water, and a permanent settlement area for refugees."[18]

While this plan is impractical for both economic and political reasons, the UN certainly could use the Sinai for arid zone research, with the cooperation of the Israeli Government and other governments facing similar problems. Here is a constructive role for an area usually considered uninhabitable and used today mainly as an arena for tank warfare. And we need not wait for a settlement between Israel and Egypt to start rehabilitating this tract of land on the highway from Cairo to Tel Aviv.

18. *Guardian*, July 14, 1967.

13 The Nuclear Threat

UN SECRETARY GENERAL U Thant has said he feels part of "a bomb-disposal team which knows the danger, hears the ticking and watches with mounting anxiety as others shake and jostle the dangerous explosive."[1]

In a very real sense, all mankind forms part of this bomb-disposal team. The most urgent problem facing the world we live in is nuclear proliferation—the danger that more and more countries will produce or obtain nuclear weapons. One need not be an academic prophet of hydrogen doom to appreciate this danger. Every human being feels it on his own skin. The awesome consequences of a nuclear war are plain to everyone, whether politically sophisticated or not. They were spelled out in classically simple terms by President John F. Kennedy in 1963, when he said:

"I ask you to stop and think what it would mean to have nuclear weapons in so many hands, in the hands of countries large and small, stable and unstable, responsible and irresponsible, scattered throughout the world. There would be no rest for anyone then, no stability, no real security, and no chance of effective disarmament."[2]

In a striking speech to the United States Senate on June 23, 1965, the late Senator Robert Kennedy brought this warning of the dangers of the spread of nuclear weapons up to date:

"Five nations now have the capacity to explode nuclear bombs.

1. Profile in London *Observer*, September 26, 1965.
2. Quoted by Senator Robert Kennedy in address to United States Senate on June 23, 1965; reported in *Congressional Record* of that date.

This capacity was developed at great cost, over the period of a generation. But at least a dozen, perhaps a score, of other nations are now in a position to develop nuclear weapons within three years.

"There can be no security," he added, "when a decision to use these weapons might be made by an unstable demagogue, or by the head of one of the innumerable two-month governments that plague so many countries, or by an irresponsible military commander, or even by an individual pilot. But if nuclear weapons spread, they may thus be set off—for it is far more difficult and expensive to construct an adequate system of control and custody than to develop the weapons themselves."[3]

Perhaps no area of the globe faces a more devastating threat from the introduction of nuclear weapons than the Middle East. In few other regions are enmities so obsessive, or the hazards imposed by geography so acute. It does not require much imagination to guess at the results of an Egyptian nuclear attack on the densely populated coastal area around Tel Aviv, with a population of well over a million. An Israeli atomic attack on the Aswan High Dam would wreck this monumental irrigation-and-power complex, which the Russians say cannot be seriously damaged by ordinary bombing, and the Nile Valley would be flooded. Thousands of people in Cairo and other places along the river would be drowned or made homeless. Nor would such nearby countries as Lebanon and Jordan emerge unscathed. A nuclear fourth round between the Arabs and Israel would turn large tracts of the Middle East into man-made, radioactive deserts.

Yet few areas in the world are so dangerously close to crossing the threshold from conventional to nuclear arms. For this reason the Middle East has featured prominently in the calls by various statesmen for a comprehensive treaty to halt nuclear proliferation. After claiming that Israel was approaching the ability to make atomic weapons, Senator Kennedy noted that "Israel and Egypt each have been deeply suspicious of the other for many years, and further Israeli progress would certainly impel the Egyptians to intensify their present efforts."

3. *Ibid.*

He added:

"There could be no stability anywhere in the world—when nuclear weapons might be used between Greeks and Turks over Cyprus; between Arabs and Israelis over the Gaza Strip; between India and Pakistan in the Rann of Kutch. But if nuclear weapons spread, it is dangerously likely that they will be so used—for these are matters of the deepest national interest to the countries concerned."[4]

In July 1965 William C. Foster, Director of the United States Arms Control and Disarmament Agency, presented what was widely accepted as the first move in the Johnson Administration's campaign to block a nuclear arms spread. Foster pinpointed India and Israel as "almost certainly the most immediate cases in point." Each of these countries was intimately involved with its neighbors. "With the present unsettled state of affairs between Pakistan and India," Foster observed, "it seems extremely improbable that either would be prepared to forgo indefinitely the acquisition of a nuclear-weapons capability once it had become apparent that the other had decided to obtain one."

"The same is true of Israel and the United Arab Republic— a point which it is to be hoped will be fully appreciated by all elements in these countries whenever the question of acquiring nuclear weapons arises. Having five nations with nuclear weapons is bad enough, and if the number is to be limited, the prospects are almost certainly better at five than at six or any higher number."[5]

Dr. Glenn Seaborg, chairman of the U.S. Atomic Energy Commission, listed Israel and Egypt among the twelve potential bomb makers. Asked whether many other countries, apart from the five atomic powers, could build atomic bombs if they put their minds to it, Dr. Seaborg replied:

"Oh, yes. A large number have the potential, over a period of years and on the basis of the scientists they have and the materials they could acquire in one way or another. I'm speaking of such countries as Japan, India, West Germany, Sweden, Italy, Canada,

4. *Ibid.*
5. *Foreign Affairs*, July 1965.

Israel and—maybe over a little longer period of time—Brazil, Switzerland, Spain, Yugoslavia, and Egypt."[6]

It remains true that there are only two Middle East states in the nuclear running: Israel and Egypt. No other country in the region has the necessary industrial base or the political motivation. This is one issue on which Egypt and Israel confront one another directly, without the other Arab countries being directly involved. So keeping nuclear weapons out of the Middle East means in practice preventing Israel and Egypt from making or importing them. Ultimately, it rests on persuading both these countries that having nuclear weapons would not increase their security and that they would not justify the large sums of money involved or the considerable political risks.

In order to estimate the chances of keeping nuclear weapons out of the Middle East, let us examine the potential of each of these countries in turn.

Israel has two atomic reactors. One, at Nahal Sorek, on the coast south of Tel Aviv, is a small 5-megawatt research plant erected in cooperation with the United States. It is under tight American safeguards, which are being transferred to the International Atomic Energy Authority in Vienna. The Nahal Sorek reactor is open to foreign students and has no military potential whatsoever, so it need not be taken into account in any assessment of Israel's ability to produce atomic weapons.

Israel's other and far larger reactor—at Dimona, in the heart of the Negev Desert—is far more important. Scarcely any other place in Israel is so off limits even to members of the Knesset and journalists. The cost of the plant's erection and maintenance has never appeared in any official budget submitted to the Knesset, and until 1962 the Knesset's Foreign Affairs and Security Committee was completely in the dark about work on the site. The Dimona reactor has strained relations between Israel and the United States and been a subject of Arab and Russian concern. A knowledge of the background of the Dimona plant is essential for any understanding of the nuclear threat in the Middle East.

The decision to build this reactor was taken in 1957, in the

6. Interview in *U.S. News & World Report*, July 19, 1965.

mood of frustration and bitterness common to France and Israel after the Sinai-Suez campaign. Discussions with France had been held as early as 1954, when the two countries began cooperating in the production of heavy water, using the process originated by Dr. Yisrael Dostrovsky at the Weizmann Institute of Science. The initial steps were taken in 1955. But actual work on the site was the direct outcome of Franco-Israel cooperation during Sinai. Dimona was conceived both as a deterrent to any future attack by Nasser and as a means of forcing the Arabs to enter into peace talks. The exact terms of the 1957 agreement covering natural uranium supplies and technical aid to Israel have never been published.

The decision to build the Dimona reactor set off a vehement controversy between the Israeli Defense Ministry and prominent scientists. The Israeli Atomic Energy Commission had been established in 1952, with Professor Ernest D. Bergman as chairman. In 1957, following the controversy over the type of reactor to be erected at Dimona, all the members of the commission, with the exception of the chairman, resigned. These leading scientists were Professors Yoel Rakach, Solly Cohen, and S. Sambursky, of the Hebrew University in Jerusalem; Professors Amos de Shalit and Yisrael Dostrovsky, of the Weizmann Institute of Science in Rehovot; and Professors Ollendorf and Rosen, from the Haifa Institute of Technology. Professor Bergman continued to hold the title of chairman of the Israeli Atomic Energy Commission, although he had no commission over which to preside. Incredibly enough, no inquiry was held into the reasons for the resignations, and no one bothered to appoint a new commission. The Knesset did not demand an explanation. The chairman continued as before to act solely within the framework of the Defense Ministry, which controlled all nuclear development in Israel for both peaceful purposes and security needs.

France and Israel kept the work at Dimona secret from the United States, which was meanwhile cooperating with Israel on the Nahal Sorek project. The first inkling Washington had that something was happening in the sands of the Negev came in May

7. Professor Gabriel Stein in *Israel-Arab States: Atom Armed or Atom Free?* (Tel Aviv: Amikam [in Hebrew]), p. 122.

and June of 1960. This initial lead was followed by various checks which finally confirmed beyond all doubt that Dimona was the site of secret atomic installations.

When taxed with this by the outgoing Eisenhower Administration, the Ben-Gurion Government at first gave evasive answers. Various American officials were given at least seven different explanations of what the reactor was—none of them accurate.

In the fall of 1960 the United States posed eight questions to Israel, in an attempt to clarify the nature of the reactor. These included a specific question in writing. Washington was not satisfied by Israel's replies, and this created tension between the two governments.

Finally, under even heavier pressure from President Eisenhower, Prime Minister Ben-Gurion made a statement in the Knesset on December 24, 1960. He revealed that the Dimona plant was a 24-megawatt nuclear reactor, fueled with natural uranium and moderated with heavy water. He added that it was intended for peaceful purposes, but gave no details of the 1957 Franco-Israel agreement. He also did not explain why, if the reactor was non-military, such elaborate secrecy had been maintained. The Americans also applied pressure to President de Gaulle, who had returned to office in 1958. De Gaulle was anxious to restore relations with the Arab world, and Franco-Israeli nuclear cooperation began slackening off from 1961 onward.

On January 20, 1961, President John F. Kennedy took office. His administration kept up the pressure on Israel to permit a visit to the Dimona site. At about this time Ben-Gurion was seeking an official invitation to the White House to meet the new President, and Dimona was one of the stumbling blocks. Eventually Ben-Gurion paid an unofficial visit first to Canada and then to the United States, ostensibly to receive an honorary degree. In May 1961 he met Kennedy in the Waldorf-Astoria Hotel in New York.

The outcome of these contacts was that Israel agreed to annual visits to Dimona by American scientists. The first of these took place in the spring of 1961. The Ben-Gurion Government permitted another visit in the summer of 1962.

In June 1963 Ben-Gurion resigned and was replaced by Levi Eshkol. No inspection took place that year.

When President Lyndon B. Johnson took office in November 1963, he continued to pursue the policy of regular spot checks at the Dimona site. Further inspections took place in 1964, after Prime Minister Eshkol's official visit to Washington, and in subsequent years.

The Americans who visited Dimona—among them some of the world's top nuclear scientists—reported to Washington that no separation plant had been erected at Dimona. This meant that plutonium-239 (military or weapons-grade plutonium) was not being extracted, and hence the plutonium produced at Dimona could not be used to manufacture weapons.

Officially, then, Washington has been reassured that Israel is not contemplating the immediate production of atomic weapons. But the United States is still keeping a watchful eye on developments at Dimona, which continues to be a source of friction between the two governments and is referred to euphemistically as *ha'noseh ha'adin* (the delicate topic). "The debate over Dimona is the major problem dividing Israel and the United States."[8]

Speculations about Israel's nuclear timetable vary widely. In his 1965 Senate speech Senator Robert Kennedy claimed that Israel and India "already possess weapons-grade fissionable material, and could fabricate an atomic device within a few months." He added: "Israel and India can make nuclear devices within a couple of months, and weapons shortly afterwards."[9]

According to the *Christian Science Monitor*, writing in the middle of 1965, Israel ("a small but sophisticated country") "is thought technologically capable of exploding a nuclear device within two and a half years."[10] *Time* expressed its belief that India could produce an atomic bomb by the end of 1966. "Experts predict that Israel may follow India into the atomic club. . . . The Israelis are getting enough plutonium to enable them to produce a modest bomb a year within five years."[11]

It is generally agreed among informed scientists that Israel

8. *Maariv*, March 26, 1966.
9. Senator Robert Kennedy, address to United States Senate, *loc. cit.*
10. *Christian Science Monitor*, July 7, 1965.
11. *Time*, July 23, 1965.

could produce atomic weapons a year or eighteen months after the political decision to go ahead had been taken. The real question today is whether Israel seeks atomic weapons and thinks they will improve its security position, particularly after the war of June 1967.

Since Ben-Gurion resigned in June 1963 there have been indications that his successor, Levi Eshkol, has been less anxious to exercise Dimona's nuclear option. Six months after Eshkol took office Professor Shimon Yiftach, the scientific director of the Defense Ministry's development programs, addressed scientific correspondents on "Atomic Reactors and Their Uses." He noted that Dimona would be an advanced research reactor, which would produce plutonium as a by-product. However, he declared, no chemical separation plant would be erected.[12]

Several prominent members of the Eshkol government have publicly expressed their desire to see the Middle East free of atomic weapons. Appearing on a National Broadcasting Company program dealing with nuclear proliferation, Foreign Minister Abba Eban said Israel "has not initiated and will not initiate the introduction of new arms or any sort of new weapons into the Middle East, conventional or nonconventional."[13] And one of the government's most authoritative spokesmen on security matters, Labor Minister Yigal Allon, put this even more clearly, when he said:

"I am aware that our efforts for the peaceful uses of nuclear power are viewed with misgivings not only by our enemies but even sometimes by our friends. I should like to take the opportunity of restating: Israel will not be the first to introduce nuclear weapons into the Middle East. May I add that Israel will not permit any of its neighbors to start this destructive race. It remains Israel's policy to do all it can not only to keep nuclear weapons out of the Middle East but also to free the region of conventional aggressive weapons."[14]

12. *Haaretz*, December 31, 1963.
13. NBC broadcast on April 17, 1966: reported by *Jewish Observer and Middle East Review*, April 22, 1966.
14. Address to the British Society for the Haifa Technion, London, December 22, 1965: reported by *Jewish Observer and Middle East Review*, December 24, 1965.

Many leading Israeli scientists and students of nuclear problems feel the prospects of blocking a Middle East nuclear race have improved since Eshkol took office. One of the heads of the Israeli Committee for a Nuclear-free Zone—a body of physicists, intellectuals from all institutions of higher learning, and public figures —has reported "a great measure of agreement with the Eshkol Government on the atomic arming of Israel and the Arab states." He noted that the committee distinguishes between the Ben-Gurion and Eshkol governments, adding: "A change has taken place for the better, although there is still not complete identity of views."[15]

The Committee for a Nuclear-free Zone—which has received powerful support from Dr. Nahum Goldmann, President of the World Zionist Organization until July 1968—argues that possessing atomic weapons will not increase Israel's security. On the contrary, it could be used by Cairo to unite the Arabs in the face of an Israeli nuclear threat. An Israeli nuclear bomb would gravely harm Israel-U.S. relations. It would not constitute a genuine deterrent, because of its low credibility factor. No one really will believe, for example, that Israel will use the bomb in reply to a Syrian border raid or insurrection inside the occupied Gaza Strip. But under pressure of Arab public opinion Egypt would be forced to turn to Moscow or Peking for a similar weapon. This would escalate the Middle East arms race into a new and highly dangerous phase.

Israel's small size and closely packed population means that it could be largely destroyed even by comparatively primitive atomic weapons. It would not have any second-strike capacity in an atomic war with Egypt. For this reason comparisons with the "balance of fear" between the United States and the Soviet Union are completely misleading.

William C. Foster, Director of the United States Arms Control and Disarmament Agency, has warned that "an atomic war in the Middle East would not be limited to the region, but might bring about an atomic holocaust which would have repercussions in the entire world."[16]

15. *Haaretz*, January 15, 1964.
16. Interview with *Maariv*'s U.S. correspondent, July 14, 1965.

And Bertrand Russell declared, in his appeal to Middle East heads of state to permit international supervision and control of nuclear plants and rocket delivery systems:

"The extension of nuclear weapons to the Middle East would be a disaster for the peace of the world. It will introduce into a desperately dangerous conflict a weapons technology operating on a hair trigger and fully capable of obliterating all the peoples of the Middle East."[17]

The Israeli Committee for a Nuclear-free Zone has called upon the Israeli Government to take the initiative in banning the manufacture or import of nuclear weapons in all the Middle East landmass. There is no question of a *unilateral* Israeli renunciation of these weapons, only of a *bilateral* agreement covering Israel and Egypt initially, and then all other states in the region. This should be backed by a Great Power guarantee and effective controls over the arms race, which would have its upper ceiling frozen beneath the nuclear danger point.

While the Eshkol Administration has not accepted the principle of a nuclear-free zone, it has moved some way toward this concept since Eshkol replaced Ben-Gurion and particularly since the Israeli Prime Minister's meeting with President Johnson in 1964. Eshkol has emphasized the need for adequate supplies of conventional arms so that Israel could maintain an effective deterrent against the Soviet-equipped United Arab Republic. Dimona, he implied, would only be brought into play if Israel could not obtain conventional arms equivalent to Egypt's and felt it was being outstripped in the arms race.

At the beginning of 1966 Eshkol finally ousted Professor Bergman from the chairmanship of the—nonexistent—Israeli Atomic Energy Commission and reconstituted the commission on a civilian basis, with himself as chairman. Later that year he indicated to President Johnson that he was ready to freeze operations at Dimona at their present limit, without exercising his nuclear option, if the United States made direct sales to Israel of

17. Appeal signed by Earl Russell, Professors Max Born, Linus Pauling, C. F. Powell, Eugene Rabinowitch, Joseph Rotblat, and Abdus Salam, Dr. Albert Schweitzer, Jean-Paul Sartre, and Danilo Dolci: published in *New Outlook*, February 1964.

conventional arms equal in quality to those Nasser was getting from Moscow. This shift in position was followed by such direct U.S. arms sales—the first to Israel since the state was established. Previous arms supplies had been made indirectly through countries like West Germany.

However, Eshkol made it clear that the activity at Dimona would not be suspended and that the plant would continue operating at its existing level. If arms supplies to Israel at any future date fell below the quantity or quality required to match Egypt's, he reserved the right to re-examine the situation and the possibility of exercising his option.

Eshkol's new posture was perfecly sensible, reasonable, and flexible. It enabled Israel to obtain direct arms from the United States for the first time, while postponing the need for any immediate decision on whether to build atomic weapons or not. But Eshkol's stand angered Ben-Gurion. Throughout 1966 he hinted darkly that Eshkol was "endangering the country's security." Although he did not detail this charge in public, Dimona was clearly in his mind.

Professor Bergman and other hard-line scientists who wanted Israel to press on and stockpile bombs also accused Eshkol of surrendering the ultimate deterrent. These circles are suspicious of even such a peaceful project as the U.S.-Israel desalting plant and its fueling with enriched uranium that Israel can obtain only from Washington. The Bergman group also fears that, in setting up this project, the United States hopes to siphon off Israeli scientific funds, manpower, and resources, in order to force a choice between Dimona and desalting when the joint burden becomes intolerable.

But despite this internal opposition by some influential scientists and many of the Dimona team, the Eshkol Government's position remains the same as in mid–1966: namely, to concentrate on obtaining enough high-quality conventional weapons to maintain a deterrent force, without going for an atomic deterrent.

In responding to Eshkol's stance, the United States was acting logically in seeking both to reassure Israel and avert any act of desperation on its part which could have followed its feeling that it was isolated. As Leonard Beaton has put it:

"If the Western Powers and, especially, the United States, insist that Israel must abjure this valuable source of security, are they prepared to make the same security available? Are they prepared to be a great deal more openhanded in making available the sophisticated non-nuclear weapons the Israelis regard as legitimate? Above all, are they prepared to offer some guarantee of Israel's integrity which might have real value?"[18]

The June 1967 war's influence on this U.S.-Israel agreement is still difficult to appraise. On the one hand, it has reduced Israel's pressing need for a crushing deterrent, because it has demonstrated Israel's complete all-round military supremacy. But, on the other hand, this very dominance shown by Israel could spur Cairo on to efforts to counter it by introducing unconventional weapons in a bid to regain lost prestige.

Egypt's nuclear potential is noticeably lower than Israel's. There is not the same broad base of technology or scientific skill. The only reactor in Egypt at present is a small Soviet research plant of 2 megawatts (thermal), which has been operating since 1961.[19] But this is not large enough to produce plutonium in militarily significant quantities.

Further, the Soviet Union has consistently refused to increase this reactor capacity or to provide Egypt with atomic warheads for its homemade missiles. West German rocket and aeronautical experts have been working on this development program, which produced the Victory and Conqueror missiles so conspicuous in Cairo military parades. But two of the scientists who directed this program, Wolfgang Pilz and Paul Goercke, have stated categorically that these missiles have no military value and were designed for purely research functions, chiefly to launch a satellite. The Egyptian threats of missiles which could reach as far as Lebanon and bombard Israeli cities were "bluff," Pilz said.[20]

It is doubtful whether, with its present economic and social difficulties, Egypt will soon attain the industrial and scientific foundation needed to produce an independent atomic weapon.

18. Leonard Beaton, *Must the Bomb Spread?* (London: Penguin Books, 1966).
19. *Ibid.*
20. Interview in *Stern: The New York Times,* October 18, 1967.

The danger is, however, that Cairo would obtain ready-made nuclear weapons, complete with delivery systems, if Israel seemed on the point of making atomic bombs. In this eventuality Egypt almost certainly would approach Moscow and—if it was refused— would turn to Peking. And there are signs that Peking would like to employ its fast-improving nuclear arsenal as a wedge for forcing its way into the Middle East, through Egypt or any other Arab country which is interested.

The *Observer* defense correspondent, Andrew Wilson, reported from Cairo in 1965 that "Chinese-Arab relations are entering a new and active phase." U.A.R. policy was still "to do everything possible to prevent nuclear proliferation in the Middle East, particularly during the difficult period of Egypt's next Five-Year Plan." But a highly placed U.A.R. source—"a close friend and adviser of President Nasser"—told Wilson that if Israel were to show signs of developing a nuclear capacity, "we would go to the Devil himself, if necessary, in order to get a bomb."[21]

Writing in similar vein, the influential editor of *Al Ahram*, Muhammed Hassanein Heikal—who is certainly "a close friend and adviser of President Nasser"—concluded an article on Israel's growing atomic potential by declaring:

"There are a number of reasons why Egypt may be unwilling to introduce nuclear weapons into the Middle East. But there is one reason why she must at all times be prepared to do so: her will to live."[22]

If Egypt were to import a Chinese nuclear device, this could not be detected by normal scientific means such as the procedures used to detect atmospheric tests. Although this device might be relatively crude by Great Power standards, it could change the Middle East security picture overnight. It would certainly compel Eshkol to change his present reasonable position on Israel's nuclear option.

It is certain that this danger of a Chinese nuclear bomb in Arab hands was in the minds of both President Johnson and Premier Kosygin when they met at Glassboro in June 1967, immediately after the Middle East war. Both men are concerned with what

21. London *Observer*, May 23, 1965.
22. *Al Ahram*, August 20, 1965.

could happen if Peking increases its influence in the Arab world, using the offer of nuclear weapons as the spearhead of its presence. This was one of the factors which led the United States and the Soviet Union to agree on the text of a nonproliferation agreement in January 1968 and to table it before the 17-nation disarmament conference in Geneva. Despite the friction caused by the Vietnam war, despite the absence of agreement on other minor issues, Washington and Moscow have recognized that a world in which Syria and Algeria could have atomic bombs would be even more dangerous to live in than it is today. The nonproliferation treaty which has been placed before the world is the last chance of preventing a flood of nuclear weapons which, if it once starts, will be worldwide.

For anyone deeply concerned with Middle East security, the question is: Will Egypt and Israel sign this nonproliferation pact?

I believe it would be in Israel's highest long-term interests to do so. I would like to see the Israeli Government setting the lead in making the Middle East a nuclear-free zone, as Latin America has become through the voluntary proclamation of all this region's countries. Israel should support the American and Russian proposal and call upon the Arab states to join in keeping nuclear weapons out of this part of the world.

No one can deny that there are formidable—perhaps insurmountable—obstacles in the way of this goal. The nonproliferation treaty itself might never be approved. Such countries as India and Japan, which are threatened by China, will not sign it unless they are guaranteed a nuclear umbrella in the event of a nuclear attack by Peking. China will of course not sign the treaty. Neither will France. Further, even if the treaty is approved in principle, it will take several years for it to come into effect. And these years of lag might be crucial for the Middle East.

Both in Israel and the Arab countries there are influential men who think atomic weapons are inevitable and want to make sure their country gets them first. We cannot tell how the ebb and flow of Middle East politics will affect the access to these weapons, whether homemade or imported. Nor can we foresee whether Israel's present balanced yet flexible policy will survive the passing of Eshkol from power. If Allon takes his place, he will probably continue the same line, but Dayan might reverse it. A lot will depend on whether Nasser stays in power and, if not, who succeeds him.

Many scientists are gloomy about the chances of averting a nuclear spread. One distinguished American told me: "In the twenty-first century every country will have atomic bombs, in the same way that every country has electric power stations today. It will be a mark of prestige. You just can't stop it."

And in January 1968 the hands of the symbolic clock on the cover of the *Bulletin of the Atomic Scientists* were moved five minutes closer to Doomsday—the first time since 1953 that they have been placed closer to the hour which symbolizes an outbreak of nuclear war. Explaining the shift from twelve minutes to midnight to seven minutes to midnight, the magazine's editor, Dr. Eugene Rabinowitch, said it had been made "in sad recognition that the past six years have brought mankind further down the road to nuclear disaster." Nations are drifting back to "preatomic pursuit of their narrow national interests," he charged, "with power politics again replacing attempts to build a stable, peaceful world society."[23]

The situation in the Middle East certainly offers little hope for any attempt to restrain the arms race, now in full force after the Arab defeat by Israel. There is a danger that either side might try to deter its enemies and increase its own military prestige by hinting at extraconventional weapons it is making or acquiring from an outside power. This could easily stampede the opposing country into a desperate bid to get the same weapons at all costs, even though the initial hint would be nothing more than part of a dangerous guessing game.

Yet, slight though the chance of success might be, we must make this attempt. Anything would be better than the present climate of rumors, veiled threats, and psychological warfare. We dare not allow our region to slide beyond the point of nuclear no return. We must seek to prevent ourselves and our neighbors in the Middle East making or getting the weapons which can destroy us all. If we must fail, let us at least fail together with the United

23. London *Times* and *International Herald Tribune*, January 9, 1968.

States and the Soviet Union in an effort to avert a world living permanently on the brink of a nuclear pit. Perhaps we and the other countries of this region still will come to our senses and realize that atomic fear and mistrust are only the most extreme form of the sterile hatreds which are poisoning the Middle East. As Adlai Stevenson so wisely said:

"It is not enough simply to do something about the weapons of destruction. Nuclear disarmament is not enough in itself. It will not suffice without emotional disarmament, too—a disarmament of the passions that can trigger the nuclear army."[24]

24. Address to the United Nations General Assembly, October 25, 1964.

14 The Meaning of Palestine

"PALESTINE," Dr. Magnes said, "is a land *sui generis*, and no one can have in Palestine everything that he wants. In all of the history of Palestine no one has had everything that he wants."[1]

During the last ten thousand years of human history this small strip of territory has indeed had an importance which cannot be explained in ordinary economic or political terms. The Holy Land was scarcely ever a dominant military power. It was not as wealthy as many of its neighbors. It did not fight wars outside its immediate arena. It was usually a province or at best a small Jewish kingdom without imperial pretensions. But no area of comparable size has had so deep and lasting influence on human history.

This land has been a great catalyst. It has transmitted ideas from Europe to the East and from Asia back to the West. It has been a "translator" in the most profound sense of this term, funneling ideas across borders of language and dogma. But it has only been able to perform this task when the lines of communication from East to West through Palestine were open. When these lines are blocked and the dialogue between the continents silenced, the Holy Land becomes only an arc of relatively infertile land open to penetration by armies from the north, east, and south and clinging to the shores of the Mediterranean as if for protection.

We live in a hard time, a modern Iron Age. We think in terms of firepower and industrial plant. We measure a country's gross national product and think this tells us its value. We try to fore-

1. Testimony to UNSCOP in 1947 (Vol. III, p. 165).

cast the outcome of the clash between Arabs and Jews by adding up their MiGs and Mirages, their Russian and American tanks, their birth rates and per capita incomes. But we seldom think about the mystery of the modern re-encounter between the two peoples. We do not contemplate the hidden meaning behind the return of the Jews to the land they lost 1,900 years ago, and the significance of this return for the Arabs. It was an Arab, Dr. Charles Malik, who reminded us:

"To dismiss the present conflict between the children of Isaac and the children of Ishmael, who are all children of Abraham, as just another ordinary politico-economic struggle, is to have no sense whatever for the awful and holy and ultimate in history."[2]

If the Jews return to the Land of Israel—return in the genuine implication of this word, which means finding the healing roots of faith and courage—they can once more play the role of catalysts for the Middle East and the world. As Dr. Louis Finkelstein has pointed out:

"Our religion is of the East and we have lived in the West. I think this is a unique phenomenon which the world happens to need."

He believes the Jews have a great national purpose: "to act as the translator of symbolic actions into word propositions. In this task, the Jews are the only people who can help. The State of Israel as a state is situated at the crossroads of the world, and its good relations with Asia and Africa may turn out to be of historic importance. . . . I think the Jews were created to play the role of interpreters, with Israel as the focus of all this and the rest of Jewry as associates."[3]

But Israel can only become a creative channel for ideas and its own original thought if the lines of communications flow freely through it. This then should be the goal of the second phase of Israel's rebirth: to reopen the contour lines of contact with the immediate environment, so that Western concepts and techniques can stream through it to the East and so that Eastern wisdom and

2. Dr. Charles Malik, "The Near East: The Search for Truth," *Foreign Affairs*, January 1952: quoted by Sylvia G. Haim, *Arab Nationalism* (Berkeley and Los Angeles: University of California Press, 1962), p. 204.
3. *Jerusalem Post*, July 9, 1965.

scholarship can flow back to the West. But Israel cannot do this if it retreats behind the present wall of distrust. It does not really matter who is to blame for putting up this wall. The true sin toward history is accepting it.

Le Monde has charted a possible path toward reconciliation between the family of Abraham—the Jews of Israel, the Arab peoples of Islam, and the Christian Arabs of the Middle East:

"In the first place, it is essential that the Arab world should emerge from its state of confusion. Let the Arab leaders accept as definitive, whether they like it or not, the existence of Israel. Let them recognize that they have hardly behaved any better toward the Jews who peopled the Arab world than Zionists have done toward the Palestinian Arabs.

"Israel, for its part, must find again its original Semitic path, so that it will no longer be a thorn in the Arabs' flesh. To be no longer artificial it must merge itself into the landscape. This in no way implies renouncing Jewish consciousness but, on the contrary, means a return to it.

"Then Israel will be able to play a capital role in history—that of a link between East and West, between countries of the Western civilization and of the Moslem world, both born of Judaism."[4]

This is a noble vision for the future—an ideal which does not negate Zionism, but expands it, turns it into a less exclusive, broader movement in which Israel and the Jews of the world can join forces with the Arabs of the Middle East and the Arab Diaspora to develop not only one Middle East country, but the entire region.

To do this Israel does not need to be a mighty military power. It is already the strongest country in the region, apart from Turkey. Some Israelis would like to see it take on almost an imperialist role, creating buffers along its borders by setting up puppet regimes. I do not think this is the path Israel should take. I too want a Greater Israel. But not an Israel with a greater area, greater tanks, greater destructive power. I want an Israel which acts with greater justice, which sets its sights at greater targets, which emulates the greatness of its past.

4. "Arabism and Zionism," Le Monde, October 19, 1965.

Lloyd George told the Jews of London in 1925: "It is small races that have been chosen for great things."[5] Israel has a specific and considerable contribution to make, like other "small" nations—the Welsh, the Irish, the Dutch. But it must accept the blessed gift of its physical smallness and divert all its energy toward the things that are truly lasting and continue the Jewish impact on the world. Guns and bombs are not an impressive monument. We need them. But an atomic bomb is not impressive. A desalting plant would be. There is nothing uniquely Jewish about buying planes from France and tanks from the United States. It is not a contribution to civilization to place Arabs under curfew, to imprison Palestinians who want self-rule, to destroy mud huts, to take "justifiable repressive measures." These things will only brutalize us. They will harm us more than they harm the people they are aimed against. They will produce "all the harsh, unhappy changes in the Israelis themselves that are the price Spartans must always pay for having Helots."[6]

What path then should Israel take?

I cannot express this better than by quoting the prophetic words of Trude Weiss-Rosmarin, editor of the *Jewish Spectator*:

"The true character of Israel can only come into its own as a product of its own geography. It is under Oriental skies, after all, that the Hebrews became a nation, and it is the Oriental world and imagery which we meet in the Hebrew Bible. It is under the impact of the Oriental influence of Arabic science, philology, and philosophy that a 'Science of Judaism' was evolved. . . . While the so-called 'Judeo-Christian civilization' is a contradiction in terms, since Christianity presses its authenticity on the claim of the abrogation of Judaism, 'Judeo-Muslim civilization' has been a blessing to both components. There is an organic bond and a natural affinity and empathy between Jewish culture and Arab-Islamic culture."

"The return of our people to its ancestral soil in the Orient," Mrs. Weiss-Rosmarin believes, "offers a unique opportunity to start anew the cycle of the Muslim Arab-Jewish symbiosis" in

5. Address to Jewish Historical Society, London, May 25, 1925.
6. Joseph Alsop, "Israeli Anti-Modernism," *International Herald Tribune*, September 20, 1967.

which, as in the past, "Jewish culture and Arab culture will blend and coalesce, while retaining their unique and distinct qualities." And once "the spirit of understanding and symbiosis" will have been initiated, there will also be the beginning of a political change and an alliance of peace with the Arab nations.[7]

When this day comes, the hope expressed by the United Nations Special Committee on Palestine in 1947 will come true:

"The Jews bring to the land the social dynamism and scientific method of the West; the Arabs confront them with individualism and intuitive understanding of life. . . .

"Palestine will remain one land in which Semitic ideals may pass into realization."[8]

Let us begin this journey back to our common past and forward to our common future.

7. Trude Weiss-Rosmarin, "Winning the Peace," *Jewish Spectator*, New York, September 1967, p. 17.
8. UNSCOP report, 1947 (Vol. I, p. 52).

Index